Alicia Yang

CROSSWORDS WORD SEARCHES
LOGIC PUZZLES & SURPRISES!

mind STRETCHERS

GOLDENROD EDITION

EDITED BY STANLEY NEWMAN

right hand
COW
left hand
COW

Reader's Digest

The Reader's Digest Association, Inc.
Pleasantville, NY / Montreal

Alicia

Alicia

Project Staff

EDITORS
Neil Wertheimer, Sandy Fein

PUZZLE EDITOR
Stanley Newman

PRINCIPAL PUZZLE AUTHORS
George Bredehorn, Stanley Newman, Dave Phillips, Peter Ritmeester

SERIES ART DIRECTOR
Rich Kershner

DESIGNERS
Tara Long, Erick Swindell

ILLUSTRATIONS
©Norm Bendel

COPY EDITOR
Leda Scheintaub

PROOFREADER
Adam Cohen

RDA Content Creation Studio

VP, EDITOR IN CHIEF
Neil Wertheimer

CREATIVE DIRECTOR
Michele Laseau

EXECUTIVE MANAGING EDITOR
Donna Ruvituso

ASSOCIATE DIRECTOR, NORTH AMERICA PREPRESS
Douglas A. Croll

MANUFACTURING MANAGER
John L. Cassidy

MARKETING DIRECTOR
Dawn Nelson

The Reader's Digest Association, Inc.

PRESIDENT AND CHIEF EXECUTIVE OFFICER
Mary G. Berner

PRESIDENT, EMERGING BUSINESSES
Alyce C. Alston

SVP, CHIEF MARKETING OFFICER PRESIDENT & CEO, DIRECT HOLDINGS
Amy J. Radin

ISBN 978-1-60652-972-0

Address any comments about *Mind Stretchers, Goldenrod Edition* to:

The Reader's Digest Association, Inc.
Editor in Chief, Books
Reader's Digest Road
Pleasantville, NY 10570-7000

To order copies of this or other editions of the *Mind Stretchers* book series, call 1-800-846-2100.

Visit our online store at **rdstore.com**

For many more fun games and puzzles, visit www.rd.com/games.

Printed in the United States of America

1 3 5 7 9 10 8 6 4 2

US 4967/L-17

Contents

Dear Puzzler,

When we began the Mind Stretchers series, we made the decision to include a title for every puzzle, large or small. Why? We think a title on a puzzle is like a "Welcome" or "Please Try Me" sign—inviting you in, so to speak.

The titles of our themed crosswords are a special case. They are additionally intended as solving aids for you—to give you indirect hints about what the longest answers in each puzzle have in common. The hints are indirect because we know that most puzzlers would rather not get too much help from the title.

If a crossword had long answers such as, say, TIE THE KNOT, SOCKS AWAY, and COAT OF PAINT, wouldn't it spoil some of the fun if we called it "Things to Wear"? We think so. That's why we usually opt for something a bit more clever—or devious, some might say. The last time I published a "clothes" theme like this, I titled it "What's On Today?".

To make optimum use of a crossword title, many experienced solvers I know try to think of possible meanings for it before they pick up their pencil. Then, after filling in the first long answer, they take another look at the title; sometimes their suspicions are confirmed, other times they discover they have to rethink. In any case, "theme guessing" undoubtedly helps speed the solving process along, and adds an extra dimension of fun to the experience. If it's not already a part of your crossword routine, I hope you'll give it a try.

The titles of other Mind Stretchers puzzles won't in themselves help you solve the puzzles, but the names of these puzzles are chosen with the same care as our crossword titles. The titles we like best involve wordplay of some sort, such as alliteration (as in "Sudoku Sum"), or the co-opting of a well-known phrase (as in "Century Marks"). My personal favorite Mind Stretchers title? The one I thought of in about half a second, the first time our maze master Dave Phillips sent me one of his puzzles that feature a bunch of armored tanks. That title would be … "Tanks a Lot" (page 76 in this edition).

Your comments on any aspect of Mind Stretchers are most welcome. You can reach me by regular mail at the address below, or by e-mail at mindstretchers@readersdigest.com.

Best wishes for happy and satisfying solving!

Stanley Newman
Mind Stretchers Puzzle Editor
c/o Reader's Digest Association
1 Reader's Digest Rd.
Pleasantville, NY 10570-7000

(Please enclose a self-addressed stamped envelope if you'd like a reply.)

■ Foreword

Meet the Puzzles!

Mind Stretchers is filled with a delightful mix of classic and new puzzle types. To help you get started, here are instructions, tips, and examples for each.

WORD GAMES

Crossword Puzzles

Edited by Stanley Newman

Crosswords are arguably America's most popular puzzles. As presented in this book, the one- and two-star puzzles test your ability to solve straightforward clues to everyday words. "More-star" puzzles have a somewhat broader vocabulary, but most of the added challenge in these comes from less obvious and trickier clues. These days, you'll be glad to know, uninteresting obscurities such as "Genus of fruit flies" and "Famed seventeenth-century soprano" don't appear in crosswords anymore.

Our 60 crosswords were authored by more than a dozen different puzzle makers, all nationally known for their skill and creativity.

Clueless Crosswords

by George Bredehorn

A unique crossword variation invented by George, these 7-by-7 grids primarily test your vocabulary and reasoning skills. There is one simple task: Complete the crossword with common uncapitalized seven-letter words, based entirely on the letters already filled in for you.

EXAMPLE							SOLUTION						
M		K			G		M	A	R	K	I	N	G
				G			I		I		G		O
		C					S	U	C	C	U	M	B
T		K					T		K		A		B
			N				A	R	S	E	N	A	L
K		H					K		H		A		E
		P	S		D		E	L	A	P	S	E	D

Hints: *Focusing on the last letter of a word, when given, often helps. For example, a last letter of G often suggests that IN are the previous two letters. When the solutions aren't coming quickly, focus on the shared spaces that are blank—you can often figure out whether it has to be a vowel or a consonant, helping you solve both words that cross it.*

Split Decisions

by George Bredehorn

Crossword puzzle lovers also enjoy this variation. Once again, no clues are provided except within the diagram. Each answer consists of two words whose spellings are the same, except for two consecutive letters. For each pair of words, the two sets of different letters are already filled in for you. All answers are common words; no phrases or hyphenated or capitalized words are used. Certain missing words may have more than one possible solution, but there is only one solution for each word that will correctly link up with all the other words.

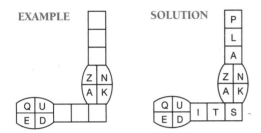

EXAMPLE   SOLUTION

Hints: Start with the shorter (three- and four-letter) words, because there will be fewer possibilities that spell words. In each puzzle, there will always be a few such word pairs that have only one solution. You may have to search a little to find them, since they may be anywhere in the grid, but it's always a good idea to fill in the answers to these first.

Triad Split Decisions

by George Bredehorn

This puzzle is solved the same way as Split Decisions, except you are given three letters for each word instead of two.

EXAMPLE   SOLUTION

Word Searches

Kids love 'em, and so do grownups, making word searches perhaps the most widely appealing puzzle type. In a word search, the challenge is to find hidden words within a grid of letters. In the typical puzzle, words can be found in vertical columns, horizontal rows, or along diagonals, with the letters of the words running either forward or backward. Usually, a list of words to search for is given to you. But

ANSWERS!

Answers to all the puzzles are found beginning on page 233, and are organized by the page number on which the puzzle appears.

to make word searches harder, puzzle writers sometimes just point you in the right direction, such as telling you to find 25 foods. Other twists include allowing words to take right turns, or leaving letters out of the grid.

Hints: One of the most reliable and efficient searching methods is to scan each row from top to bottom for the first letter of the word. So if you are looking for "violin" you would look for the letter "v." When you find one, look at all the letters that surround it for the second letter of the word (in this case, "i"). Each time you find a correct two-letter combination (in this case, "vi"), you then scan either for the correct three-letter combination ("vio") or the whole word.

NUMBER GAMES

Sudoku

by Conceptis Ltd.

Sudoku puzzles have become massively popular in the past few years, thanks to their simplicity and test of pure reasoning. The basic Sudoku puzzle is a 9-by-9 square grid, split into 9 square regions, each containing 9 cells. Each puzzle starts off with roughly 20 to 35 of the squares filled in with the numbers 1 to 9. There is just one rule: Fill in the rest of the squares

EXAMPLE

8	4					7	1	
3			7	1	8			9
		5	9		3	6		
	9	7	8		1	2	3	
	6							9
	3	1	2		9	7	6	
		4	3		2	9		
1			5	9	4			6
9	8						5	3

SOLUTION

8	4	9	6	2	5	3	7	1
3	2	6	7	1	8	5	4	9
7	1	5	9	4	3	6	8	2
5	9	7	8	6	1	2	3	4
2	6	8	4	3	7	1	9	5
4	3	1	2	5	9	7	6	8
6	5	4	3	8	2	9	1	7
1	7	3	5	9	4	8	2	6
9	8	2	1	7	6	4	5	3

with the numbers 1 to 9 so that no number appears twice in any row, column, or region.

Hints: *Use the numbers provided to rule out where else the same number can appear. For example, if there is a 1 in a cell, a 1 cannot appear in the same row, column, or region. By scanning all the cells that the various 1 values rule out, you often can find where the remaining 1 values must go.*

Hyper-Sudoku

by Peter Ritmeester

Peter is the inventor of this unique Sudoku variation. In addition to the numbers 1 to 9 appearing in each row and column, Hyper-Sudoku also has four 3-by-3 regions to work with, indicated by gray shading.

EXAMPLE										SOLUTION								
1	4	5	9			7				1	4	5	9	3	6	7	2	8
		7	5	8	4	1				9	2	7	5	8	4	1	3	6
3				7	2		5			3	8	6	1	7	2	9	5	4
5	9		4	2	7					5	9	3	4	2	7	8	6	1
	6		8					7		2	6	1	8	5	9	3	4	7
	7	4				2	9	5		8	7	4	6	1	3	2	9	5
	1						8			7	1	9	3	6	5	4	8	2
	5		2			6				4	5	8	2	9	1	6	7	3
6			7			5				6	3	2	7	4	8	5	1	9

LOGIC PUZZLES

Find the Ships

by Conceptis Ltd.

If you love playing the board game Battleship, you'll enjoy this pencil-and-paper variation! In each puzzle, a group of ships of varying sizes is provided on the right. Your job: Properly place the ships in the grid. A handful of ship "parts" are put on the board to get you started. The placement rules:

1. Ships must be oriented horizontally or vertically. No diagonals!

2. A ship can't go in a square with wavy lines; that indicates water.

3. The numbers on the left and bottom of the grid tell you how many squares in that row or column contain part of ships.

4. No two ships can touch each other, even diagonally.

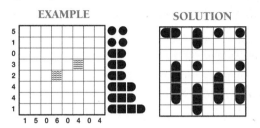

Hints: *The solving process involves both finding those squares where a ship must go and eliminating those squares where a ship cannot go. The numbers provided should give you a head start with the latter, the number 0 clearly implying that every square in that row or column can be eliminated. If you know that a square will be occupied by a ship, but don't yet know what kind of ship, mark that square, then cross out all the squares that are diagonal to it—all of these must contain water.*

ABC

by Peter Ritmeester

This innovative new puzzle challenges your logic much in the way a Sudoku puzzle does. Each row and column in an ABC puzzle contains exactly one A, one B, and one C, plus one blank (or two, in harder puzzles). Your task is to figure out where the three letters go in each row. The clues outside the puzzle frame tell you the first letter encountered when moving in the direction of an arrow.

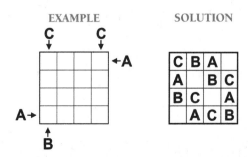

Hints: *If a clue says a letter is first in a row or column, don't assume that it must go in the first square. It could go in either of the first two squares (or first three, in the harder puzzles). A good way to start is to look for where column and row clues intersect (for example, when two clues look like they are pointing at the same square). These intersecting clues often give you the most information about where the first letter of a row or column must go. At times, it's also possible to figure out where a certain letter goes by eliminating every other square as a possibility for that letter in a particular row or column.*

Fences

by Conceptis Ltd.

Lovers of mazes will enjoy these challenges. Connect the dots with vertical or horizontal lines, so that a single loop is formed with no crossings or branches. Each number indicates how many lines surround it; squares with no number may be surrounded by any number of lines.

EXAMPLE   SOLUTION

Hints: *Don't try to solve the puzzle by making one continuous line—instead, fill in the links (that is, spaces between two dots) you are certain about, and then figure out how to connect those links. To start the puzzle, mark off any links that can't be connected. That would include all four links around each 0. Another good starting step is to look for any 3 values next or adjacent to a 0; solving those links is easy. In time, you will see that rules and patterns emerge, particularly in the puzzle corners, and when two numbers are adjacent to each other.*

Number-Out

by Conceptis Ltd.

This innovative new puzzle challenges your logic in much the same way a Sudoku puzzle does. Your task is to shade squares so that no number appears in any row or column more than once. Shaded squares may not touch each other horizontally or vertically, and all unshaded squares must form a single continuous area.

EXAMPLE   SOLUTION

Hints: *First look for all the numbers that are unduplicated in their row and column. Those squares will never be shaded, so we suggest that you circle them as a reminder to yourself. When there are three of the same number consecutively in a row or column, the one in the middle must always be unshaded, so you can shade the other two. Also, any square that is between a pair of the same numbers must always be unshaded. Once a square is shaded, you know that the squares adjacent to it, both horizontally and vertically, must be unshaded.*

Star Search

by Peter Ritmeester

Another fun game in the same style of Minesweeper. Your task: find the stars that are hidden among the blank squares. The numbered squares indicate how many stars are hidden in squares adjacent to them (including diagonally). There is never more than one star in any square.

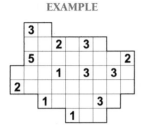
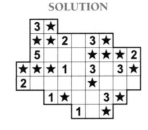

EXAMPLE   SOLUTION

Hint: If, for example, a 3 is surrounded by four empty squares, but two of those squares are adjacent to the same square with a 1, the other two empty squares around the 3 must contain stars.

123

by Peter Ritmeester

Each grid in this puzzle has pieces that look like dominoes. You must fill in the blank squares so that each "domino" contains one each of the numbers 1, 2, and 3, according to these two rules:

EXAMPLE   SOLUTION

1. No two adjacent squares, horizontally or vertically, can have the same number.

2. Each completed row and column of the diagram will have an equal number of 1s, 2s, and 3s.

Hints: Look first for any blank square that is adjacent to two different numbers. By rule 1 above, the "missing" number of 1-2-3 must go in that blank square. Rule 2 becomes important to use later in the solving process. For example, knowing that a 9-by-9 diagram must have three 1s, three 2s, and three 3s in each row and column allows you to use the process of elimination to deduce what blank squares in nearly filled rows and columns must be.

Throughout *Mind Stretchers* you will find unique mazes, visual conundrums, and other colorful challenges, each developed by maze master Dave Phillips. Each comes under a new name and has unique instructions. Our best advice? Patience and perseverance. Your eyes will need time to unravel the visual secrets.

In addition, you will also discover these visual puzzles:

Line Drawings

by George Bredehorn

George loves to create never-before-seen puzzle types, and here is another unique Bredehorn game. Each Line Drawing puzzle is different in its design, but the task is the same: Figure out where to place the prescribed number of lines to partition the space in the instructed way.

Hint: Use a pencil and a straightedge as you work. Some lines come very close to the items within the region, so being straight and accurate with your line-drawing is crucial.

One-Way Streets

by Peter Ritmeester

Another fun variation on the maze. The diagram represents a pattern of streets. A and B are parking spaces, and the black squares are stores. Find a route that starts at A, passes through all the stores exactly once, and ends at B. (Harder puzzles use P's to indicate parking spaces instead of A's and B's, and don't tell you the starting and ending places.) Arrows indicate one-way traffic for that block only. No

EXAMPLE   SOLUTION

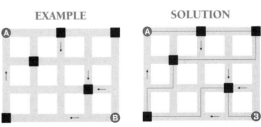

block or intersection may be entered more than once.

Hints: The particular arrangement of stores and arrows will always limit the possibilities for the first store passed through from the starting point A and the last store passed through before reaching ending point B. So try to work both from the start and the end of the route. Also, the placement of an arrow on a block doesn't necessarily mean that your route will pass through that block. You can also use arrows to eliminate blocks where your path will not go.

BRAIN TEASERS

To round out the more involved puzzles are more than 150 short brain teasers, most written by our puzzle editor, Stanley Newman. Stan is famous in the puzzle world for his inventive brain games. An example of how to solve each puzzle appears in the puzzle's first occurrence (the page number is noted below). You'll find the following types scattered throughout the pages.

* Invented by and cowritten with George Bredehorn

** By George Bredehorn

But wait...there's more!

At the top of many of the pages in this book are additional brain teasers, organized into three categories:

• **QUICK!**: These tests challenge your ability to instantly calculate numbers or recall well-known facts.

• **DO YOU KNOW** ...: These more demanding questions probe the depth of your knowledge of facts and trivia.

• **HAVE YOU** ... and **DO YOU** ...: These reminders reveal the many things you can do each day to benefit your brain.

For the record, we have deliberately left out answers to the **QUICK!** and **DO YOU KNOW** ... features. Our hope is that if you don't know an answer, you'll be intrigued enough to open a book or search the Internet for it!

■ Meet the Authors

STANLEY NEWMAN (puzzle editor and author) is crossword editor for *Newsday,* the major newspaper of Long Island, New York. He is the author/editor of over 125 books, including the autobiography and instructional manual *Cruciverbalism* and the best-selling *Million Word Crossword Dictionary.* Winner of the First U.S. Open Crossword Championship in 1982, he holds the world's record for the fastest completion of a *New York Times* crossword— 2 minutes, 14 seconds. Stan operates the website www.StanXwords.com and also conducts an annual Crossword University skill-building program on a luxury-liner cruise.

GEORGE BREDEHORN is a retired elementary school teacher from Wantagh, New York. His variety word games have appeared in the *New York Times* and many puzzle magazines. Every week for the past 20 years, he and his wife, Dorothy, have hosted a group of Long Island puzzlers who play some of the 80-plus games that George has invented.

CONCEPTIS (www.conceptispuzzles.com) is a leading supplier of logic puzzles to printed, electronic, and other gaming media all over the world. On average, ten million Conceptis puzzles are printed in newspapers, magazines and books each day, while millions more are played online and on mobile phones each month.

DAVE PHILLIPS has designed puzzles for books, magazines, newspapers, PC games, and advertising for more than 30 years. In addition, Dave is a renowned creator of walk-through mazes. Each year his corn-maze designs challenge visitors with miles of paths woven into works of art. Dave is also codeveloper of eBrainyGames.com, a website that features puzzles and games for sale.

PETER RITMEESTER is chief executive officer of PZZL.com, which produces many varieties of puzzles for newspapers and websites worldwide. Peter is also general secretary of the World Puzzle Federation. The federation organizes the annual World Puzzle Championship, which includes difficult versions of many of the types of logic puzzles that Peter has created for *Mind Stretchers.*

■ Master Class: **Tournament Crosswords**

How I Became a Crossword Champion

In February 1981, a little over five years after I graduated from Rutgers University with a master's degree in statistics, I was gainfully employed at a Wall Street firm as a bond analyst—an intellectually challenging job, to be sure, but not exactly a psychically fulfilling one. Back then, crosswords and puzzles were nothing more than a pastime for me. I would solve the *New York Times* crossword on the commuter train to work and, when occasional chunks of spare time presented themselves, I might work my way through a puzzle magazine for some pleasant mental exercise. Little did I know that my career path was about to veer off in a most unexpected direction.

It can all be traced to a small ad that appeared on the *Times* puzzle page, for a crossword contest that was to be held on an upcoming weekend at a hotel in Stamford, Connecticut: "The Fourth Annual American Crossword Puzzle Tournament" (ACPT). Since I thought I could solve crosswords pretty well, I decided to enter—just to see how my skills compared to everyone else's. But this was by no means an easy decision for me to make.

Similar ads for the tournament had appeared in the *Times* in previous years, but I'd never been interested in participating before. I had what I thought was an excellent reason: *abject fear*. You see, in the mid-1970s, I had entered two Scrabble tournaments. Scrabble had been a lifelong hobby for me, and I thought I was good at it. So, I assumed I would do pretty well. Well, I didn't do very well, either time. Not very well at all. I discovered, to my horror, that the skill level of the contestants was far beyond my own, and I lost nearly all of the games I played in both competitions. Seeing what would be involved to substantially improve my skills (most importantly, learning and memorizing thousands of obscure words I didn't know), I decided to permanently retire from Scrabble competition.

So, you can probably understand my hesitancy about returning to any sort of word-game competition after those Scrabble fiascos. Why did I finally decide to give crossword contests a try? I hoped that the different abilities needed for successful crossword solving as compared to Scrabble (knowledge of word meanings and trivia, quick recall, hand-eye coordination) might lead to a different result for me.

My First Crossword Tournament

About 125 people competed in that 1981 ACPT. The director of the event, who'd founded it three years before, and who was at that time the puzzle editor of *Games* magazine, was a gentleman who in later years would gain far more prominence in the puzzle world—Will Shortz.

The tournament consisted of seven puzzles of varying difficulty solved by everyone: three on Saturday morning, three on Saturday afternoon, and—appropriately—a Sunday-size crossword on Sunday morning. Then, a championship playoff would be held later Sunday, among the top three finishers overall. Scoring was based on both speed and accuracy, weighted more or less equally.

How did I do? Surprisingly, not too badly; I finished in 13th place—in other words, in the top 10 percent (though just barely). Once the full scoring and standings were posted, I could see that I was one of the fastest solvers in the room, but hadn't finished higher because I had made careless mistakes in several puzzles. In my haste to complete each puzzle as quickly as possible, I wasn't watching the crossing words as closely as I should have. Since I had never solved puzzles against the clock before, I wasn't at all prepared for the different mind-set that it required. Also, there were quite a few answer words in the various puzzles that I wasn't familiar with, and I discovered all too many meanings of commonly seen "crossword words" that were new to me.

So I left Stamford on Sunday afternoon, not in a glum "coulda, woulda, shoulda" mood, but rather feeling exhilarated and filled with optimism. Because, unlike with Scrabble, I felt strongly that I could improve my skills in crossword "speed solving" enough to do a lot better in the following year's tournament. And, even before I returned to my Brooklyn home that day, I had a pretty good idea how I was going to go about it.

My Crossword "Strength Training" Program

The most important thing that I needed to work on: finding my "optimum" puzzle-solving speed. That is, slowing myself down just enough to avoid careless mistakes. After only a couple of weeks of experimentation (using the daily *New York Times* and some books of older *Times* puzzles), I hit upon that speed, training myself to always look at the Down words formed as I filled in Across words (and vice versa). In other words, applying the same rule followed by careful pedestrians navigating their way through urban thoroughfares: Look both ways when crossing! To my surprise, I discovered that this slower speed typically added only a few extra seconds to my solving time. With severe scoring penalties for incorrect answers in the tournament, this was a very inexpensive "insurance policy" indeed.

To beef up my crossword-useful vocabulary, I began to keep track of all the clues and answers that were new to me. I would circle any of these that I found in every puzzle I did, then I'd look up these words in my unabridged dictionary and I'd enter the information on index cards. (This was several years before my first personal computer. A word processor would have made this task much easier.)

Checking the printed solution to every crossword I solved became an integral part of my new solving routine—to provide immediate reinforcement for my attempts at complete accuracy, as well as to confirm answers I wasn't sure about.

As it turned out, I didn't have to wait a year (till the next ACPT) to see if my training regimen was working. Only one month after my first crossword tournament, there was another one scheduled, at Grossinger's, an upstate New York resort hotel. Once again, Will Shortz was the tournament director. About 50 people competed, and I finished in fifth place. (Hmm ... top 10 percent once again, just barely.) But I knew my month of training had paid off. Not only did I make fewer errors than in the previous month's tournament, but several words I had just learned had been in the puzzles.

Buoyed by this improvement, I spent the next months solving crosswords every day, continuing the program I'd created for myself. By the time 1981 turned into 1982, I had solved more than 1,500 crosswords, and my file-card box had more than 2,500 words in it. To be sure I really knew all these new words and meanings, I would review them every few weeks.

1982: Contest #1
By a quirk in the scheduling, the first crossword tournament scheduled for 1982 wasn't the ACPT in March, but another contest at Grossinger's in February. There were about 50 competitors once again (including the previous year's champ, a gracious lady named Miriam), and Will Shortz was in charge again. The event consisted of four crosswords on Saturday. To my surprise, I completed each of the puzzles a few seconds faster than Miriam. When the results were posted Sunday morning, I discovered that Miriam and I both had perfect solutions to all four puzzles, but my speed gave me the victory. The prize—a future weekend at Grossinger's.

To me, the prize wasn't nearly as important as the win. I can't adequately describe the excitement I felt in experiencing the success of my self-styled training program. But there was no time for laurel-resting. The next ACPT was just one month away.

1982: Contest #2
The format of the March 1982 ACPT was the same as the previous year. During the six puzzles of the Saturday morning and afternoon sessions, I could see I was doing a lot better than just a year ago. Though I was solving the puzzles more slowly and more carefully, my solving times had actually improved—because many more words were familiar to me than in 1981, and I found myself at many fewer "stopping points" than before. I was very pleased to see that I was finishing most of the puzzles faster than the top finishers of the year before.

The next morning, the standings were posted, and I found myself in second place! I honestly couldn't believe it. My knees got weak, and I had to sit down and take deep breaths. In first place was Philip, the previous year's winner. The scores were fairly close, clustering about the top six competitors. To maintain my position in the top three (and make it to the championship round), I would have to regain my composure and complete the seventh puzzle with no mistakes that morning. And, somehow, I did!

The finalists were Philip, newcomer Joe, and myself. We were all positioned at tables with overhead projectors, so the audience could follow our solving progress on the final puzzle—a very tricky themeless. Rules for this puzzle were different from the other seven. Only accuracy counted, with time of completion to be used as the tiebreaker if necessary. Though I kept my cool and solved the puzzle as quickly and carefully as I could,

Philip shouted "Done!" to indicate his completion of the puzzle a few seconds before I had finished. (Joe didn't complete the puzzle in the time limit.) I was sure I had lost, but tournament director Will Shortz announced that Philip had two wrong letters, and my solution was completely correct. I had won!

First prize was $500 (not a small sum, especially in those days) and a big championship trophy, both of which were handed to me by puzzledom's grande dame: Margaret Farrar, first crossword editor of the *New York Times*. And it just so happened that *People* magazine was covering the event this year, and so the article that appeared in the magazine a week later was all about ... me!

Clearly, it was my training program that made it all possible. I found out later that I was the first ACPT contestant ever to "go into training" this way, but most definitely not the last. Yes, I was breathing some very rarefied air that weekend. But the best was yet to come.

1982: Contest #3

Inspired by the burgeoning success of the ACPT, Will Shortz convinced his employer, *Games* magazine, to sponsor the first truly nationwide crossword tournament in 1982—the First U.S. Open Crossword Puzzle Championship. More than 10,000 people submitted the qualifying puzzle that appeared in the magazine. All entrants who completed this first puzzle without error were sent four tiebreaker puzzles to solve. Out of those submitting solutions, the top 250 would be invited to the final round in New York City in August.

Naturally, I entered. And, not only did I obtain a coveted invitation to the final round, I was one of only 11 people who completed all four tiebreaker puzzles completely correctly. Naturally, I intensified my training regimen, with two additional wrinkles: I organized two

tournament-like practice sessions with three others who had qualified as contestants; and I stepped up the quantity of difficult themeless puzzles, to gain as much practice as possible in interpreting tricky clues.

The format of the one-day final round was similar to the ACPT—five puzzles of various sizes throughout the day, with a final puzzle for the top three finishers. This time, the finalists would work standing at giant Plexiglas boards on stage, rather than seated at overhead projectors.

Those additional five months of practice, learning hundreds more new words and meanings, undoubtedly raised my solving skills even higher than they were in March. As the preliminary rounds of the event were going on, I could tell things were going well for me. Though 250 of the nation's best crossworders were present, I finished two of those first five puzzles at least a full minute faster than anyone else in the room! And I felt myself to be in complete control accuracy-wise as well.

After a wait of several hours, the top 10 finishers were announced in reverse order. Finally, I heard my name—I was in first place going into the championship round! Even though I had one letter wrong in one of the puzzles (not a careless mistake, just two crossing words I didn't know), what the *Games* article on the tournament later called my "dazzling speed" gave me a substantial lead over the second and third place finishers.

The final puzzle was a themeless toughie, all right, by puzzlemaster Merl Reagle. Luckily for me, it had four not-so-easy words I had just learned in past few months, all of which I filled in right away. While I did get stuck for a few seconds here and there, I completed the puzzle first, with a little time to spare. I called "Done!" and sat down on the edge of the platform—numb and exhausted!

Though I had one letter wrong, the

next-closest finalist had eight wrong, making me the winner. The photographers and press immediately descended upon me. What an experience that was! The moment I best remember: being unable to correctly spell my last name when asked by a CBS-TV reporter. And guess what? That was the bit broadcast nationwide that evening, introduced by anchorman Charles Osgood.

First prize this time was a hefty $1,500, plus a six-foot pencil trophy. Of the two, guess which one I still have?

Aftermath

As Will Shortz himself once put it, in the introduction to my 100th book, "In one year, Stan had gone from being a nobody to a star in the puzzle world." And nobody was more surprised about that than me. But it was gratifying, you can be sure.

After each of my three tournament wins in 1982, I went right back to work at my Wall Street job the following Monday as though nothing had happened. My first tentative steps into the "business end" of puzzles weren't to happen for a little while yet, but none of that would have come to pass if it weren't for what happened to me in 1982.

What I taught myself way back then became the basis of the talks I give today about improving one's crosswording ability, not to mention quite a few *Mind Stretchers* Master Classes on various aspects of puzzle solving. Having helped thousands of people over the years at all levels to get better at it, I know that anyone can do it.

I hope I've given you a little inspiration here to try it for yourself.

—Stanley Newman

★ Nothing to Drink by Sally R. Stein

ACROSS

1 Bath-powder ingredient
5 Walked on
9 Prohibits
13 Black-and-white cookie
14 Garden tool
15 So all can hear
17 Remainder
18 Role model
19 Roadside eatery
20 Toward the right, on a map
21 Ingredient that helps dough rise
23 More than
25 Beginning
26 Types of steaks
29 Feel sorry for
31 Kitchen appliance
32 Ebb
33 Skiing surface
37 Up and about
38 Attila follower
39 Place on a scale
40 Unskilled worker
41 Hug partner
42 Verbal greeting
43 9 EEE or 42 regular
44 Cash in
45 Phase
49 Window glass
50 Sets sail
53 Percussion instrument
57 Expert
58 All the time
59 Barrett of gossip
60 Wide awake
61 Start a card game
62 __ Honor (address for a judge)
63 Former Mach 2 fliers: Abbr.
64 A portion (of)
65 TV award

DOWN

1 Ripped
2 Neck of the woods
3 Not so much
4 Eli Whitney invention
5 Big families
6 Plane tracker
7 "Got it, stop nagging!"
8 Sandwich shop
9 Villain
10 Most favored group
11 Prohibited things
12 Shoe material
16 "Darn it!"
22 Short letter
24 Change course suddenly
26 Ensnare
27 Pedestal bottom
28 Not fooled by
29 DVD-player button
30 Rural hotels
32 Expert, slangily
33 8 Down bread
34 Cleopatra's river
35 Stare at
36 For __ the Bell Tolls
39 A question of time
41 Do-it-yourselfer's buys
43 Aromas
44 Baby's toy
45 __ mater
46 Closes with glue
47 Installs, as a driveway
48 Chris of tennis
49 Kind of tournament
51 Writing tablets
52 Margarine
54 Den or dinette
55 E pluribus __
56 Lamb owner of rhyme

★ Looped Path

Draw a continuous, unbroken loop that passes through each of the red, blue, and white squares exactly once. Move from square to square in a straight line or by turning left or right, but never diagonally. You must alternate passing through red and blue squares, with any number of white squares in between.

CENTURY MARKS

Select one number in each of the four columns so that the total adds up to exactly 100.

Example: $\dfrac{6}{⑧} + \dfrac{⑮}{73} + \dfrac{㊵}{61} + \dfrac{29}{㊲} = 100$

$$\begin{array}{c} 53 \\ \hline 26 \end{array} + \begin{array}{c} 12 \\ \hline 24 \end{array} + \begin{array}{c} 17 \\ \hline 41 \end{array} + \begin{array}{c} 33 \\ \hline 7 \end{array} = 100$$

★ O to Be in England

Find these British place names that are hidden in the diagram, either across, down, or diagonally.

OADBY	ORTON
OAKHAM	OSGODBY
OAKSHOTT	OSSETT
ODDER	OSTERLEY
ODSTOCK	OSWESTRY
OKEHAMPTON	OTFORD
OLDHAM	OTLEY
OLD ROMNEY	OTTERBURN
OLLERTON	OTTERY ST. MARY
OLNEY	OULSTON
ONSLOW	OUNDLE
ORBY	OVER
ORCOP	OVINGTON
	OXFORD
	OXLODE
	OXTON

INITIAL REACTION

Identify the well-known proverb from the first letters in each of its words.
Example: L.B.Y.L. Answer: Look Before You Leap

F. T. F. _____

★ Sudoku

Fill in the blank boxes so that every row, column, and 3x3 box contains all of the numbers 1 to 9.

9	5	0	3	1	6	4	2	7
6	7	1	0	4	9	2	4	3
0	6	3	4	7	5	8	1	2
5	1	9	2	8	3	7	6	4
7	2	6	1	9	4	3	8	5
1	0	4	5	2	7	9	3	6
4	8	7	6	3	1	2	5	9
3	4	2	7	0	8	5	9	1
4	0	5	9	3	2	6	7	8

MIXAGRAMS

Each line contains a five-letter word and a four-letter word that have been mixed together (the order of the letters in each word has not been changed). Unmix the two words on each line and write them in the spaces provided. When you're done, find a two-part answer to the clue by reading down the letter columns in the answers. Example: D A R I U N V E T = DRIVE + AUNT

CLUE: Parting words

B E L V E U N' E T = _ _ _ _ _ + _ _ _ _

M A L I X S I M P = _ _ _ _ _ + _ _ _ _

W A G I N S U T S = _ _ _ _ _ + _ _ _ _

B A S T E C E S H = _ _ _ _ _ + _ _ _ _

★ **Lazy Day** by Gail Grabowski

ACROSS

1 Poisonous snake
4 Discard
9 Very stylish
13 Make a fool of
14 Investigate
15 Round of applause
16 Buffalo's lake
17 Is the boss
18 Household pests
19 Hotel barroom
22 "Roses __ red ..."
23 Elevations: Abbr.
24 Tornado or hurricane
26 Soup server
28 Spine-tingling
32 Numero __
33 401(k) alternative: Abbr.
35 Research room
36 Wineglass feature
37 "I'll take what's left"
41 Sound quality
42 __ Jima
43 Heavy weight
44 Overhead trains
45 Blissful spots
47 Engaged in battle
51 Grownup
53 Meat department abbr.
55 Poem of praise
56 "Comfort food" main course
61 For guys only
62 Small stream
63 Border
64 Solemn vow
65 Throw with force
66 Turn sharply
67 Author Harte
68 Deed holder
69 Proof-of-age items, for short

DOWN

1 __ borealis (northern lights)
2 Added seasonings to
3 Quick look
4 No-fat Jack
5 Vacation on a vessel
6 Breadbasket item
7 Cain's brother
8 Mexican coin
9 Monotonous song
10 Favorite social spots
11 Web surfer's medium
12 Long-term S&L investments
13 Window sticker
20 In that place
21 Place into service
25 May honoree
27 Not prerecorded
29 Pop singer __ John
30 College cheer
31 Skeptic's remark
34 Surrounded by
36 Mailed out
37 Kindergartener's award
38 Protect from heat loss
39 Fleecy female
40 Cook in the oven
41 Herbal brew
45 And so on: Abbr.
46 Part of a jacket
48 Covered with trees
49 Wise sayings
50 Pertain (to)
52 Far from strenuous
54 Bread maker
57 Canyon sound
58 Sketched
59 Not at all nice
60 Strauss of jeans
61 Weep audibly

★ Fences

Connect the dots with vertical or horizontal lines, so that a single loop is formed with no crossings or branches. Each number indicates how many lines surround it; squares with no number may be surrounded by any number of lines.

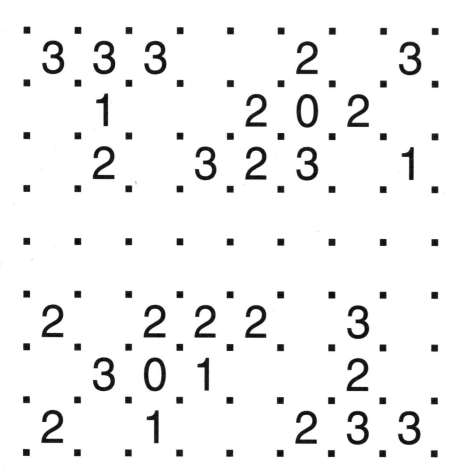

WRONG IS RIGHT

Which of these four words is misspelled?

     A) jinx   B) lynx

     C) larinx   D) minx

★★ Line Drawing

Draw three straight lines, each from one edge of the square to another edge, so that each of the six regions contains a different amount of money.

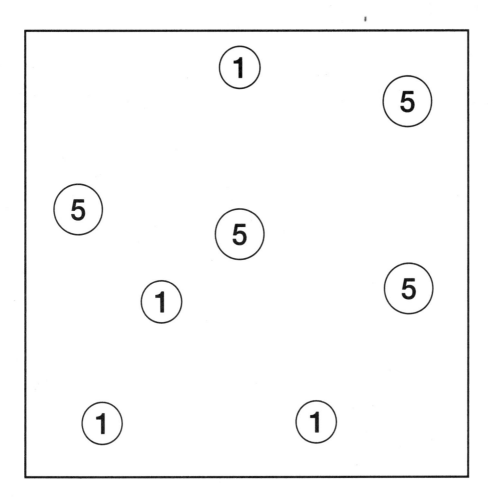

THREE OF A KIND

Find the three hidden words in the sentence that go together in some way.
Example: Chefs were <u>bus</u>ily slicing <u>car</u>rots and <u>cab</u>bage (Answer: bus, car, cab).

A simple answer shows limited thinking ability.

★ Dig In!

Find these culinary words that are hidden in the diagram, either across, down, or diagonally. (FIRST and COURSE are hidden separately.) There's one additional 11-letter answer in the category, not listed below, that's also hidden in the diagram. It's something that every cook needs. What's that word?

```
T E C U A S V L E D I S C C S G
R R N F P O S E I A T S O N E N
A R E Q U U T N G N T O O K R I
R H H S O J N T E E K I U S V T
C N C R S E E M A I T N N A I A
R N T U R E I K N R B A O O N E
O U I O F D D G O S R A B R G M
A L K C N I E P I C E R S L P U
S C O O K E R Y T R A Y G D E A
T U C W P X G S E Y K W A L A S
S U P P E E N G T D F L S T E V
M Z A P F T I U B G A R N I S H
E L O R E S S A C S S H C N U L
A H C O U R S E K I T C H E Z M
L I N G R E D I E N T A P R O O
```

APRON
BREAKFAST
CASSEROLE
CHEF
CONDIMENTS
COOKERY
COOKING
DESSERT
DINNER
EATING
FIRST COURSE
GARNISH
KITCHEN
LUNCH
MEAL
PORTION
RECIPE
ROAST
SALAD
SAUCE
SERVING
SOUP
STEAK
STEW
SUPPER
TRAY
VEGETABLES

WHO'S WHAT WHERE?

The correct term for a resident of Dubuque, Iowa, is:

     A) Dubuquer   B) Dubuquite

     C) Dubuquonian   D) Dubuquian

★ For a Song by Gail Grabowski

ACROSS

1 Wrestling surfaces
5 Young male horse
9 Heelless shoes
14 Margarine
15 At a distance
16 Vowel group
17 Top-ranked
19 À la ___ (menu option)
20 Electrical unit
21 Wild brawl
22 High-class tie
23 Scored 100 on
24 Castro of Cuba
26 Elk's horn
29 Window section
30 Historic time
33 Pan-fry
34 Large coffee vessel
35 Equitable
36 Cone-bearing tree
37 Does damage to
39 Vampire novelist Rice
40 Hardly ___ (rarely)
41 King Kong, for one
42 Lock of 37 Down
43 Teachers' org.
44 Use a dishtowel
45 Something confidential
46 Oyster product
48 Regal address
49 ___ con carne
51 Corrects copy
53 Female deer
56 Minimal amount
57 One bit at a time
59 Golfer Palmer's nickname
60 Shakespeare villain
61 Two-band, as a radio
62 Beau
63 Primary school: Abbr.
64 Flagmaker Betsy

DOWN

1 ___ Lisa
2 College grad
3 Office sub
4 Weep loudly
5 Life's work
6 Days ___ (yore)
7 Country byway
8 Timbered land for commercial use
9 False front
10 Rental agreement
11 Ventilation-system filter
12 Wizard of Oz dog
13 Birdseed ingredient
18 Game-show host
23 Shorten, as slacks
25 Rural stopovers
26 Colorado resort
27 Unsophisticated
28 Adjust the baby grand
29 Blender setting
31 Remove the soapsuds from
32 Take ___ (relax)
35 Mockery
37 Beauty-salon sweeping
38 All-American dessert
42 Briefly stated
44 Restaurant worker
45 Seinfeld or Cheers
47 Borden's cow
48 Military campaign
49 Cat's weapon
50 War honoree
52 Clock face
53 Test-driven vehicle
54 Clumsy ones
55 Shade providers
58 Feb. follower

★ Number-Out

Shade squares so that no number appears in any row or column more than once. Shaded squares may not touch each other horizontally or vertically, and all unshaded squares must form a single continuous area.

4	1	5	5	3
5	4	5	2	4
3	3	1	1	2
5	3	2	1	4
1	3	4	1	5

THINK ALIKE

Unscramble the letters in the phrase BED VIAL to form two words with the same or similar meanings. Example: The letters in BEST RATING can be rearranged to spell START and BEGIN.

_____   _____

★ Pipe Down

Which pipe was laid down in the middle, having the same number of pipes below it as above it?

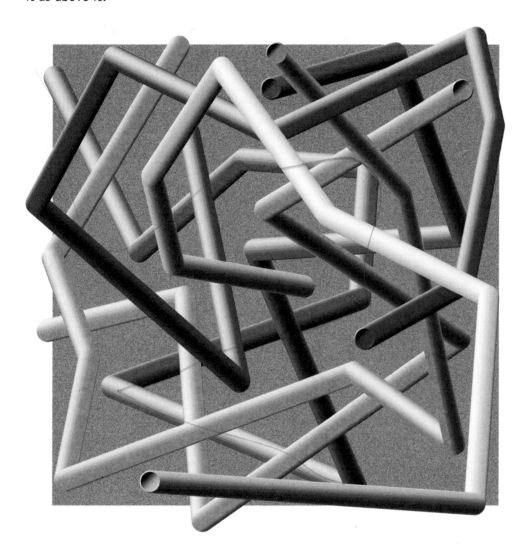

SMALL CHANGE

Change one letter in each of these two words, to form a common two-word phrase.
Example: PANTRY CHEW Answer: PASTRY CHEF

WIDE GUN

★ Theme Park by Sally R. Stein

ACROSS

1 Women's golf org.
5 "Hey, you!"
9 Jeans or slacks
14 Considerably
15 Diminutive suffix
16 Really love
17 Veal or venison
18 Took to court
19 Actress Sophia
20 Chronological records
23 Tiny bit
24 Dictation taker
25 Postage-stamp backing
26 Advanced college degs.
27 Top of the Capitol
29 Ten Commandments obtainer
31 Find a sum
34 Sheet of ice on the sea
36 Devour
39 Treacherous one
43 Less healthy-looking
44 Serene
45 Lab-maze runner
46 Buttes' relatives
49 Demeanor
51 Read electronically
53 City-related, for short
55 Push gently
59 Like the Sahara
60 Genealogy diagrams
62 Author Zola
64 Parcel (out)
65 HS seniors' exams
66 Online message
67 Religious image
68 A Great Lake
69 Group of experts
70 Change for a $20 bill
71 Former fast planes: Abbr.

DOWN

1 End-table light sources
2 Skirt fold
3 Rant and rave
4 Go to, as a class
5 Annoying one
6 Caviar source
7 Take feloniously
8 Boredom
9 Close friends
10 Fuss
11 Bright light in the night sky
12 Tire surface
13 Ships off
21 Top-of-house workers
22 Summer zodiac sign
26 Bosc or Bartlett
28 1051, to Caesar
30 Film clip
31 Poisonous snake
32 Genetic-fingerprint material
33 Firehouse dog, often
35 And so on: Abbr.
37 Country s. of Canada
38 Seattle clock setting: Abbr.
40 Well-sharpened
41 Portrait on 70 Across
42 Inventor Whitney
47 Drs.' group
48 Mountaintop
50 Hospital professionals
51 Ram or lamb
52 List-dividing punctuation mark
54 Sister's daughter
56 Cherished people
57 "Understand?"
58 Double-curve letters
60 Keeled over
61 Cravings
63 Be deceitful

★ One-Way Streets

The diagram represents a pattern of streets. A and B are parking spaces, and the black squares are stores. Find the route that starts at A, passes through all stores exactly once, and ends at B. Arrows indicate one-way traffic for that block only. No block or intersection may be entered more than once.

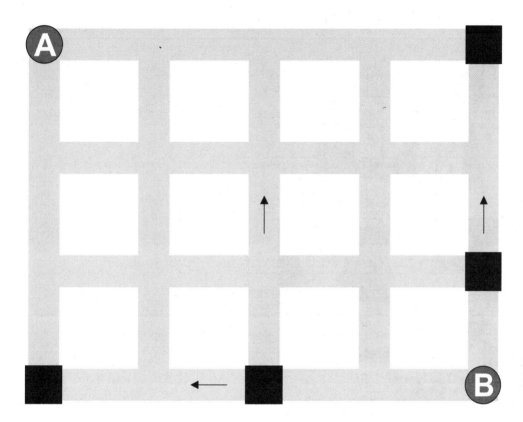

SOUND THINKING

There is only one common uncapitalized word whose consonant sounds are Z, L, and Y, in that order. What is it?

_____

★★ Split Decisions

In this clueless crossword puzzle, each answer consists of two words whose spellings are the same, except for the consecutive letters given. All answers are common words; no phrases or hyphenated words are used. NOTE: Answers include one familiar capitalized word. Some of the clues may have more than one solution, but there is only one word pair that will correctly link up with all the other word pairs.

TRANSDELETION

Delete one letter from the word WHALES and rearrange the rest, to get something to wear.

_____

★ Star Search

Find the stars that are hidden in some of the blank squares. The numbered squares indicate how many stars are hidden in the squares adjacent to them (including diagonally). There is never more than one star in any square.

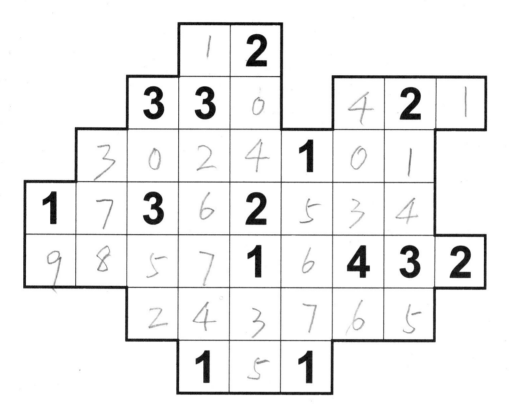

CHOICE WORDS

Form three six-letter words from the same category, by selecting one letter from each column three times. Each letter will be used exactly once.

Example: B A B C O T   Answer: BOBCAT, JAGUAR, OCELOT
          J O E U A R
          O C G L A T

P A P D A N   _ _ _ _ _ _

B O N Y E R   _ _ _ _ _ _

L I N L A N   _ _ _ _ _ _

★★ "Express" Yourself

Try to find these synonyms for various meanings of "express" that are hidden in the diagram either across, down, or diagonally, and you'll find that one of them rushed off and isn't there. What's the missing word?

```
K E F A S S V N M R E V E Z L
C P T H X W E A B Y D E O L V
I R O A C O N V E Y I H E O E
U W E I I I T E T E S T I F T
Q T U V F C U C D E C L A R E
H Q T E E A N N T E L D K A E
P I S E T A L U M R O F S G Y
O T G T R V L O N H S S L F B
T T D H F T L N S E E U I R R
S E E F S I T N C R V T I Q E
N S N L P P W A T I S W I F I
O S O G J A E S D E K S I R B
N A T S A F R E T R A P I D O
M S E F I N A M D E C L A R H
```

ANNOUNCE
ASSERT
BRISK
CONVEY
DECLARE
DENOTE
DISCLOSE
DIVULGE
ENUNCIATE
FAST
FORMULATE
HIGH-SPEED
MANIFEST
NON-STOP
QUICK
RAPID
REVEAL
SHOW
STATE
SWIFT
TELL
TESTIFY
UTTER
VENT

IN OTHER WORDS

There is only one common uncapitalized word that contains the consecutive letters KAC. What is it?

_____

★ Rough Road by Gail Grabowski

ACROSS

1 In need of directions
5 Video-game maker
10 Strikebreaker
14 Competent
15 Not at all interested
16 Marching-band instrument
17 Reaction to a ghost story
19 Flows back
20 Colonist
21 Brit's cavalry sword
22 Young men
23 __ Way galaxy
25 Makes a trade
27 Ali __
28 Was in possession of
31 Backbone
32 Artist's cap
33 Poem of praise
34 Smooch
35 Minimum amount
36 Narrow valley
37 Frozen water
38 Up, on most maps
39 Gets ready, for short
40 Christmas mo.
41 Yours and mine
42 Elaborate meal
43 All set
45 Shortly
46 Reduce drastically, as prices
48 Arctic plains
52 Chest muscles, briefly
53 Stones removed from maraschinos
56 Paul who sang "Puppy Love"
57 Approximately
58 Like __ of bricks
59 Like a snoop
60 June or July
61 Tree fluids

DOWN

1 Falls behind
2 Woodwind instrument
3 Opening for a coin
4 Nuclear-treaty subjects
5 Monks' homes
6 Guided vacations
7 Sleeve filler
8 Sales agent, briefly
9 Proof-of-age items, for short
10 Rib eye or porterhouse
11 Small, snug spaces
12 Etc., for one
13 Military installation
18 Marry secretly
21 Venetian-blind part
23 Wetland
24 Skeptic's remark
25 Cinnamon or ginger
26 Sarcastic remarks
27 Is victorious over
29 Skilled
30 Cozy rooms
31 Lose control on a slippery road
32 Fruit on a bush
35 Noisy
36 Mom and Dad's dads
38 Ark builder
39 Fragrant spring flower
42 __ of July
44 English-class assignment
45 Pompous walk
46 Stretch across
47 Prime-time TV host
49 Actress Hayworth
50 Perched on
51 Some paycheck IDs
53 Machine part
54 TV movie channel
55 Long period of time

★ Hyper-Sudoku

Fill in the blank boxes so that every row, column, 3x3 box, *and* each of the four 3x3 gray regions contains all of the numbers 1 to 9.

6	1	8	9	4	3	7	5	2
7	3	4	2	8	5	9	6	1
2	9	5	8	6	1	3	7	4
9	8	2	7	3	2	5	4	6
3	2	9	4	1	7	6	5	8
1	4	0	6	2	9	7	8	3
5	7	6	3	9	4	1	2	0
	6	0	1	7	8	4	3	5
	5	3	8	0	6	2	4	7

MIXAGRAMS

Each line contains a five-letter word and a four-letter word that have been mixed together (the order of the letters in each word has not been changed). Unmix the two words on each line and write them in the spaces provided. When you're done, find a two-part answer to the clue by reading down the letter columns in the answers.

CLUE: Bus bargain

F I S H R U N G E = _ _ _ _ _ + _ _ _ _

A N A W A T A L Y = _ _ _ _ _ + _ _ _ _

F R I L U S E K E = _ _ _ _ _ + _ _ _ _

A F E T O N E R S = _ _ _ _ _ + _ _ _ _

★★ Slipper

Which numbered picture is the true reflection of Scrooge slipping on the ice?

BETWEENER

What three-letter word belongs between the word at left and the word at right, so that the first and second word, and the second and third word, each form a common compound word?

UPPER __ __ __ BACK

★ 123

Fill in the diagram so that each rectangular piece has one each of the numbers 1, 2, and 3, under these rules: 1) No two adjacent squares, horizontally or vertically, can have the same number. 2) Each completed row and column of the diagram will have an equal number of 1s, 2s, and 3s.

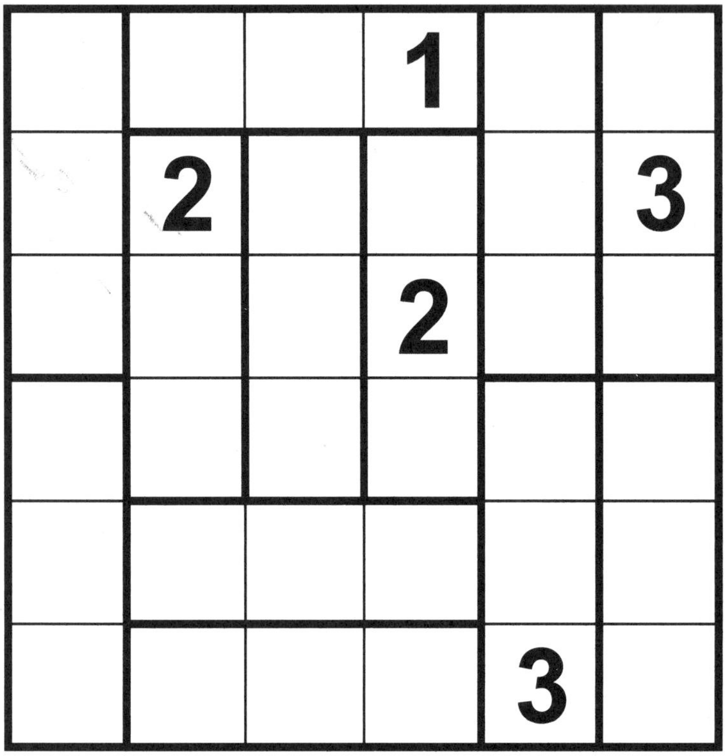

			1		
	2				**3**
			2		
				3	

SUDOKU SUM

Fill in the missing numbers from 1 to 9, so that the sum of each row and column is as indicated.

EXAMPLE

	12	14	19
6			3
17	6		
22		8	

ANSWER

	12	14	19
6	1	2	3
17	6	4	7
22	5	8	9

	15	12	18
10	5		
20		9	
15			8

★ No Kidding by Sally R. Stein

ACROSS

1 Donkey sound
5 Hive dwellers
9 Out of whack
14 Make simpler
15 Jane Austen novel
16 Last baseball inning, usually
17 Wicked
18 Quantities: Abbr.
19 From the sun
20 *Survivor* or *The Apprentice*
23 __ out a living
24 Belittle, slangily
25 Made a home, as a hawk
27 Tried to rip open
31 Despicable one
33 From Dublin
34 Be a nag
35 Scandinavian capital
39 Situation's essential truth
42 Dog pest
43 Laundry appliance
44 Donald Duck nephew
45 Piece of dinette furniture
47 Bearlike zoo beasts
48 Erase
51 Recruiting-poster Uncle
52 Ecology agcy.
53 "Honestly ..."
60 Must, slangily
62 Crowd sound
63 Diva's performance
64 Intermission follower
65 63 Across, for example
66 Tie tightly
67 Luster
68 Business envelope abbr.
69 Is a spectator at

DOWN

1 Beverage on tap
2 Enthusiastic review
3 Where India is
4 Scream
5 "Get lost!"
6 Television awards
7 CPR experts
8 Wide belt
9 Exam-sheet entry
10 *"O Sole __"*
11 Small bay
12 Amount bet
13 Destroy, as documents
21 It's east of Oregon
22 Lunch time, at times
26 Exactly right, to a Brit
27 Spat
28 Type of vaccine
29 Cereal grain
30 Many-acred residence
31 Nevada/California lake
32 Small songbird
34 Computer-keyboard key
36 Cuff link alternative
37 *Star Wars* princess
38 Miner's discoveries
40 __-optic cable
41 San Antonio attraction
46 Reach, as a goal
47 Store customer
48 French painter Edgar
49 Historical period
50 Coffeehouse order
51 Ten Commandments verb
54 __ Major (Big Dipper)
55 Car-horn sound
56 Keep __ on (watch)
57 Cleveland's lake
58 Poem unit
59 Young fellows
61 All-even game

★ ABC

Enter the letters A, B, and C into the diagram so that each row and column has exactly one A, one B, and one C. The letters outside the diagram indicate the first letter encountered, moving in the direction of the arrow. Keep in mind that after all the letters have been filled in, there will be one blank box in each row and column.

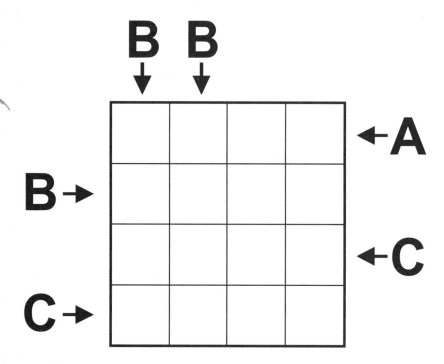

CLUELESS CROSSWORD

Complete the crossword with common uncapitalized seven-letter words, based entirely on the letters already filled in for you.

★ Find the Ships

Determine the position of the 10 ships listed to the right of the diagram. The ships may be oriented either horizontally or vertically. A square with wavy lines indicates water and will not contain a ship. The numbers at the edge of the diagram indicate how many squares in that row or column contain parts of ships. When all 10 ships are correctly placed in the diagram, no two of them will touch each other, not even diagonally.

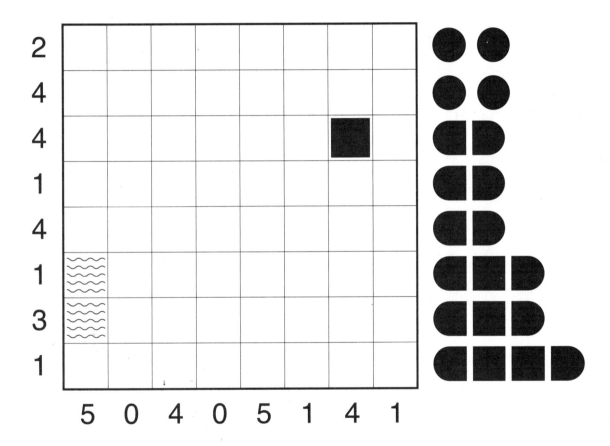

TWO-BY-FOUR

The eight letters in the word QUIVERED can be rearranged to form a pair of common four-letter words in only one way, if no four-letter word is repeated. Can you find the two words?

— — — —   — — — —

★ Bright Lights

Find the names of these famous thinkers that are hidden in the diagram, either across, down, or diagonally.

```
A N I K W A D E D G M L H C A M
E R E P M A A I N N E N E J U J
N E W T O N V R E I R I N B O I
Z N E R O L Y U S E C V G U O L
R E P E P L U C N T A L L E I N
C O P E R N I C U S T E W N R N
P H U B B L E H B N O K N L E F
D A E C A L V I N I R A E G B L
A S S T S H O P B E E R T R O E
R N G T L Y L P C U E N A H P M
W I N P E U T A S U O H Z A M I
I K I L N U A R Q R E L P E K N
N W L A O Y R C L U M I E R E G
O A U N B H E H U Y A D A R A F
H D A C Q B M U D O P P L E R M
V O P K L E N S E R F H E R T Z
```

AMPÈRE
BECQUEREL
BRAHE
BUNSEN
CALVIN
COPERNICUS
CULPEPER
CURIE
DARWIN
DAVY
DAWKINS
DOPPLER
EINSTEIN
FARADAY
FLEMING
FOUCAULT
FRESNEL
GEIGER
HALLEY

HERTZ
HIPPARCHUS
HUBBLE
JOULE
KELVIN
KEPLER
LINNAEUS
LORENZ
LUMIÈRE
MACH
MERCATOR
NEWTON
NOBEL
OHM
PASTEUR
PAULING
PLANCK
RÖNTGEN
VOLTA

INITIAL REACTION

Identify the well-known proverb from the first letters in each of its words.

S. W. R. D. _____

★ Spring Gardening by Gail Grabowski

ACROSS

1 Flat-topped elevation
5 Hawaiian garlands
9 Escapade
14 Historical times
15 In addition
16 Residence
17 Lamp-socket insert
19 Used an oar
20 Golf-ball platform
21 Is an omen of
22 Smooths (out)
23 Tiresome speaker
24 Spud
26 Car motor
29 Floor-washing implements
30 Workstation machines, for short
33 Glanced (at)
34 Mine product
35 Chimney duct
36 Diarist __ Frank
37 Chinese-restaurant sauce
38 Uncommon
39 Sock parts
40 Advanced degree: Abbr.
41 Gift-giver's request
43 Superlative suffix
44 Pod vegetables
45 "Am not!" retort
46 Hr. after noon
48 Slip and slide
49 Does modeling work
51 Auto-club suggestion
53 Hosp. workers
56 Bring to bear
57 Go beyond, as a target
59 Christopher of *Superman*
60 Formally transfer
61 Italian wine region

62 Below
63 Leg joint
64 Psychic reader

DOWN

1 Thaw
2 One of the Great Lakes
3 Wise person
4 Campfire residue
5 Worked hard
6 Evade
7 Spot of land in the sea
8 Tearful tale
9 Insertion marks

10 Higher than
11 Electricity source
12 Biblical paradise
13 Crimson and scarlet
18 Steakhouse selection
23 Two-wheelers
25 King Kong, for one
26 Fill with joy
27 Forbidden acts
28 Deteriorated
29 States of mind
31 Antique-shop collectible
32 Take care of

35 Released
37 Irish emblem
40 Energy
41 Acorn producer
42 Uses a lever
44 Annoy
47 Coward's lack
48 Jacket material
49 Lima's country
50 Yoked animals
52 Pizzeria appliance
53 Valentine's Day flower
54 Brief memo
55 Recipe direction
58 Owns

★ Sequence Maze

Enter the maze at top, pass through all the squares exactly once, then exit,
all without retracing your path.

SMALL CHANGE

Change one letter in each of these two words, to form a common two-word phrase.

HOW NEAT

★ Fences

Connect the dots with vertical or horizontal lines, so that a single loop is formed with no crossings or branches. Each number indicates how many lines surround it; squares with no number may be surrounded by any number of lines.

```
0    1         2
2 3           3 3
        3 2 3     2
3 3               2
1               2 3
2     1 3 0
2 1             3 2
  2         2   3
```

★ Play It Again

All these words hidden in the diagram either across, down, or diagonally, pertain to a well-known play, whose title is also hidden in the diagram.

```
Y M C I R O Y R F V K G E E N D O J
I O O G H O S X S R U T G C U B I I
G E R T R U D E U I A N E E N R T L
D T N I C A S T L E E N F L S I A E
E R E Q C U E D L V F F C O M S R H
N A L S D K E L E K I N G I A A O P
M G I Z T N A R C N E S O R S F H O
A E U G S E E L R Q C L B S E C D B
R D S T R Y A O A K I N D U A L O E
K Y E T N U Y I M F I Y J I A C P R
I R E A D G V O L T E M A N D I T N
N S L I S C H P R E A U Y O F R A A
W D U Y A W R O N X H E H L E S R R
W S O H G H F G S I R P M O U O O D
E R O N I S L E Z T K E O P V T H O
```

BERNARDO
CASTLE
CLAUDIUS
CORNELIUS
DENMARK
ELSINORE
FEUD
FORTINBRAS
FRANCISCO
GERTRUDE
GHOST
GUILDENSTERN
HORATIO
KING
LAERTES
MARCELLUS
NORWAY
OPHELIA
OSRIC
POLONIUS
PRINCE
REVENGE
REYNALDO
ROSENCRANTZ
TRAGEDY
VOLTEMAND
YORICK

WHO'S WHAT WHERE?

The correct term for a resident of the U.S. territory of Guam is:

A) Guamite   B) Guamero

C) Guamanian   D) Guaman

★ Patriotic Fish by Sally R. Stein

ACROSS

1 Cookie's chocolate morsel
5 Unsuccessful film
9 D sharp's alias
14 The Dalai __
15 Eve's second son
16 Portion of pizza
17 African snakes
18 Acting job
19 Sentence-clauses separator
20 Proofreading notation
21 Popular seafood selection
23 King's residence
25 Have an evening meal
26 Lotion additive
29 Use the microwave, maybe
34 British nobles
38 "That's too bad!"
40 Opera solo
41 *Jaws* menace
44 Hidden valley
45 Sedan or station wagon
46 No longer in fashion
47 Very serious
49 Poet Pound
51 An hour after noon
53 Zealous
58 Large sport fish
64 Sandwich-cookie name
65 Airplane walkway
66 Take a chance with
67 Type of vaccine
68 Varnish ingredient
69 Fashion mag
70 Repetitive learning method
71 Pop, as a balloon
72 Turned to blonde
73 Mailbox opening

DOWN

1 Hold tightly
2 "__ la vista!"
3 Urge forward
4 Ziti or spaghetti
5 Large beer container
6 Woodwind instrument
7 Card-game grouping
8 Sanctify
9 Make a getaway
10 Unsuccessful film
11 Like a wet dishrag
12 High point
13 Rip
22 Hospital professional
24 Acting group
27 Honolulu's locale
28 Privileged group
30 "Very funny!"
31 Historical periods
32 Ventilates
33 Subtract, with "away"
34 Henhouse products
35 Singer Guthrie
36 Fishing-line holder
37 Narrow street
39 From __ (completely)
42 "I don't __ go!" (kid's protest)
43 Practice for a boxing match
48 Unspecific brief period
50 Placed in order
52 Made a blunder
54 Entryways
55 Actor Flynn
56 "Swell!"
57 Apartment sign
58 Stinging remark
59 In __ of (instead of)
60 Khrushchev's country: Abbr.
61 Yale students
62 Easter flower
63 Cruise-ship stop, often

★ Sudoku

Fill in the blank boxes so that every row, column, and 3x3 box contains all of the numbers 1 to 9.

0	2	8	9	3	4	1	3	5
1	4	3	5	6	8	9	2	7
7	1	9	3	2	0	4	6	8
6	3	4	2	1	7	5	9	3
1	8	5	9	3	6	7	4	2
2	6	1	6	4	7	2	5	9
3	9	2	7	8	0	6	1	4
4	5	6	2	9	3	8	7	1
9	4	7	1	5	2	3	8	6

MIXAGRAMS

Each line contains a five-letter word and a four-letter word that have been mixed together (the order of the letters in each word has not been changed). Unmix the two words on each line and write them in the spaces provided. When you're done, find a two-part answer to the clue by reading down the letter columns in the answers.

CLUE: Newspaper area

F O R C E A L A D = _ _ _ _ _ + _ _ _ _

W A X H O O P L E = _ _ _ _ _ + _ _ _ _

B R E I P E A L S = _ _ _ _ _ + _ _ _ _

M A L E Y A K O R = _ _ _ _ _ + _ _ _ _

★ 123

Fill in the diagram so that each rectangular piece has one each of the numbers 1, 2, and 3, under these rules: 1) No two adjacent squares, horizontally or vertically, can have the same number. 2) Each completed row and column of the diagram will have an equal number of 1s, 2s, and 3s.

2	4	5	6	7	8
4	5	**3**	7	8	**1**
1	2	4	3	9	7
3	1	6	4	**1**	5
5	6	7	**2**	3	4
6	**3**	9	8	4	**3**

ADDITION SWITCH

Switch the positions of two of the digits in the incorrect sum at right, to get a correct sum.

Example: 955+264 = 411. Switch the second 1 in 411 with the 9 in 955 to get: 155+264 = 419

```
  435
+ 291
-----
  836
```

★ LP Collection by Gail Grabowski

ACROSS

1 Thorny flower
5 Wild guess
9 Some young horses
14 Creme-filled cookie
15 Something prohibited
16 Luau greeting
17 Backyard bash
19 Opponent
20 Overhead railroads
21 Formal ceremonies
22 Major happening
23 Piece of kitchen flooring
24 Nestling's noise
26 Narrow valleys
28 Lion's sound
29 Early afternoon hour
32 Highest part of a wave
33 Not at home
34 Perched on
35 Emcee
36 Skydiver's need, for short
38 Low-calorie, in product names
39 Simple
40 Sombrero, for example
41 Boutique or grocery
42 L-P link
43 Identical
44 Alan Ladd western
45 Gets closer to
47 Keg contents
48 Answer a Help Wanted ad
50 "Go fly __!"
52 Auto-club offering
55 Type of race
56 Full retail cost
58 Angry
59 Hand-cream ingredient
60 Gumbo veggie
61 Desert mounds
62 Fully cooked
63 Wall-calendar line

DOWN

1 Actor's part
2 Verbal
3 Puts in a hem
4 Long period of time
5 Slow-moving mollusks
6 Rich cake
7 Poker-hand starter
8 Merit-badge wearer
9 Life's work
10 Martini garnish
11 Magical romantic brew
12 As compared to
13 Pretzel topping
18 Write with block letters
23 Short-tempered
25 Despise
26 Reaction to a bad joke
27 Teacher's guideline
28 Auto-club suggestion
30 __ Dame (Indiana university)
31 Fencing weapon
32 HS science course
34 Church platform
36 Scorch
37 Sandwich filler
41 Woolly animal
43 Give one's permission
44 Small sofa
46 Fill with joy
47 American buffalo
48 Bone-dry
49 Lima's country
51 Prefix meaning "thousand"
52 Emcee's need
53 Land measurement
54 Mountaintop
57 Use an oar

★ One-Way Streets

The diagram represents a pattern of streets. A and B are parking spaces, and the black squares are stores. Find the route that starts at A, passes through all stores exactly once, and ends at B. Arrows indicate one-way traffic for that block only. No block or intersection may be entered more than once.

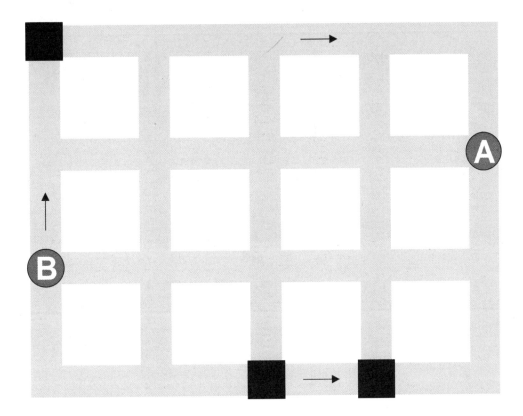

SOUND THINKING

The longest common uncapitalized word whose consonant sounds are B, K, and T, in that order, has seven letters. What is it?

★ Missing Links

Find the three rings that are linked together, but linked to no others on the page.

SAY IT AGAIN

What three-letter word can be either a "polite" verb or a part of a ship?

— — —

★ Star Search

Find the stars that are hidden in some of the blank squares. The numbered squares indicate how many stars are hidden in the squares adjacent to them (including diagonally). There is never more than one star in any square.

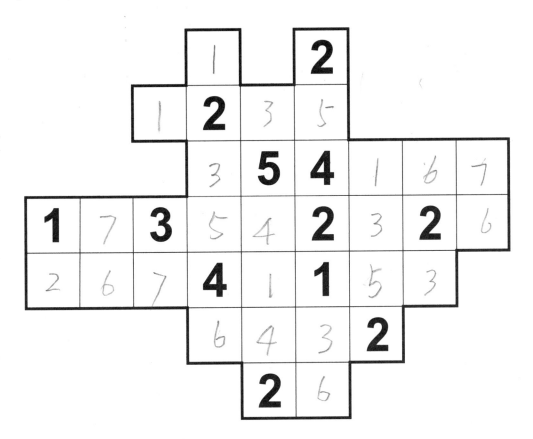

CHOICE WORDS

Form three six-letter words from the same category, by selecting one letter from each column three times. Each letter will be used exactly once.

```
O   A   N   A   O   I     _ _ _ _ _ _
K   R   W   G   A   N     _ _ _ _ _ _
H   A   E   S   I   S     _ _ _ _ _ _
```

★ Capital Idea by Sherry S. Lucas

ACROSS

1 Mama's spouse
5 Young male horse
9 Desirable quality
14 "Very sorry!"
15 Opera solo
16 Intent look
17 Midwest state capital
20 Go in
21 Competent
22 Sparrow's home
23 Gas used in store signs
25 Cozy
27 Fully attentive
30 By way of
32 Minor quake
36 Actress Thurman
37 Takes in some sun
39 Prepare, as pizza cheese
40 Midwest state capital
43 Frogs' relatives
44 Strait-laced
45 Obviously embarrassed
46 Completed, as a crossword
48 Germane
49 Well ventilated
50 Auction-sale condition
52 Annoying one
54 Graceful bird
57 53, in old Rome
59 Epic tale by Homer
63 Midwest state capital
66 Autumn flower
67 __ Major (Big Dipper)
68 Skinny
69 The ones close by
70 Third son of Adam
71 Perfect scores in gymnastics

DOWN

1 Lose color
2 Actor Alda
3 Breathe quickly
4 Agreement
5 Tuna or soup holder
6 Life forms
7 Arm or leg
8 Coin-toss call
9 Campfire residue
10 "Business ends" of bees
11 Wise person
12 Important periods
13 Circus structure
18 Angry emotion
19 Penny
24 Roundish shape
26 Pressed for
27 Corrodes, as metal
28 "Are not!" response
29 Concerning Benedict XVI
31 Dog originally from Japan
33 New Zealand native
34 Aquatic mammal
35 All set
37 Mass-transit vehicles
38 Most lively
41 Moves forward
42 Evening, on marquees
47 Pickle flavoring
49 Finally
51 Nasal cavity
53 Title for Lancelot
54 Chair piece
55 What a genie might grant
56 Poker-hand starter
58 Concerning, in memos
60 Aruba or Maui
61 Similar
62 River blockers
64 Miner's find
65 "__, humbug!"

★ Let's Get Together

Find these "group" words that are hidden in the diagram, either across, down, or diagonally.

```
H G N B G S E S S I O V D S M
I A E O N C S M A S S R N X J
P V R G I E F A S S E M B L Y
Y O A V R T M T E H G R O U A
B N R G E O N T D W O R C B Q
K A N C H S H E E R O B M A J
M O N C T R T N V G N O R H T
C E N D A U S D F N N O M Y M
E U E B G E G A L M O H E R R
B D B T M B N N O L I C E H A
C L R B I A A C C D S T T U W
E R L O E N G E K D S M I D S
H E R W H T G D R U E O N D B
C O M P A N Y O L H S P Z L A
L S E R G N O C G R O U P E M
```

ASSEMBLY
ATTENDANCE
BAND
BEVY
BUNCH
CLUSTER
COMPANY
CONGRESS
CONVENTION
CROP
CROWD
ENSEMBLE
FLOCK
GANG
GATHERING
GROUP
HARVEST
HERD
HORDE
HUDDLE
JAMBOREE
MASS
MEETING
MOB
RABBLE
SESSION
SWARM
THRONG

IN OTHER WORDS

Not counting ALBS (the church vestments), there is only one common uncapitalized word that contains the consecutive letters LBS. What is it?

_____

bRain BREAtHer
R_X FOR REDUCING HOSPITAL ERRORS

A 1999 report found that between 50,000 and 100,000 Americans die in hospitals each year, not from the medical conditions they checked in for, but from preventable medical errors. Below are recommendations from the Agency for Healthcare Research and Quality for things patients can do to reduce medical errors, both in and out of the hospital.

Be an active member of your health care team When your doctor hands you a prescription or says you need surgery, don't just nod. Question everything, including the results of pertinent studies and your doctor's experience doing your particular procedure.

Make sure all your doctors know everything you're taking—including prescription drugs, OTC meds, vitamin and herb supplements, *and any illegal drugs.* Don't worry—your doctor is bound by confidentiality rules not to disclose the information to anyone.

Always ask for detailed info about any medications that are prescribed Make sure to ask: What's this medicine for? How do I take it and for how long? What are likely side effects? What do I do if they occur? Is this medicine safe to take with my other meds and supplements? What food, drink, and/or activities should I avoid while taking this medicine?

If you're having surgery, be sure that you, your doctor, and your surgeon agree on exactly what will be done For example, the American Academy of Orthopedic Surgeons urges its members to initial the surgery site—say, your left knee—and then double-check that it's correct.

When your doctor writes you a prescription, make sure you can read it If you can, the pharmacist probably can, too—reducing the chance of medication errors.

Make sure you understand medication labels For example, does "four doses daily" mean a dose every six hours or just during regular waking hours?

If you have a test, don't assume that no news is good news If you don't hear from your doctor, get in touch with him/her and ask for the results.

When you're discharged from the hospital, ask about your treatment plan, including, in particular, details about the meds you'll be taking and precise instructions about when you can resume your regular activities.

Make sure that there's one person, such as your primary care doctor, who's in overall charge of your care This is especially important if you have many health problems or are in the hospital.

Ask a family member or close friend to be with you at the hospital and to act as your advocate (someone who can help get things done and speak up for you if you can't).

★★ Line Drawing

Draw three straight lines, each from one edge of the square to another edge, so that the words in each of the four regions have something in common.

TEARS

RATES

CARTE

STARE   REACT

ASTER

CARET

CRATE

TRACE

CATER

TIERS

TRIES

RITES

TIRES

STEER

TREES   RESET

THREE OF A KIND

Find the three hidden words in the sentence that go together in some way.

On a whim, I learned another theme song.

★ ABC

Enter the letters A, B, and C into the diagram so that each row and column has exactly one A, one B, and one C. The letters outside the diagram indicate the first letter encountered, moving in the direction of the arrow. Keep in mind that after all the letters have been filled in, there will be one blank box in each row and column.

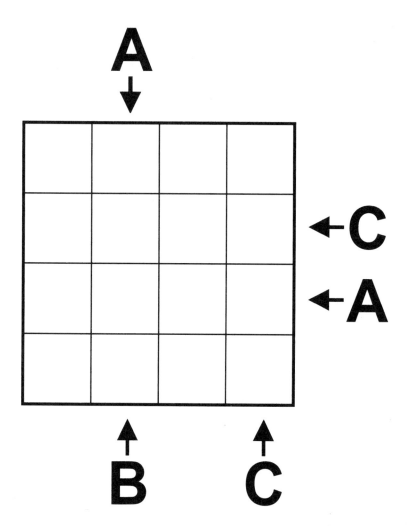

NATIONAL TREASURE

Of the common uncapitalized six-letter words that can be formed from the letters in BELGIAN, only one is an adjective. What is it?

__ __ __ __ __ __

★ Celebrities of the Month by Sally R. Stein

ACROSS

1 What cowboys call ladies
5 Retired fast planes: Abbr.
9 Panama waterway
14 Spheroid hairdo
15 Lotion additive
16 Make joyful
17 Letterhead symbol
18 Fence opening
19 Allow entry
20 *Little Women* author
23 Dictation taker
24 Volcanic outflow
25 Wide gap
28 Alexander __ Bell
33 24-hr. cash source
36 Minestrone and chicken noodle
39 Nebraska neighbor
40 "Lonely" guy of TV commercials
44 Albacore, for one
45 Reject
46 Center of a hurricane
47 Puts on, as a play
50 Poor grades
52 Scent detector
55 Group of mountains
59 Minnesota clinic founders
65 Great disorder
66 Raucous
67 Chimps and gorillas
68 Fully awake
69 __-European (language group)
70 Hourly charge
71 Improves, as one's muscles
72 Fabric worker
73 Word of regret

DOWN

1 Shopping centers
2 In progress
3 Bicker
4 Sounding like a cow
5 Epic story
6 Door-shutting sound
7 Sum
8 Informal farewell
9 Basement
10 Actor Baldwin
11 US alliance
12 Take a crack __
13 Gave temporarily
21 March king John Philip
22 Student's stat.
26 Captain's journal
27 Mink and sable
29 Atmosphere
30 At one's residence
31 Not at one's residence
32 Horse's hair
33 Quantities: Abbr.
34 Fully stretched
35 Talking bird
37 Vigor
38 Potato, slangily
41 "You're it!" game
42 Exist
43 Not moving
48 Makes into law
49 __ sauce (Chinese condiment)
51 African desert
53 Three-dimensional
54 Black hardwood
56 Himalayan land
57 Garbo of films
58 Slalom curves
59 The one over there
60 Angelic topper
61 Having a smooth surface
62 Additional
63 Far from polite
64 Aroma

★★ Five by Five

Group the 25 numbers in the grid into five sets of five, with each set having all of the numbers 1 through 5. The numbers in each set must all be connected to each other by a common horizontal or vertical side.

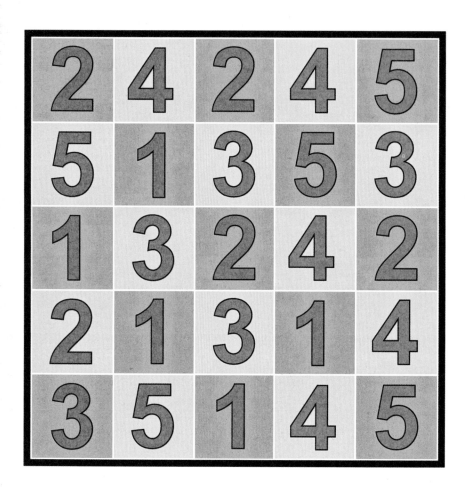

BETWEENER

What three-letter word belongs between the word at left and the word at right, so that the first and second word, and the second and third word, each form a common compound word?

TIP _ _ _ NAIL

★ Health Spa Whodunit

Solve this mystery by discovering which one of these six suspects, six weapons, and six locations is missing from the diagram. The others are all hidden either across, down, or diagonally. The individual words of all multiple-word answers are hidden separately. Ignore words contained within parentheses.

DIEGO (the) DIETITIAN	ACUPUNCTURE NEEDLE	COUCH
HERMIONE (the) HERBALIST	BATHROBE BELT	POOL
HOMER (the) HOMEOPATH	ESSENTIAL OIL VIAL	RESTAURANT
MARCIA (the) MASSEUSE	FORK	SAUNA
OSBORNE (the) OSTEOPATH	POISONED GREEN TEA	SHOWER
RALPH (the) REFLEXOLOGIST	TOWEL	TREATMENT ROOM

```
V V L V N A D L G W T H P O I S O N E D L
I I I O N O I J H R N E T O W E M H Y A R
A A A U O O E N A O E A I A S H O R C I T
I L A T V P T U H F M K R H P M O U O S E
E S S E N T I A L M T E N U E O P M I F S
T N A R U A T S E R A E O O A U E L E E U
O E E L A R I N B U E R P P N T A T N R E
M S F E S O A X E D R A C C A B S O S S S
A O B W F B N Z L E T O T I R T I E H O S
R I N O I M R E H D R U F E G M H O R P A
C C R T R D I E G O R G H A R E W O H S M
I K S A U N R T R E A T M E N E O B S O O
A M O O R N E E D L V O H T Q P O E T S O
```

INITIAL REACTION

Identify the well-known proverb from the first letters in each of its words.

N. P. N. G. _____

★ Find the Ships

Determine the position of the 10 ships listed to the right of the diagram. The ships may be oriented either horizontally or vertically. A square with wavy lines indicates water and will not contain a ship. The numbers at the edge of the diagram indicate how many squares in that row or column contain parts of ships. When all 10 ships are correctly placed in the diagram, no two of them will touch each other, not even diagonally.

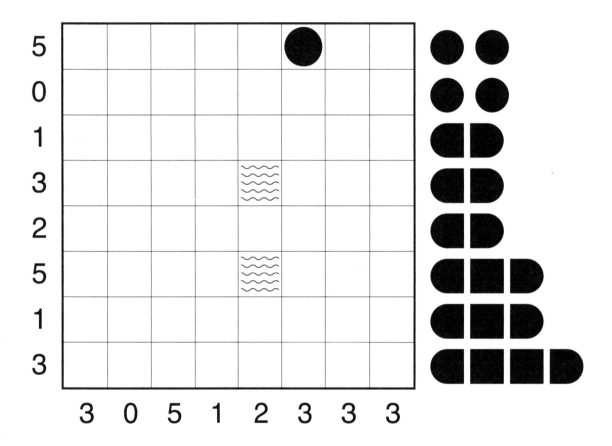

TWO-BY-FOUR

The eight letters in the word RAPIDITY can be rearranged to form a pair of common four-letter words in two different ways, if no four-letter word is repeated. Can you find both pairs of words?

— — — —   — — — —

— — — —   — — — —

★★ Sudoku

Fill in the blank boxes so that every row, column, and 3x3 box contains all of the numbers 1 to 9.

	1					4		
6			2	4	7		3	
				9		6		5
	4		9				6	
	5	2				9	8	
	7				5	2		
4		7		2				
	8		6	7	1			3
		3					5	

MIXAGRAMS

Each line contains a five-letter word and a four-letter word that have been mixed together (the order of the letters in each word has not been changed). Unmix the two words on each line and write them in the spaces provided. When you're done, find a two-part answer to the clue by reading down the letter columns in the answers.

CLUE: Crab

F I N O C C H U S = _ _ _ _ _ + _ _ _ _

P L O T U T O R E = _ _ _ _ _ + _ _ _ _

C O B L E T O R A = _ _ _ _ _ + _ _ _ _

S P I M E L C E D = _ _ _ _ _ + _ _ _ _

★ Influential by Gail Grabowski

ACROSS

1 Balance-sheet item
6 Opera highlight
10 Heavy weights
14 __ con carne
15 "Me neither!"
16 Something hilarious
17 Car-engine measure
19 Prefix for freeze
20 Lamb's mom
21 Zeus and Apollo
22 Outdoor-chair material
24 Superhero's garment
25 Fishhook attachment
26 Words on a dirty car
29 Stuffed pasta
32 Lauder of cosmetics
33 Birthday-party dessert
34 Poison-ivy reaction
36 Pilots' announcements: Abbr.
37 Night before
38 Heap
39 Hit, as with hailstones
40 Snow glider
41 Piano technician
42 Sends again, as a letter
44 Young hooters
45 Remove, as a knot
46 "Neato!"
47 Virtuous
50 Has an evening meal
51 Lawn material
54 College military org.
55 Swimming method
58 Verbal exam
59 Spiny houseplant
60 Squirrel snack
61 Walk in water
62 Lab-maze runners
63 Rushed toward

DOWN

1 Feel sore
2 Broadway production
3 Regal address
4 Overhead trains
5 Reason for extra innings
6 Battery terminal
7 Lines of theater seats
8 Anger
9 Broadcasting signal
10 County-fair contest
11 Pigpen sound
12 Brief letter
13 Recipe direction
18 Vatican City leader
23 Three, on a sundial
24 Pec, more formally
25 Used the oven
26 Sob
27 Late-blooming flower
28 No longer fresh
29 Rants and __
30 Singer Frankie
31 Tiny spot of land
33 Stringed instrument
35 That woman's
40 Private courtroom conference
41 Like a so-so movie rating
43 Pantry pest
44 "How clumsy of me!"
46 Pickled veggies
47 Cornfield bird
48 Israeli dance
49 Just slightly
50 Glasgow native
51 Any minute now
52 Cajun vegetable
53 Fender-bender result
56 Pie __ mode
57 Zenith competitor

★ Fences

Connect the dots with vertical or horizontal lines, so that a single loop is formed with no crossings or branches. Each number indicates how many lines surround it; squares with no number may be surrounded by any number of lines.

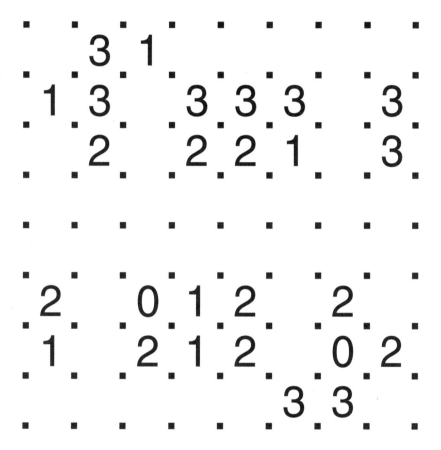

★★ Triad Split Decisions

In this clueless crossword puzzle, each answer consists of two words whose spellings are the same, except for the consecutive letters given. All answers are common words; no phrases or hyphenated or capitalized words are used. Some of the clues may have more than one solution, but there is only one word pair that will correctly link up with all the other word pairs.

TRANSDELETION

Delete one letter from the word RERUNS and rearrange the rest, to get an occupation.

_____

★ 123

Fill in the diagram so that each rectangular piece has one each of the numbers 1, 2, and 3, under these rules: 1) No two adjacent squares, horizontally or vertically, can have the same number. 2) Each completed row and column of the diagram will have an equal number of 1s, 2s, and 3s.

					2
			2		
		3			3
1					

SUDOKU SUM

Fill in the missing numbers from 1 to 9, so that the sum of each row and column is as indicated.

	14	17	14
10			1
18		4	
17	2		

★ Hankerings by Gail Grabowski

ACROSS

1 Chinese-food staple
5 Health resorts
9 Tea variety
14 Fan-mail recipient
15 Payment method
16 Fencing move
17 Whine and complain
19 On __ (winning)
20 Unhappy
21 Playful aquatic mammal
22 Short messages
23 Cashews and pecans
24 Most minuscule
26 Higher than
28 Horn sound
29 "Absolutely!"
32 Keen-witted
33 Finished first
34 Whitish gemstone
35 __ story (biography)
36 Coffee-to-go topper
37 All-knowing
38 Environmental science: Abbr.
39 Stovetop vessel
40 Acquired a tan
42 "__ the land of the free ..."
43 Small taste
44 Prepare to propose
45 Fill with joy
47 Ponytail material
48 Shoe parts
50 Actor George C.
52 Words from the sponsor
55 States openly
56 New bride and groom's trip
58 Granter of wishes
59 More than
60 Prefix for social
61 Uneasy feeling
62 Ties the knot

63 Annoying one

DOWN

1 Barbecue favorites
2 Creative thought
3 Like Antarctica
4 Letter after kay
5 Toss randomly, as seeds
6 Treaties
7 Tennis great Arthur
8 Robin Hood's forest
9 Venus or Mars
10 Italian coins
11 Paneling wood
12 Make eyes at
13 Electrified swimmers
18 "__ got to be kidding!"
23 Fictional work
25 Very long time
26 Wonderland girl
27 Pretty soon
28 Packing string
30 Artist's stand
31 Winter vehicle
32 Nile queen, for short
34 Deed holder
36 TV program for night owls

39 Center of a peach
40 Ice Capades performers
41 Togetherness
43 Long-eared hound
46 Clark's exploration partner
47 Sharpened
48 Lengthy story
49 Baking appliance
51 Sheltered inlet
52 Top-notch
53 Round specks
54 Grumpy mood
57 Traveler's guide

★ Number-Out

Shade squares so that no number appears in any row or column more than once. Shaded squares may not touch each other horizontally or vertically, and all unshaded squares must form a single continuous area.

3	2	5	1	1
5	2	4	5	1
4	2	2	5	3
3	5	1	5	4
1	3	3	4	5

THINK ALIKE

Unscramble the letters in the phrase BAGEL RIG to form two words with the same or similar meanings.

_____   _____

★ No Three in a Row

Enter the maze, pass through all the squares exactly once, then exit, all without retracing your path. You may not pass through three squares of the same color consecutively.

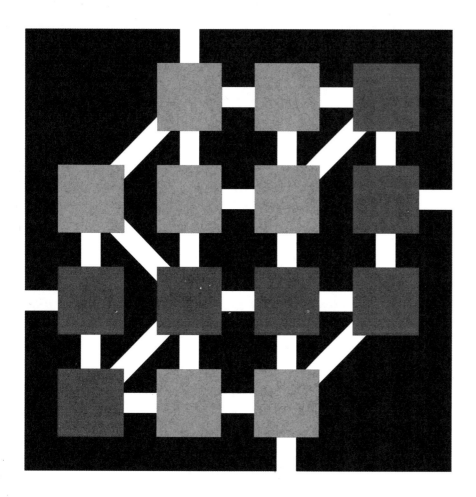

SAY IT AGAIN

What three-letter word can be mean either "proper" or "in good health"?

— — —

★ Northern Exposure

Find these Canadian places and things that are hidden in the diagram, either across, down, or diagonally. Individual words of all two-word phrases are hidden separately. Ignore words contained within parentheses.

```
D A J K C U G S N B S S F E D N A R G H E
R N H A T A E N A J A E E L O N D O N R L
I O A M S V N S I S L S A I T O C S E N A
V T R L L P I A K K K N T L T V Y I A I N
E T N O D N E A D O C A N E S N U A N A O
R A W O M N T R R A N I T S B Q U U B G I
Q W Z P S C U N H O J D K O N J V O U A T
H A F S H W M O R L E A F O O I P L M R A
A L B E R T A O F T X N J M K N F W W A N
X Y W M E L C D Z W F A K I T C H E N E R
T A L O G G E R S R E C B U D D S P A R T
N I N U I T E R E E D N I E R N R X E O R
I C S N C L U N I S L A N D O A A S C C O
F N H T P O C O N O K U Y W I Z H F O K P
F O G A B H S D A L C H U R C H I L L I M
A V M I R U Y I W U E F I N K W O L L E Y
B A R N E L B K P T B E S T H G C R D S P
P A I S V M O J C I Z A E T M E B I S R L
C A R R U A P T S O Q H I M R P C A O E E
H O R L O A N O T N R U K B A I E V N S L
I T O K C T N I G E L D S C N N I T O F E
L C Y I N O C O G A T S U E C N I O T K F
L N F E A H N I Q E Y O H T C I G T I U X
S I A W V T N I V Y R N W E O W T D O Y B
C G V H A X A F I L A H S N F R N C E B D
L A B R A D O R R B G V I G S O O L R O A
O Q I E E N J K U R L I B T L G L N O A W
P O K K G K N I H I A S N K K A N W T A B
C E B E U Q A I T T C I V K V U C I J O E
T H R E E N I L R I A N W O L E K I R E A
L A E R T N O M A S E D M O N T O N E P R
D Q C C H A P P Y H S L L A F T R O F R S
```

ALBERTA
ARCTIC
BAFFIN
  ISLAND
BANFF
BEARS
BISON
BRITISH
  COLUMBIA
CALGARY
CANADA
CANADIANS
CARIBOU
CHARLOTTE-
  TOWN
CHURCHILL
CORONATION
  GULF
DAWSON CREEK
EDMONTON
FORT
  RESOLUTION
FRENCH
GLACIER
GOOSE BAY
GRANDE
  PRAIRIE
HALIFAX
HAPPY
  VALLEY

HOT SPRINGS
HUDSON (Bay)
HUSKIES
INUIT
INUVIK
IQALUIT
JASPER
JONQUIERE
KAMLOOPS
KELOWNA
KICKING HORSE
  RIVER
KITCHENER
KLONDIKE
LABRADOR
  BASIN
LOGGERS
LONDON
MANITOBA
MAPLE LEAF
MEDICINE HAT
MONTREAL
MOOSE JAW
MOUNTIES
NAHANNI
  BUTTE
NATIONAL
  PARK
NEWFOUND-
  LAND

NIAGARA
  FALLS
NOVA
  SCOTIA
ONTARIO
OTTAWA
PACIFIC OCEAN
PORT ARTHUR
PROVINCES
QUEBEC
REGINA
REINDEER LAKE
ROCKIES
ROCKY
  MOUNTAINS
SAINT JOHN
SASKATCHEWAN
SASKATOON
SEALS
SNOW
THREE HILLS
TORONTO
VANCOUVER
VICTORIA
WINNIPEG
WOLVES
WOOD
YELLOWKNIFE
YUKON

WHO'S WHAT WHERE?

The correct term for a resident of Minneapolis, Minnesota, is:

A) Minneapolitan
B) Minneapolite
C) Minneapoler
D) Minneapian

★ Regret-Full by Sally R. Stein

ACROSS

1 Doozies
5 "__ want for Christmas is ..."
9 "When You Wish Upon __"
14 Considerably
15 Low-quality
16 Compassion
17 Regretful remark
20 Houston pro baseballer
21 The USA: Abbr.
22 __ out a living (just gets by)
23 Bearded farm animal
25 Acquire
27 Japanese and Koreans
30 Ruckus
31 Ran into
34 Mercedes-__
35 Window ledge
37 Bit of broccoli
39 Regretful remark
42 Long look
43 Concerning, in memos
44 Shoemaker's tools
45 Tee preceder
46 Business envelope abbr.
48 Dusk
50 General vicinity
51 A portion of
52 Have the belief
55 On the summit of
57 Location
61 Regretful remark
64 Brainy
65 Film __ (somber cinematic genre)
66 Spiny houseplant
67 Small food sample
68 Understands
69 Physicians, familiarly

DOWN

1 Mama's mate
2 Misfortunes
3 Verse writer
4 Astronomer, often
5 Gorilla, for one
6 Lite, on food labels
7 Weaving machine
8 Not perfect, as discounted new clothing
9 "What a good boy __"
10 Early evening
11 Hard journey
12 Summit
13 Sandwich breads
18 Any day now
19 Mardi __
24 Helper: Abbr.
26 "This __ sudden!"
27 Make humble
28 Religious groups
29 Ancient Peruvians
30 Swashbuckling actor Errol
31 Cat sounds
32 Hawk relative
33 Secret meeting
36 Acting like
38 What a Boeing 747 can hold
40 Fleshy fruit
41 Mexican coin
47 Rip up
49 Baseball judges
50 On the ball
51 Divide
52 Boxer's weapon
53 Actress Thompson
54 Airport-board displays: Abbr.
56 Woodwind instrument
58 Singer Guthrie
59 Gator's kin
60 Potato features
62 Hwy.
63 Decade fractions: Abbr.

★★ One-Way Streets

The diagram represents a pattern of streets. A and B are parking spaces, and the black squares are stores. Find a route that starts at A, passes through all stores exactly once, and ends at B. Arrows indicate one-way traffic for that block only. No block or intersection may be entered more than once.

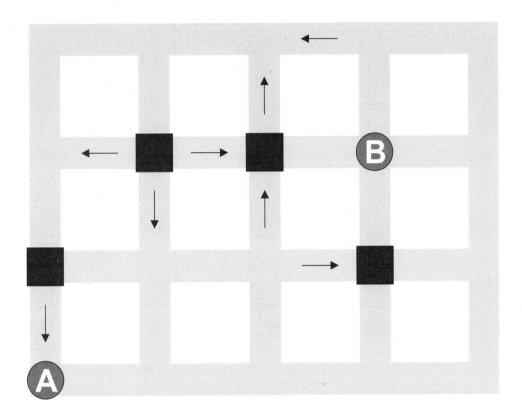

SOUND THINKING

The consonant sounds in the word CHIPS are CH, P, and S. What two-word phrase for a popular ethnic-food dish is pronounced with the same consonant sounds in the same order?

_____

★ Hyper-Sudoku

Fill in the blank boxes so that every row, column, 3x3 box, *and* each of the four 3x3 gray regions contains all of the numbers 1 to 9.

2	1	2	3	5	6	7	8	9
3	5	4	6	8	2	9	7	1
1	3	9	8	4	1	8	5	6
8	7	1	2	6	4	5	9	3
10	2	3	9	7	8	10	1	4
6	8	5	3	9	10	5	4	7
3	10	8	4	1	9	3	6	5
4	6	10	7	2	5	1	3	8
9	0	7	5	10	3	2	0	10

CENTURY MARKS

Select one number in each of the four columns so that the total adds up to exactly 100.

$$\boxed{\frac{33}{25}} + \boxed{\frac{19}{28}} + \boxed{\frac{39}{40}} + \boxed{\frac{7}{11}} = 100$$

★ Star Search

Find the stars that are hidden in some of the blank squares. The numbered squares indicate how many stars are hidden in the squares adjacent to them (including diagonally). There is never more than one star in any square.

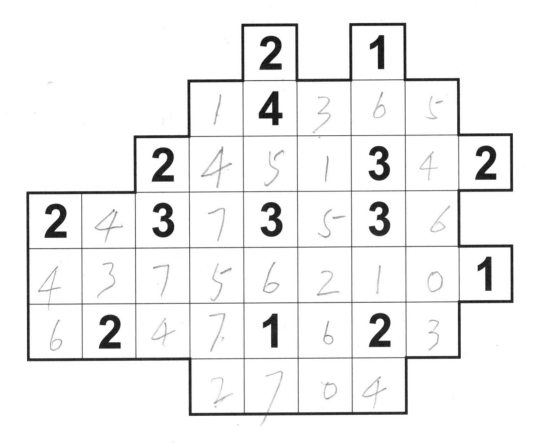

CHOICE WORDS

Form three six-letter words from the same category, by selecting one letter from each column three times. Each letter will be used exactly once.

D	Y	T	T	G	D	_ _ _ _ _ _
M	E	S	H	E	N	_ _ _ _ _ _
S	E	S	I	O	M	_ _ _ _ _ _

★ Choice Desserts by Sally R. Stein

ACROSS

1 Polish, as shoes
5 Encounters
10 Jail room
14 Where Dayton is
15 Of the eyes
16 Opera solo
17 Panasonic competitor
18 Small quantity of salt
19 Wheat or soybeans
20 Rich dessert
22 Heavy weights
23 __ la la
24 Computerized messages
26 Golden Rule pronoun
28 School-team arguer
32 Provides a staff for
34 __ go (release)
35 Warn
40 Dessert with ice cream
44 Telecast's sound portion
45 Brain scan: Abbr.
46 College official
47 Inhale and exhale
51 Corporate execs.
52 Right away, slangily
55 Meadow
57 Historical periods
58 Desserts in a box
64 Clock sound
65 Des Moines native
66 Enjoy a carousel
67 Tennis great Arthur
68 Annoy
69 __ of the above
70 Display
71 Double-curve letters
72 Break sharply

DOWN

1 Type of pear
2 "Yikes!"
3 Adjusted precisely
4 Entrance hall
5 Sulk
6 Grand-scale story
7 Sicilian volcano
8 Box-office buy
9 Sneaky plan
10 Arizona plants
11 Flynn of film
12 Kings of the jungle
13 Track circuits
21 Unhappy
25 Jordanian, for one
26 Community pool locale: Abbr.
27 Honolulu's island
29 Inventor Whitney
30 Honey maker
31 In between ports
33 __ Lanka
36 Jar cover
37 Height of a mountain
38 Gather, as grain
39 Change for a $20 bill
41 Steals from
42 Boeing product
43 Cry of discomfort
48 Cookbook entry
49 Reverberations
50 Right-angle shape
52 From Dublin
53 Mexican snack chip
54 Out of kilter
56 Merits
57 Schedule stats.
59 Is indebted to
60 Stalactites' locale
61 Change for a $5 bill
62 Writer Ferber
63 Ooze

★ ABC

Enter the letters A, B, and C into the diagram so that each row and column has exactly one A, one B, and one C. The letters outside the diagram indicate the first letter encountered, moving in the direction of the arrow. Keep in mind that after all the letters have been filled in, there will be one blank box in each row and column.

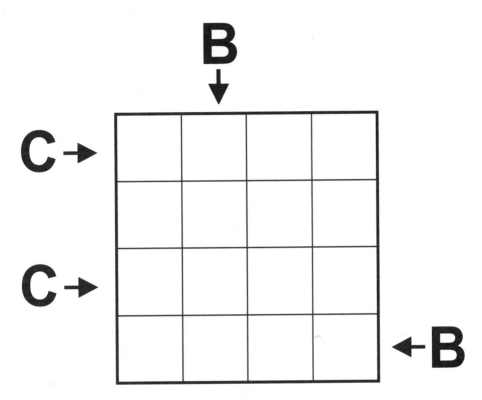

CLUELESS CROSSWORD

Complete the crossword with common uncapitalized seven-letter words, based entirely on the letters already filled in for you.

★★ Tanks a Lot

Enter the maze, pass over all tanks from behind (thereby destroying them), then exit. You may not pass through any square more than once, and may not enter a square in the line of fire of a tank you have not yet destroyed.

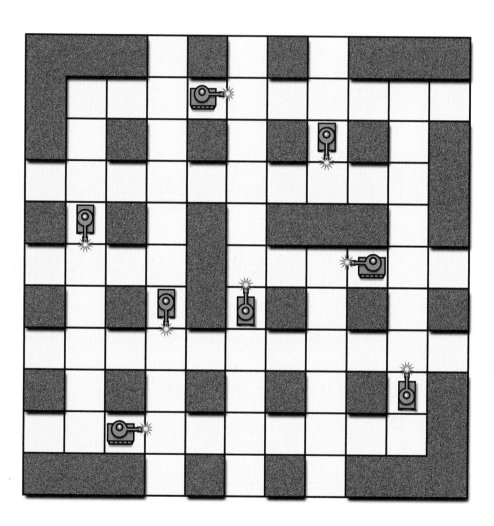

BETWEENER

What three-letter word belongs between the word at left and the word at right, so that the first and second word, and the second and third word, each form a common compound word?

UNDER ___ ___ ___ COAST

★★ Sudoku

Fill in the blank boxes so that every row, column, and 3x3 box contains all of the numbers 1 to 9.

10	9	5	3	1	4	6	8	2
5	7	8	2	3	9	1	4	6
0	1	7	5	6	3	4	2	10
7	2	3	4	5	10	8	6	9
1	3	2	8	7	5	3	9	5
4	5	6	9	8	1	5	3	1
6	0	9	7	3	2	4	1	8
8	4	10	1	2	3	2	0	7
3	8	1	6	4	7	10	5	1

MIXAGRAMS

Each line contains a five-letter word and a four-letter word that have been mixed together (the order of the letters in each word has not been changed). Unmix the two words on each line and write them in the spaces provided. When you're done, find a two-part answer to the clue by reading down the letter columns in the answers.

CLUE: Tank dweller

G U F I L A T C H = _ _ _ _ _ + _ _ _ _

O I N K C E Y A N = _ _ _ _ _ + _ _ _ _

S L A P D U E N R = _ _ _ _ _ + _ _ _ _

D O T H T U R L Y = _ _ _ _ _ + _ _ _ _

★ Birthday Offerings by Gail Grabowski

ACROSS

1 By oneself
5 Ram's offspring
9 Pesto herb
14 On the peak of
15 Creme-filled cookie
16 E on a gas gauge
17 Ability to speak persuasively
19 Honking birds
20 Retired fast plane: Abbr.
21 McCartney and Revere
22 "If __ I had known"
23 Fill completely
24 Tennis great Ivan
26 College field of study
29 Stockholm native
31 Expert on IRS forms
34 Approximately
35 Strange
36 "Faster __ a speeding bullet"
37 College cheers
38 Rocking toy, to a child
40 Wagon-train direction
41 Sicilian volcano
42 Belly muscles
43 Prickly plants
44 Capitol Hill VIP
45 Desirable quality
47 Goes backpacking
48 Ritzy boat
50 Small songbird
52 Glasgow native
53 Sign before Taurus
55 Ghost's greeting
58 Practices for a bout
59 Untrustworthy poker player
61 Must
62 Easter bloom
63 Computer operator
64 Allen or Frome

65 "Anything __?"
66 Flat-topped elevation

DOWN

1 Droops
2 Soul singer Redding
3 Barn's upper level
4 Select, with "for"
5 Diet-food label claim
6 Squabbles (with)
7 More than just a snack
8 Winter Olympics vehicles
9 Old-style "Scram!"
10 Change, as a law
11 Word-processor feature

12 __-bitsy
13 Caustic chemical
18 Dizzying gallery hangings
23 Composer John Philip
25 Whirlpool
26 Stallions' mates
27 Die down
28 "I Walk the Line" singer
30 More unfavorable
32 Adhesive substance
33 Naysayers
36 Tom Sawyer creator
38 Corned-beef concoction

39 Roadblock
43 Game of kings and castles
45 Takes, as advice
46 Manipulates, as a baton
49 Major blood vessel
51 Change the color again
52 Petty quarrel
54 Train-track part
55 Military installation
56 Mine extracts
57 Cajun veggie
58 That woman
60 Engine sound

★★ Line Drawing

Draw three straight lines, each from one edge of the square to another edge, so that the letters in each of the six regions spell a three-letter word.

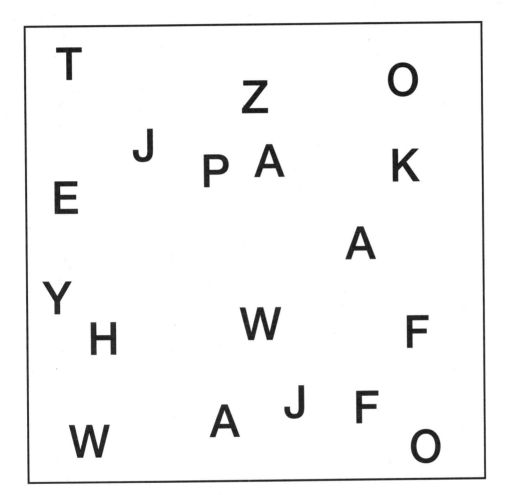

THREE OF A KIND

Find the three hidden words in the sentence that go together in some way.

Honey, it would be great to scuba dive at Plymouth Reef.

★★ Find the Ships

Determine the position of the 10 ships listed to the right of the diagram. The ships may be oriented either horizontally or vertically. A square with wavy lines indicates water and will not contain a ship. The numbers at the edge of the diagram indicate how many squares in that row or column contain parts of ships. When all 10 ships are correctly placed in the diagram, no two of them will touch each other, not even diagonally.

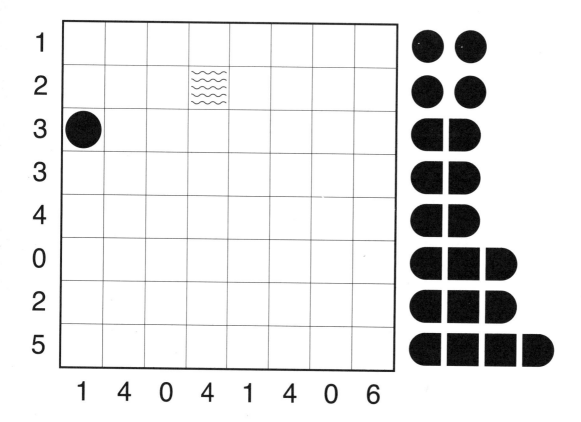

TWO-BY-FOUR

The eight letters in the word TWILIGHT can be rearranged to form a pair of common four-letter words in two different ways, if no four-letter word is repeated. Can you find both pairs of words?

— — — —   — — — —

— — — —   — — — —

★★ Fences

Connect the dots with vertical or horizontal lines, so that a single loop is formed with no crossings or branches. Each number indicates how many lines surround it; squares with no number may be surrounded by any number of lines.

```
2  1  2     1     1

1     0

2     2        3  3

3  1



         1  2

0  2     1     3

         2     3

3     3     3  2  2
```

ADDITION SWITCH

Switch the positions of two of the digits in the incorrect sum at right, to get a correct sum.

```
  808
+ 114
─────
  722
```

★ Urging On by Gail Grabowski

ACROSS

1 Without a warranty
5 Draped Delhi garments
14 Butterfly relative
15 Battery terminal
16 College girl
17 Telemarketer's tool
20 James Bond, for one
21 High cards
22 Afternoon nap in Acapulco
23 Matures
24 Bands' bookings
25 Performers' platforms
28 Steals from
29 NFL six-pointers
32 Add up
33 Shopping center
34 Singer Diamond
35 Interview with news reporters
38 Pronto, in a memo
39 Spheres
40 Brought some relief to
41 Preschooler
42 Flushed, as cheeks
43 Affectionate touch
44 Small pooch, for short
45 Lays down a lawn
46 Italian cheese
49 Penny
50 Female deer
53 Completely unplanned
56 Low-lying area
57 Picture holder
58 Actor Baldwin
59 Beseeched
60 Ambulance warning
61 Saucer or dinner plate

DOWN

1 Sound boosters
2 Minestrone, for example
3 __-bitsy
4 "No talking!"
5 Pasta toppings
6 Poker-pot fees
7 Goes bad
8 Wedding words
9 Down-to-earth
10 Feels sore
11 Pigeon sounds
12 Circus structure
13 Creative thought
18 Breakfast rolls
19 Sty dwellers
23 Short of breath
24 Plays 18 holes
25 Mar. 17 honoree
26 Sculpted figure
27 Eroded
28 Went quickly past
29 Form of a verb
30 Cuts into cubes
31 Winter vehicles
33 Telegraph inventor
34 Gets closer to
36 Culinary contests
37 Entertain, as with a story
42 Nevada city
43 Scam artists
44 Used a vegetable peeler
45 Teacher's request
46 Invitation initials
47 Whitish gemstone
48 Stubborn animal
49 Burn slightly
50 Sandwich shop
51 Singles
52 Draw with acid
54 Prefix meaning "three"
55 Irate

★★ Knot or Not?

When plugged in, which TVs will have knotted cords, and which will not?

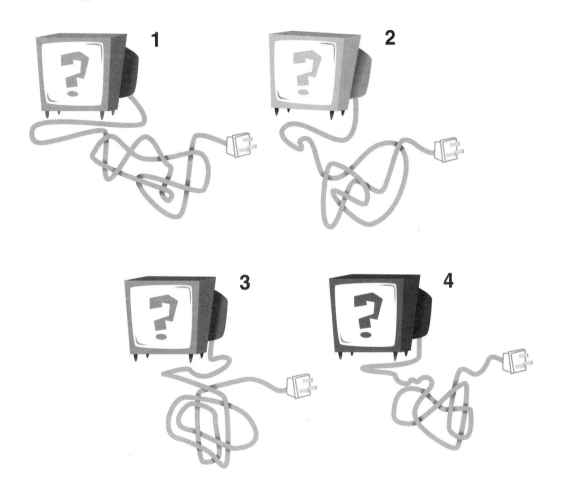

SMALL CHANGE

Change one letter in each of these two words, to form a common two-word phrase.

WISH CASE

_____

★★ 123

Fill in the diagram so that each rectangular piece has one each of the numbers 1, 2, and 3, under these rules: 1) No two adjacent squares, horizontally or vertically, can have the same number. 2) Each completed row and column of the diagram will have an equal number of 1s, 2s, and 3s.

WRONG IS RIGHT

Which of these four words is misspelled?

A) competitor   B) compatable

C) camaraderie   D) Camembert

★ Number-Out

Shade squares so that no number appears in any row or column more than once. Shaded squares may not touch each other horizontally or vertically, and all unshaded squares must form a single continuous area.

4	3	2	2	1
5	4	3	1	4
1	4	2	3	5
3	4	5	1	3
4	1	4	5	3

THINK ALIKE

Unscramble the letters in the phrase MONEY FEE to form two words with the same or similar meanings.

_____   _____

★ Graduation Day by Sally R. Stein

ACROSS

1 Cushy
5 Dog protection org.
10 Slightly open, as a door
14 "Stop, horse!"
15 Constellation components
16 Entice
17 Med.-school course
18 Casual shirts
19 Is deceitful
20 Arctic formation
23 Lion or leopard
24 Boat in Genesis
25 Remark of uncertainty
27 "Leatherneck" soldier
31 Book of maps
33 Go __ for the ride
34 Nastase of tennis
35 Naval leaders: Abbr.
39 Not as much
42 Raison d'__
43 Roll-call response
44 Dough-rising ingredient
45 Bird sound
47 Far-reaching views
48 Tidbit of food
51 Catch some rays
52 Air-quality agcy.
53 Woman's formal wear
60 Talk wildly
62 Turk's neighbor
63 Opera solo
64 Ceramic repair need
65 Middling poker pair
66 Patsies
67 Sports cable network
68 Grind, as teeth
69 Courtroom statement

DOWN

1 Make a trade
2 Cry of dread
3 Baby horse
4 "So long!"
5 Have ambitions
6 Carry in inventory
7 Devoid of color
8 Gator relative
9 Attacked vigorously
10 Everyone
11 Morning beverage
12 Neighborhoods
13 Takes it easy
21 End-to-end measure

22 Tiger Woods' grp.
26 Common practices
27 Husband or wife
28 Frequently
29 Loud crowd sound
30 Small bays
31 On the ball
32 Bike wheel
34 Phrase of understanding
36 "Darn it!"
37 Butte's larger cousin
38 Adjusts, as a clock
40 Placing into a bookcase

41 Examining
46 Very small
47 Disappear suddenly
48 Join forces
49 Milky gems
50 Accumulated, as debts
51 Fork prongs
54 Ireland nickname
55 Grandma
56 Sound of fright
57 Nonwritten exam
58 Help with the dishes
59 Space Shuttle org.
61 Midmorning

★★ Sty Writing

Enter the maze where indicated at bottom, pass through all the stars exactly once, then end at the pig's snout. You may not retrace your path.

SAY IT AGAIN

What three-letter noun can be either something that comes from a tree, or a synonym for "fool"?

— — —

★★ Split Decisions

In this clueless crossword puzzle, each answer consists of two words whose spellings are the same, except for the consecutive letters given. All answers are common words; no phrases or hyphenated or capitalized words are used. Some of the clues may have more than one solution, but there is only one word pair that will correctly link up with all the other word pairs.

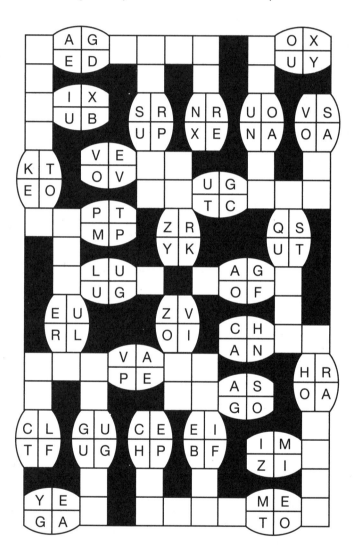

TRANSDELETION

Delete one letter from the word EMERALD and rearrange the rest, to get a term for someone in charge.

_____

★ Hyper-Sudoku

Fill in the blank boxes so that every row, column, 3x3 box, *and* each of the four 3x3 gray regions contains all of the numbers 1 to 9.

5	6						4	
8	3	9		4		2		
							9	5
	8	1			4			
	5	2			6	1		4
			2	1		5		
			3	8	1	4		
			4	5	7		2	3
	4						5	1

MIXAGRAMS

Each line contains a five-letter word and a four-letter word that have been mixed together (the order of the letters in each word has not been changed). Unmix the two words on each line and write them in the spaces provided. When you're done, find a two-part answer to the clue by reading down the letter columns in the answers.

CLUE: Grist for DeMille

D E T H F E I R Y = _ _ _ _ _ + _ _ _ _

E T O M P I T A Z = _ _ _ _ _ + _ _ _ _

E L G E I T L E S = _ _ _ _ _ + _ _ _ _

C R Y C L I M E E = _ _ _ _ _ + _ _ _ _

★ What's Now? by Sally R. Stein

ACROSS

1 Scotch and __ (bar order)
5 Native of England, for short
9 Ready for use
14 Mouse-catching device
15 Mystical glow
16 Cello's smaller cousin
17 Freeway exit
18 Word of regret
19 Sign up
20 Now
22 Takes out a lease
23 Mexican coins
24 Mexican nap
26 "__ was saying ..."
28 Speak unclearly
32 Milwaukee's loc.
35 Comparatively angry
39 Use oars
40 Now
43 Gun owners' org.
44 Ship's steering device
45 Sandwich breads
46 One receiving a loan
48 Pronounce
50 Short, as a play
54 Gotten up
58 Largest mammal
61 Now
63 Made sharper
64 Black-and-white cookie
65 Ultimate objective
66 Surpass
67 Lemon peel
68 Golden Rule preposition
69 Fire-setting crime
70 Indicates agreement
71 Ball-__ hammer

DOWN

1 Handbag handle
2 Give a speech
3 Moistens
4 Get close to
5 Sheep sounds
6 Bylaws
7 Teheran resident
8 Sample of food
9 Capsize
10 Work-shift start, often
11 Ripped
12 Very often
13 Buddies

21 Double-curve letter
25 Mascara mishaps
27 Confident comment
29 Donkey sound
30 Theater level
31 Rams' mates
32 Gust or gale
33 Concerning
34 Wild guess
36 Find a sum
37 Papa
38 Change the color of
41 Attached, as some patches
42 Evaporating

47 Ohio city
49 Exist
51 Squirrel food
52 Collector's item
53 Current style
55 Carved in __ (unchangeable)
56 Gladden
57 Hosiery fabric
58 Horse-stopping shout
59 Appointment-book line
60 Picnic spoilers
62 Window-curtain holders

★ Tool Time

Find these specific and generic terms that are hidden in the diagram, either across, down, or diagonally. There are two additional words in the category (one specific, one generic), not listed below, that are also hidden in the diagram.

```
S  E  S  S  A  H  U  F  E  H  C  T  A  H  E
N  A  X  C  S  T  D  T  L  E  W  O  R  T  T
W  S  P  A  D  E  R  T  E  L  L  A  M  N  V
T  O  R  L  A  H  I  R  U  N  S  C  E  H  E
W  O  I  P  U  C  L  L  A  Q  S  M  C  A  M
X  B  O  E  L  T  T  K  P  L  U  I  L  M  U
A  P  P  L  I  A  N  C  E  R  M  E  L  M  R
L  G  J  S  V  H  Y  V  T  P  S  O  W  E  T
X  E  A  A  N  W  E  S  L  I  R  R  X  R  S
S  F  V  D  A  B  N  E  H  L  E  L  W  A  N
N  I  R  O  G  I  M  C  D  N  I  Y  G  N  I
E  V  A  L  H  E  S  O  C  R  L  R  A  V  A
T  E  S  A  N  S  T  H  D  Z  P  M  D  I  W
U  D  P  T  D  E  V  I  C  E  B  E  V  E  P
```

ANVIL
APPLIANCE
AWL
AXE
BEVEL
CHISEL
DEVICE
DRILL
GADGET
HATCHET
INSTRUMENT
MALLET
PLIERS
RASP
SAW
SCALPEL
SHOVEL
SPADE
TOOL
TROWEL
UTENSIL
WRENCH

IN OTHER WORDS

There is only one common uncapitalized word that contains the consecutive letters MPP. What is it?

_____

bRain BREAtHer
CRIME: IT'S NOT ALL BAD

Yes, of course crime is bad. But we bet these observations about it will make you smile!

Anytime four New Yorkers get into a cab together without arguing, a bank robbery has just taken place.

—JOHNNY CARSON

Thus the metric system did not really catch on in the States, unless you count the increasing popularity of the nine-millimeter bullet.

—DAVE BARRY

Obviously crime pays, or there'd be no crime.

—G. GORDON LIDDY

People say New Yorkers can't get along. Not true. I saw two New Yorkers, complete strangers, sharing a cab. One guy took the tires and the radio; the other guy took the engine.

—DAVID LETTERMAN

It's ridiculous to set a detective story in New York City. New York City itself is a detective story.

—AGATHA CHRISTIE

The number one rule of thieves is that nothing is too small to steal.

—JIMMY BRESLIN

In England, if you commit a crime, the police don't have a gun and you don't have a gun. If you commit a crime, the police will say, "Stop, or I'll say stop again."

—ROBIN WILLIAMS

The towels were so thick there I could hardly close my suitcase.

—YOGI BERRA

★★ One-Way Streets

The diagram represents a pattern of streets. P's are parking spaces, and the black squares are stores. Find the route that starts at a parking space, passes through all stores exactly once, and ends at the other parking space. Arrows indicate one-way traffic for that block only. No block or intersection may be entered more than once.

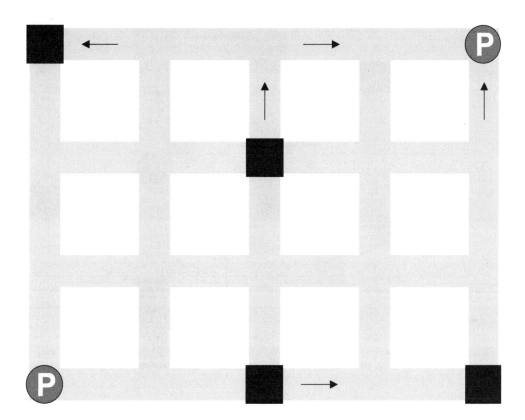

SOUND THINKING

There is only one common uncapitalized word whose consonant sounds are D, R, and W, in that order. What is it?

_____

★ Giving Way by Gail Grabowski

ACROSS

1 Ink smudge
5 "Get lost!"
10 Fuzzy image
14 Teeming (with)
15 Got out of bed
16 Huron or Erie
17 Get __ the ground floor
18 Many-stop train
19 Chills, as a drink
20 Pants-accessory clasp
22 Bird's dwelling
23 Breaks up, informally
24 Give temporarily
26 Beast seen by Goldilocks
29 Not as loud
33 Impolite look
37 Fail to catch
39 "Me, too!"
40 Eiffel Tower locale
42 Fruit drink
43 Spanish national hero
44 Mashed-potatoes topper
45 Borscht veggie
47 Lavish affection (on)
48 Agreement
50 Gumbo ingredient
52 Gather, as crops
54 Prerecorded
59 Thick slice
62 Investment stat
65 Bring under control
66 Folklore being
67 Enjoying a cruise
68 Smooth out
69 "I'll do that!"
70 Wander
71 Magician's stick
72 English-class assignment
73 Rental units: Abbr.

DOWN

1 Illegal payment
2 Tablecloth fabric
3 From way back
4 Campsite shelters
5 Greeted, military-style
6 Gator kin
7 Boulder
8 Big __ outdoors
9 Brawls
10 Pin the Tail on the Donkey accessory
11 Doily material
12 Luau instruments, for short
13 Take a breather
21 Baby's neckwear
25 Snoop (around)
27 Saudi citizen, for one
28 Bronco-riding event
30 Filled tortilla
31 Give off
32 Amusement-park feature
33 Women's links org.
34 Corn units
35 Historical times
36 Curve in the Mississippi
38 Quick look
41 "Auld Lang __"
46 Streetcar of yore
49 Snitch
51 "__ questions?"
53 Skin features
55 Jeweled crown
56 Ancient fable teller
57 Fabric fold
58 Dutch cheeses
59 Beef dish
60 Volcanic flow
61 Prayer ending
63 Little kids
64 __ mater

★★ Two-Color Maze

Enter the maze, pass through all the color squares exactly once, then exit, all without retracing your path. You must alternate between red and blue squares.

SMALL CHANGE

Change one letter in each of these two words, to form a common two-word phrase.

LIGHT OIL

★★ Star Search

Find the stars that are hidden in some of the blank squares. The numbered squares indicate how many stars are hidden in the squares adjacent to them (including diagonally). There is never more than one star in any square.

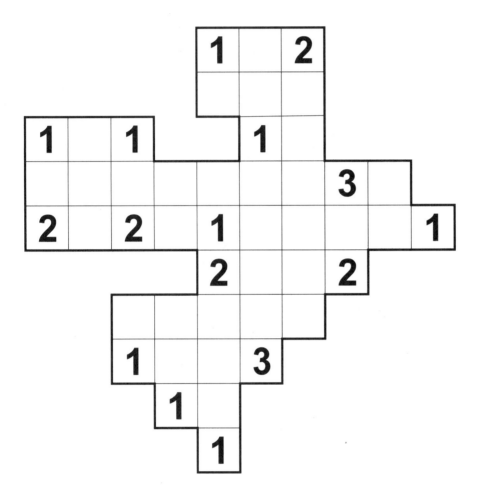

CHOICE WORDS

Form three six-letter words from the same category, by selecting one letter from each column three times. Each letter will be used exactly once.

L	A	I	S	E	N	_ _ _ _ _ _
D	A	S	D	I	L	_ _ _ _ _ _
M	A	M	S	E	E	_ _ _ _ _ _

★★ Triad Split Decisions

In this clueless crossword puzzle, each answer consists of two words whose spellings are the same, except for the consecutive letters given. All answers are common words; no phrases or hyphenated or capitalized words are used. Some of the clues may have more than one solution, but there is only one word pair that will correctly link up with all the other word pairs.

TRANSDELETION

Delete one letter from the word SUCTION and rearrange the rest, to get someone who might attend a reunion.

_____

★★ Catch of the Day by Daniel R. Stark

ACROSS

1 Need an aspirin
5 Spike, as punch
9 Holy terrors
14 Skiff or sloop
15 Horror-film servant
16 Ignited again
17 Radar blip
18 Bangkok resident
19 In a strange way
20 Excessive-interest collector
22 Potter's device
23 Subtraction word
24 Pick up on
25 Drive bananas
29 More to the point
32 Well-__ (rich)
34 Bit of brandy, say
35 Wander
39 Deliver via chute
41 Loud enough
43 Alliance
44 Shale extract
46 "No" answer
47 Jibes
50 Artist's negotiator
51 Extent
54 Joyride
56 Paraffin-based
57 Fine fellow
62 Mandate
63 Kitchen ending
64 Art-sch. subject
65 Zeal
66 Greek letters
67 Related
68 Like tall grass
69 French peak
70 Small bills

DOWN

1 Biblical shepherd
2 Chanel nickname
3 Tee-hee cousin
4 Harrow rival
5 Like a contortionist
6 Appalled
7 Make rougher
8 *Phantom of the Opera* lead
9 Look casually
10 False lead
11 Priscilla's suitor
12 Roofing pieces
13 Vogue
21 More cunning
25 Melville captain
26 Astronaut Armstrong
27 Fictional sleuth Wolfe
28 Patti Page tune
30 Southwestern creek
31 Tater
33 Way out
36 Stage award
37 Novelist Paton
38 Cheesy sandwich
40 Chart shape
42 Senior members
45 Nation surrounded by South Africa
48 Aristocracy
49 Very accurate, in London
51 Give testimony
52 Skilled force
53 Common compound
55 That is: Lat.
57 Microbe
58 Green Hornet sidekick
59 Ever's partner
60 Narrative
61 Sched. listings

★★ ABC

Enter the letters A, B, and C into the diagram so that each row and column has exactly one A, one B, and one C. The letters outside the diagram indicate the first letter encountered, moving in the direction of the arrow. Keep in mind that after all the letters have been filled in, there will be two blank boxes in each row and column.

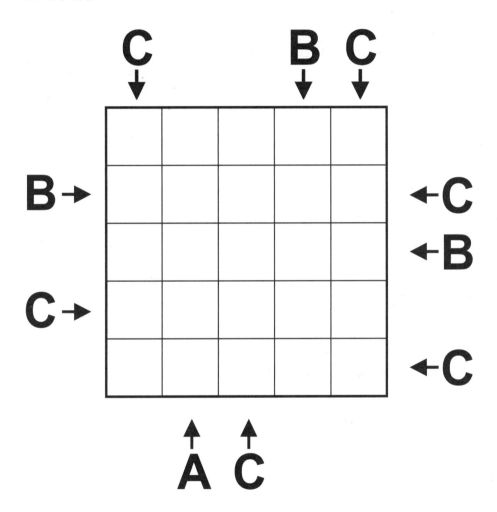

NATIONAL TREASURE

Of the common uncapitalized seven-letter words that can be formed from the letters in PAKISTANI, only one is a noun that doesn't end in S. What is it?

— — — — — — —

★★ Find the Ships

Determine the position of the 10 ships listed to the right of the diagram. The ships may be oriented either horizontally or vertically. A square with wavy lines indicates water and will not contain a ship. The numbers at the edge of the diagram indicate how many squares in that row or column contain parts of ships. When all 10 ships are correctly placed in the diagram, no two of them will touch each other, not even diagonally.

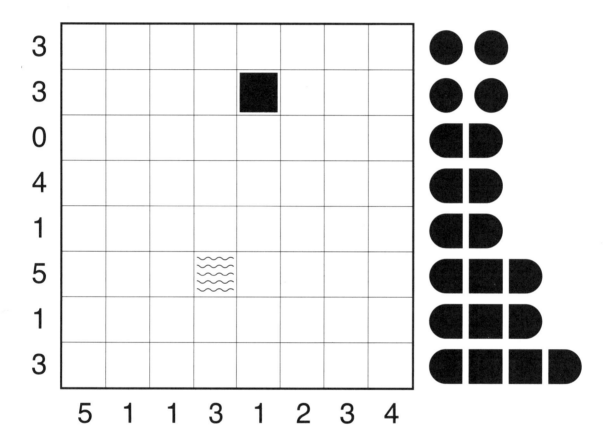

TWO-BY-FOUR

The eight letters in the word UNBUCKLE can be rearranged to form a pair of common four-letter words in two different ways. Can you find both pairs of words?

__ __ __ __   __ __ __ __

__ __ __ __   __ __ __ __

★★ Choose Your Weapon by Shirley Soloway

ACROSS

1 Barber's concern
6 Type of radio
10 Very long time
14 Just not done
15 Airline-seat attachment
16 Seaside formation
17 Sinclair Lewis novel
19 "What's __ for me?"
20 Niftily
21 Not much time
23 Shade tree
24 Virgo preceder
26 Optimistic
27 Where a frat might meet
30 Sunblock letters
33 Not very good
36 Warm up, for short
37 Stamp-saving service
39 Demote
41 Ending for project
42 Designer Nina
43 Form of oxygen
44 German's "one"
46 Three-person card game
47 __ capita
48 One of Arthur's knights
51 WWII turning point
53 __ Tin Tin
54 Fawn's mother
57 Attaches firmly
60 Three-legged stands
62 Pork cut
63 Leads, as a project
66 Blotter's home
67 Vexes
68 Dragon puppet of '50s TV
69 Very pale
70 Sandwich breads
71 Tops of heads

DOWN

1 Cabinet department
2 December song
3 James __ Garfield
4 Ill-gotten gains
5 '90s Joint Chiefs chairman
6 S&L device
7 High-tech med. test
8 Thomas Waller's nickname
9 Movie damsel's grateful cry
10 Lone Ranger's farewell
11 Big bag for grain
12 Oklahoma city
13 Detonates, with "off"
18 Escort inside, perhaps
22 One with potential
25 Leno successor
27 Cinematic brothers' surname
28 Ancient souvenir
29 Kitchen device
31 Printer's width
32 Skim along
33 Hog food
34 Flow slowly
35 Oceanic predator
38 Fine rain
40 Chill out
45 Comparatively cagy
49 Sailor's affirmative
50 How a ground ball may be caught
52 Penny-ante
54 Traded
55 Any Errol Flynn film
56 Slalom curves
57 *The West Wing* actor
58 Opposite sides of a fight
59 Energetic
61 Actress Ward
64 __ out a living
65 Beast of burden

★★ Two Pairs

Among the 16 pictures below, find the two pairs of pictures that are identical to each other.

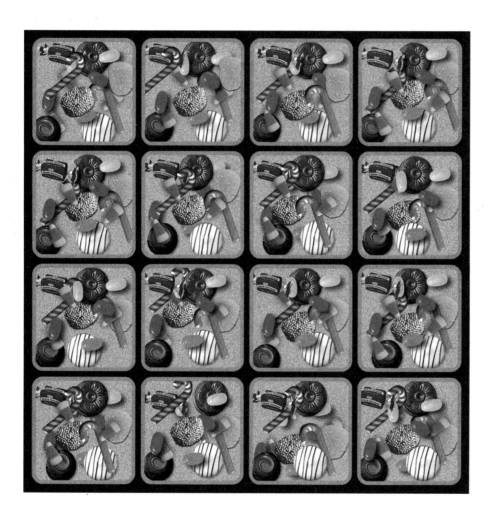

BETWEENER

What four-letter word belongs between the word at left and the word at right, so that the first and second word, and the second and third word, each form a common compound word?

HORSE __ __ __ __ PEN

★★ Sudoku

Fill in the blank boxes so that every row, column, and 3x3 box contains all of the numbers 1 to 9.

7	8						6	5
4		1		2		9		3
	9			7			2	
			2		6			
9								7
			7		4			
	3			6			8	
2		5		8		6		1
8	4						9	2

MIXAGRAMS

Each line contains a five-letter word and a four-letter word that have been mixed together (the order of the letters in each word has not been changed). Unmix the two words on each line and write them in the spaces provided. When you're done, find a two-part answer to the clue by reading down the letter columns in the answers.

CLUE: Thin man

S W A B O G U P S	=	_ _ _ _ _	+	_ _ _ _
S E R I E C L O T	=	_ _ _ _ _	+	_ _ _ _
A T O N G R I L Y	=	_ _ _ _ _	+	_ _ _ _
C A N A F I E V E	=	_ _ _ · _	+	_ _ _ _

★★ Fences

Connect the dots with vertical or horizontal lines, so that a single loop is formed with no crossings or branches. Each number indicates how many lines surround it; squares with no number may be surrounded by any number of lines.

```
 .  .  .  .  .  .  .  .  .
    0     2 1 3     3
 .  .  .  .  .  .  .  .  .
      2   2         2
 .  .  .  .  .  .  .  .  .
  2                     1
 .  .  .  .  .  .  .  .  .
        2       2     3
 .  .  .  .  .  .  .  .  .
  2     1       3
 .  .  .  .  .  .  .  .  .
  2                   2
 .  .  .  .  .  .  .  .  .
  3         3     2
 .  .  .  .  .  .  .  .  .
  3     2 1 3     0
 .  .  .  .  .  .  .  .  .
```

WRONG IS RIGHT

Which of these four words is misspelled?

    A) spatula   B) sparcity

    C) spartan   D) spatial

★★ **Award Winners** by Fred Piscop

ACROSS

- **1** Start fishing
- **5** "Slung" fare
- **9** Mandolin cousins
- **14** Mouse pusher
- **15** Rights org.
- **16** Chip away at
- **17** Take a hack
- **18** Stay away from
- **19** Sharpshooter Oakley
- **20** Charlie McCarthy's voice
- **23** Cash on the Ginza
- **24** Furrow fillers
- **25** Just __ (slightly)
- **27** __-Tzu (Chinese philosopher)
- **28** Arizona explorer
- **32** "None of the above"
- **35** Place to dock
- **36** Frosty's makeup
- **37** Bud's comic pal
- **38** __ of hand (magician's forte)
- **41** Playwright Akins
- **42** Abode, informally
- **44** Some sushi fare
- **45** Got wind of
- **47** Hobbyists' racers
- **49** Penn. neighbor
- **50** __ up (add muscle)
- **51** TV studio equipment
- **55** Designer monogram
- **57** Wisecracking pianist
- **60** Full of substance
- **62** Cameo-shaped
- **63** Voting no
- **64** Hidden store
- **65** __ Scotia
- **66** Stadium section
- **67** Part of FAQ
- **68** Meadow mothers
- **69** Wraps up

DOWN

- **1** Makes better
- **2** Out of the way
- **3** Marsh plant
- **4** Spinning-wheel pedal
- **5** Maker of G.I. Joe
- **6** Needs aspirin
- **7** Disparaging remark
- **8** Nailed to the wall
- **9** Simple shelter
- **10** Java holder
- **11** *Who's the Boss?* star
- **12** Falco of *The Sopranos*
- **13** In the public eye
- **21** Brings up
- **22** You're on it
- **26** Ques. reply
- **28** Mattress innards
- **29** Assns.
- **30** A way in
- **31** Was in the hole
- **32** Early automaker
- **33** Slave away
- **34** FDR Supreme Court appointee
- **35** Use a spyglass
- **39** Radiator problems
- **40** Topic
- **43** Alphabetic quartet
- **46** Jack up
- **48** Was too sweet
- **49** SMU locale
- **51** Have a yen for
- **52** Took to jail
- **53** Chipped in
- **54** Mixes by hand
- **55** Village People tune
- **56** Salty septet
- **58** Traffic-lane marker
- **59** Declare frankly
- **61** Everyday article

★★ Number-Out

Shade squares so that no number appears in any row or column more than once. Shaded squares may not touch each other horizontally or vertically, and all unshaded squares must form a single continuous area.

2	3	5	4	4	4
2	6	5	5	1	3
5	1	3	1	6	1
6	1	4	3	5	6
3	1	6	2	6	5
1	5	2	4	2	6

THINK ALIKE

Unscramble the letters in the phrase FIND SHINE to form two words with the same or similar meanings.

_____   _____

★★ Hyper-Sudoku

Fill in the blank boxes so that every row, column, 3x3 box, *and* each of the four 3x3 gray regions contains all of the numbers 1 to 9.

	1		7			3		
8						9	7	
	6				8			
7	9	8	2			1		
			9	8		7	6	4
						2		
5				2				
		3	6		7			
					5	4		

CENTURY MARKS

Select one number in each of the four columns so that the total adds up to exactly 100.

$$\frac{22}{18} + \frac{24}{38} + \frac{26}{37} + \frac{17}{15} = 100$$

★★ Number Twos by Fred Piscop

ACROSS

1 Sheets, tablecloths, etc.
6 Actress Lollobrigida
10 Seemingly endless
14 Put up with
15 Planets, to poets
16 Toledo's lake
17 Seal tightly
19 A handful
20 Builders
21 Suppresses
23 Aussie bounder
24 Begins the bidding
25 Fancy neckwear
29 LP player, briefly
32 French composer
33 Go yachting
34 Consider, with "on"
38 Golden-__ (senior)
39 Tricky pitch
40 Crinkly veggie
41 Stinging remark
42 Small snack
43 In itself
44 Pallid-looking
46 Sporting a topper
47 Second-year students
50 Prickly husk
51 Aries, familiarly
53 Huge amount, as of vitamins
58 __ avis
59 Electronic casino game
61 Greek love god
62 Emily of etiquette
63 Calculus pioneer
64 Decline gradually
65 Drags to court
66 __-fatty acids

DOWN

1 Wash up
2 Structural beam
3 "Way to go!"
4 Part of HEW: Abbr.
5 Not taking sides
6 Enter the NFL draft
7 Saving options, for short
8 *The Office* network
9 Shows curiosity
10 Place for a fob
11 Sprang up
12 *American Idol* judge
13 Many mall rats
18 Not worth debating
22 Charged atom
25 Curmudgeonly sort
26 Sitar tune
27 State firmly
28 "Drop a hint," e.g.
29 Birthday do
30 Drone's home
31 Corrida cry
33 Interview wear
35 Doe's mate
36 "If all __ fails ..."
37 Lawn intruder
39 *Gunsmoke* network
43 Defensive wall
45 Fit __ fiddle
46 Quasimodo's creator
47 Scatter about
48 *GWTW* surname
49 Former leader of Argentina
50 Borscht veggies
52 NBA award recipients
53 Dept.-store goods
54 Ill-humored
55 Tulsa's locale: Abbr.
56 Observed
57 Botches one
60 Debtor's letters

★ Golden

Find these synonyms of various meanings of "golden" (plus "golden" itself) that are hidden in the diagram, either across, down, or diagonally.

```
P R E C I O U S G I L D S D G
K F E C E X C E L L E N T A N
N L I S U S B A U X S J F Z I
E A T D P U H F U U Q L T Z M
G X F E L L S I O R O B N L A
G E H L G S E I N U I W A I E
U N I G E G R N R I O C I N L
N O I C I O U I D L N B L G G
N L C S L L S N L E M G L D B
T U O G I H L E P E N G I E L
S V I R I M Y I N G O T R D O
E L U N S U O R T S U L B L N
Y A G R I A F R I N G O A I D
N E D L O G R W P F A I Z G T
```

AURIC
BLOND
BRILLIANT
BULLION
DAZZLING
EXCELLENT
FAIR
FLAXEN
FLOURISHING
GILDED
GILT
GLEAMING
GLORIOUS
GOLDEN
INGOT
LUSTROUS
NUGGET
PRECIOUS
PROMISING
RESPLENDENT
SHINING
SUCCESSFUL
YELLOW

INITIAL REACTION

Identify the well-known proverb from the first letters in each of its words.

W. B. I. H. D. _____

★★ Sets of Three

Group all the symbols into sets of three, with each set having either all the same shape and three different colors, or all the same color and three different shapes. The symbols in each set must all be connected to each other by a common horizontal or vertical side.

SAY IT AGAIN

What four-letter word can be something a driver often does, or a place to play?

— — — —

★★ Shipping News by Randall J. Hartman

ACROSS

1 Lawn cover
6 Robin Cook thriller
10 Crooner Perry
14 Like haunted houses
15 Lena of *Chocolat*
16 Kind of exam
17 Devilfish
18 Doll's word
19 Unimportant
20 Part of some addresses
23 Cove's big brother
24 Yoko __
25 Supple
29 Magician's prop
31 Poker prize
34 Messages on a screen
35 Contained
36 Speak unclearly
37 Travel-agent offering
40 Swelled heads
41 Signs of approval
42 Supple
43 Author Deighton
44 Catch sight of
45 Train stations
46 Wrestling surface
47 Santa __, CA
48 An essential ingredient
55 Sidewalk border
56 Type of tide
57 Yuletide tune
59 "__ Wanna Do" (Sheryl Crow tune)
60 Engage in telemarketing
61 Join forces
62 Online journal
63 Novelist Wiesel
64 On pins and needles

DOWN

1 Amethyst, e.g.
2 Harvest
3 River to the Ligurian Sea
4 Poses
5 Passenger restraint
6 Warm and snug
7 Norwegian saint
8 Actress Rogers
9 Snake of the Amazon
10 Jazz group
11 Billion-selling cookie
12 *Duck Soup* surname
13 Corrida cheer
21 Boat propeller
22 Extremity
25 Carpenter's device
26 Publicist's concern
27 Peach State city
28 Partiality
29 *Peter Pan* girl
30 *Sound of Music* scenery
31 Student of Socrates
32 Should, with "to"
33 Kilmer poem
35 Free-throw target
36 Leave out
38 Example
39 Quite definite
44 Consume
45 Some forensic evidence
46 Crime boss
47 Still-life fruit
48 Skeet-shooter's shout
49 Singer Guthrie
50 Patricia of *Hud*
51 Surrealist Salvador
52 Short staff
53 Green land
54 A whole bunch
55 Metered vehicle
58 Golf pro Trevino

★★ One-Way Streets

The diagram represents a pattern of streets. P's are parking spaces, and the black squares are stores. Find the route that starts at a parking space, passes through all stores exactly once, and ends at the other parking space. Arrows indicate one-way traffic for that block only. No block or intersection may be entered more than once.

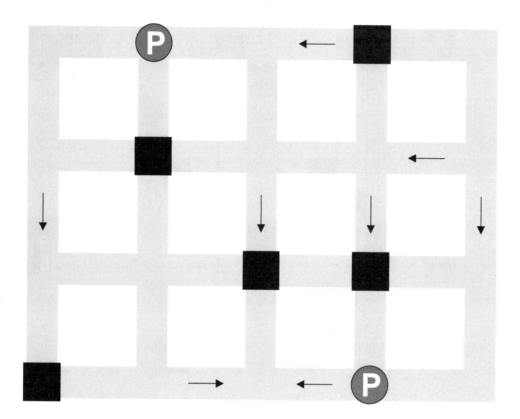

SOUND THINKING

There is only one common uncapitalized word whose consonant sounds are F, R, M, and S, in that order. What is it?

_____

★★ 123

Fill in the diagram so that each rectangular piece has one each of the numbers 1, 2, and 3, under these rules: 1) No two adjacent squares, horizontally or vertically, can have the same number. 2) Each completed row and column of the diagram will have an equal number of 1s, 2s, and 3s.

SUDOKU SUM

Fill in the missing numbers from 1 to 9, so that the sum of each row and column is as indicated.

	20	16	9
20		9	
8			2
17	8		

★★★ Line Drawing

Draw two straight lines, each from one edge of the square to another edge,
so that the "numbers" in each of the four regions have something in common.

SIX THOUSAND

FOUR HUNDRED

NINETY

TWENTY-ONE   FOUR

TWENTY

TWELVE

THIRTEEN

SEVEN HUNDRED

ONE

FIFTEEN THOUSAND

TWENTY-SEVEN

THREE OF A KIND

Find the three hidden words in the sentence that go together in some way.

Hey, guys—want to head over to the bowling alley?

★★ Find a Seat by Kevin Donovan

ACROSS

1 Ethereal instruments
6 Male deer
11 *60 Minutes* network
14 Hello, in Hilo
15 Soup server
16 Primitive abode
17 Police informant
19 "__ you kidding?"
20 Frog cousin
21 Sign of agreement
22 Angry feeling
23 Pupa protection
26 Fitting-room fixture
28 Earth-friendly prefix
29 Unadorned
33 Afternoon refresher
34 Alphabetic trio
35 French Sudan, today
36 Monumental
39 Diplomat's requirement
41 Some Mozart melodies
43 Therefore
44 For a specific purpose
46 Caused to separate
47 __ Paulo
48 Tour organizer, for short
49 Eye annoyances
51 Make a choice
52 Raisin portions
55 Soap-opera parts
57 Car-floor accessory
58 One __ time
60 Soft or silver follower
61 *Wheel of Fortune* purchase
62 Seldom-used substitute
67 Piece of land
68 Carpentry device
69 Concerto instrument

70 Summer sign
71 Borden's cow
72 Run-down

DOWN

1 Retains
2 Keyboard key
3 Aussie marsupial
4 Reminder of times past
5 Western hangout
6 Skidded
7 Luggage attachment
8 Yemeni port
9 Sad state
10 Passing along

11 Meeting leader
12 Prospector's animal
13 Maneuver the rudder
18 Nicaragua neighbor
23 Jai alai basket
24 Group of eight
25 Loafer of a sort
27 Hard to find
30 Go-__ (kids' vehicles)
31 "Untouchable" Ness
32 Personal journal
37 With dropped jaw
38 Horn honks
40 Like some orders
42 Playground piece

45 Competent
50 Dog's breakfast, maybe
52 T-shirt size
53 River runner
54 Sneak off, with "away"
56 Like King's work
59 Social bugs
60 Amusement-park sound
63 Third-to-last Greek letter
64 Ginnie __
65 NFL position
66 Country singer Clark

★★ Star Search

Find the stars that are hidden in some of the blank squares. The numbered squares indicate how many stars are hidden in the squares adjacent to them (including diagonally). There is never more than one star in any square.

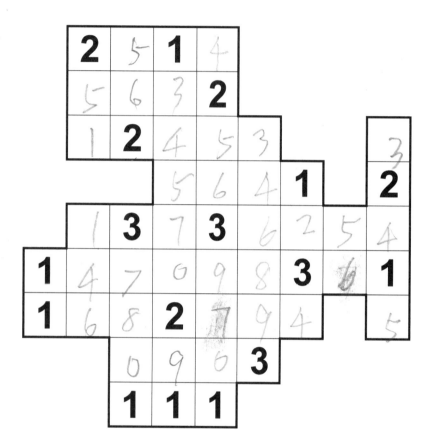

CHOICE WORDS

Form three six-letter words from the same category, by selecting one letter from each column three times. Each letter will be used exactly once.

E	W	N	L	T	N	_ _ _ _ _ _
N	L	E	E	E	E	_ _ _ _ _ _
T	I	E	V	V	Y	_ _ _ _ _ _

★★ Dicey

Group the dice into sets of two or more whose sums equal nine. The dice in each set must be connected to each other by a common horizontal or vertical side.

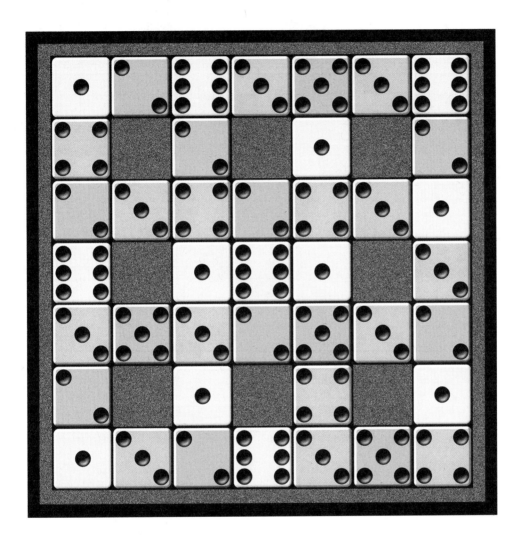

SMALL CHANGE

Change one letter in each of these two words, to form a common two-word phrase.

TRUE SLUMP

★★ Up to Speed by Daniel R. Stark

ACROSS

1 Nightclubs
6 Sarcastic comment
10 __ shui (architectural art)
14 No longer together
15 Burglar's take
16 Jai __
17 Japanese-American
18 Sicilian spewer
19 Sorts
20 After deductions
21 London newspaper district
24 Hawk's gripper
26 Vogues
27 Glossy finish
29 Pipe wood
31 Ivory Coast neighbor
32 Fragrant flowers
34 Disencumber
37 Karaoke singers' needs
39 Fond du __, WI
40 Exciting
42 Pacino and Unser
43 Main points
46 Fraternal org.
47 Singer Della
48 Is of benefit
50 Make beloved
53 Correct a text
54 Free-flowing metal
57 Mushroom top
60 Sudden impulse
61 Falco of *The Sopranos*
62 Pointy roof
64 Defects and all
65 Ponce de __
66 Gobbled up
67 Telescope part
68 Typeface
69 Wood nymph

DOWN

1 Eve's eldest
2 Church area
3 Tries to deceive
4 Poetic preposition
5 Quell
6 Luster
7 After midnight
8 First cousin's mom
9 Credit cards, slangily
10 Less cloudy
11 Actress Burstyn
12 Frequent adjective for "truth"
13 Main points
22 Laze around
23 Dumpster contents
25 Jacques' girlfriend
27 Jane Austen heroine
28 Catch in the act
29 Point the finger at
30 Ethnicity
33 Seine vistas
34 South Dakota town
35 Role model, maybe
36 Salon bottles
38 Vegan's taboo
41 Diplomat Abba
44 Feminine pronoun
45 Alike
47 Grade schooler's break
49 Experienced (in)
50 Peer
51 Clinic worker
52 "Hearty appetite!"
53 Happening
55 Prefix meaning "thought"
56 Pride member
58 Zone
59 Remain undecided
63 Golfers' benchmark

★★ Hyper-Sudoku

Fill in the blank boxes so that every row, column, 3x3 box, *and* each of the four 3x3 gray regions contains all of the numbers 1 to 9.

2	9	7	8	1	3	6	4	5
7	1	8	5	6	4	2	3	6
8	2	3	7	5	1	4	6	9
9	3	0	6	2	7	1	5	4
6	4	1	4	3	0	9	2	8
0	6	4	2	8	9	5	7	3
3	5	9	0	6	1	7	1	2
4	7	5		4	2	3	9	1
1		2	3	9	5	0	8	7

MIXAGRAMS

Each line contains a five-letter word and a four-letter word that have been mixed together (the order of the letters in each word has not been changed). Unmix the two words on each line and write them in the spaces provided. When you're done, find a two-part answer to the clue by reading down the letter columns in the answers.

CLUE: Boston's nickname

R O S T I B R E D = _ _ _ _ _ + _ _ _ _

S T O C H E M K E = _ _ _ _ _ + _ _ _ _

S L E W A S I G H = _ _ _ _ _ + _ _ _ _

L A I N T E N E N = _ _ _ _ _ + _ _ _ _

★★ ABC

Enter the letters A, B, and C into the diagram so that each row and column has exactly one A, one B, and one C. The letters outside the diagram indicate the first letter encountered, moving in the direction of the arrow. Keep in mind that after all the letters have been filled in, there will be two blank boxes in each row and column.

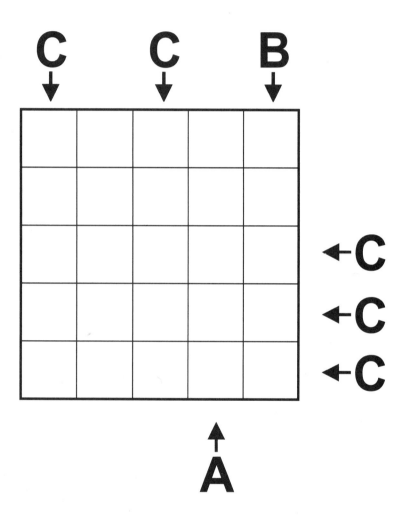

NATIONAL TREASURE

Find the one common six-letter word that can be formed from the letters in LITHUANIAN.

— — — — — —

★★ **Poolside** by Fred Piscop

ACROSS

1 Euro fractions
6 Basilica part
10 Meadow musing
13 Birdlike
14 Locket shape
15 Pack in
16 Entrée with paper frills
18 Big-eared hopper
19 Show contempt for
20 Prime example
22 Stadium section
24 Spiral-horned antelope
25 Be important
29 Taken __ (surprised)
32 Pungent-smelling
33 Easy job
34 Hack
38 __ to none (long odds)
39 Navigational aid
40 Slack-jawed
41 Whopping
42 __ the Great (fictional boy sleuth)
43 Biological copy
44 Fiji neighbor
46 Gertrude Stein colleague
47 Up to now
50 Folk singer Joan
52 Numero uno
55 European news agency
60 Racetrack boundary
61 Words before exiting
63 Prod
64 Charged particles
65 Wear down
66 Beatnik exclamation
67 *Cosby Show* daughter
68 Like interstates

DOWN

1 Showroom selections
2 The second Senator Bayh
3 Not naughty
4 Walk off with
5 Sounded indignant
6 Nick of *Cape Fear*
7 An ex of Frank
8 Silent-screen siren
9 Exile isle
10 Actress Sonia
11 Brother of Moses
12 Rephrase
15 Grid coach's lecture
17 So-so
21 VCR button
23 Owed at the bar
25 Crush
26 Rights org.
27 High-school math
28 Train-station freebie
30 Unconcealed
31 Quick to learn
33 Carpet type
35 MP's quarry
36 TV's "Warrior Princess"
37 Bad day for Caesar
39 Paula Zahn's former channel
43 Mexican resort
45 It needs refining
46 Links areas
47 Use a pick
48 *Pal Joey* playwright
49 Pretend to have
51 Dilettantish
53 Commotion
54 Ten C-notes
56 Supermodel Banks
57 Milton Friedman's subj.
58 Far from polite
59 Parakeet meal
62 "Go on ..."

★★ Flaky

Which of the numbered snowflakes has been made from each of the three stamps?

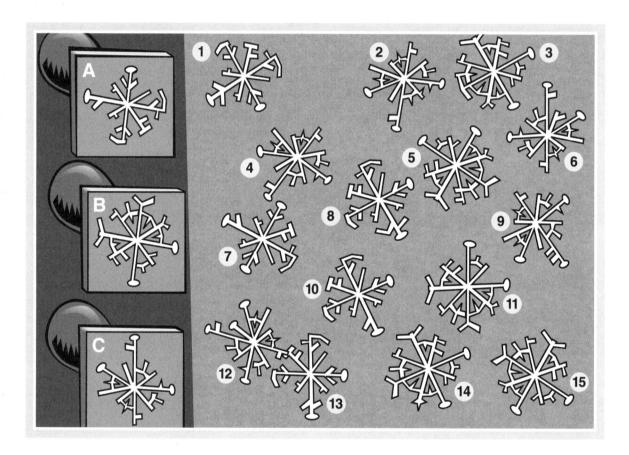

BETWEENER

What four-letter word belongs between the word at left and the word at right, so that the first and second word, and the second and third word, each form a common compound word?

WILD _ _ _ _ BLOOD

★★ Find the Ships

Determine the position of the 10 ships listed to the right of the diagram. The ships may be oriented either horizontally or vertically. A square with wavy lines indicates water and will not contain a ship. The numbers at the edge of the diagram indicate how many squares in that row or column contain parts of ships. When all 10 ships are correctly placed in the diagram, no two of them will touch each other, not even diagonally.

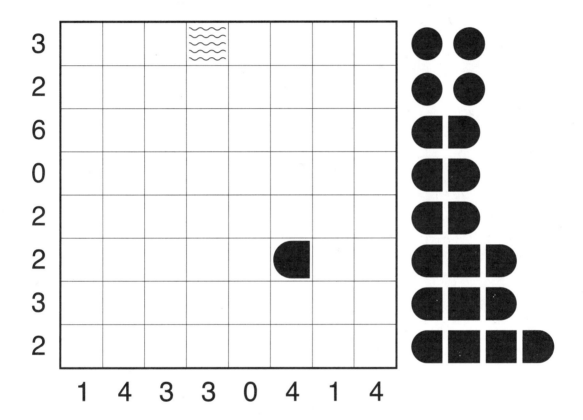

TWO-BY-FOUR

The eight letters in the word VAULTING can be rearranged to form a pair of common four-letter words in only one way. Can you find the two words?

— — — —   — — — —

★★ Triad Split Decisions

In this clueless crossword puzzle, each answer consists of two words whose spellings are the same, except for the consecutive letters given. All answers are common words; no phrases or hyphenated or capitalized words are used. Some of the clues may have more than one solution, but there is only one word pair that will correctly link up with all the other word pairs.

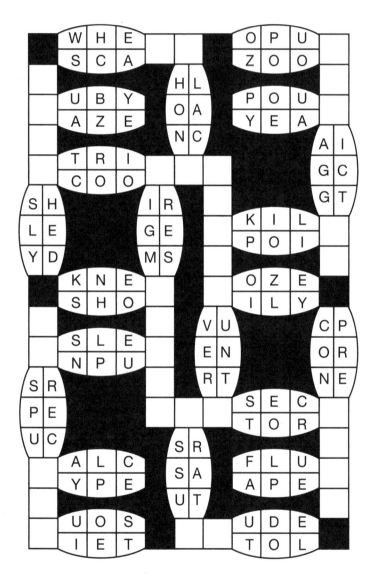

TRANSDELETION

Delete one letter from the word PELICAN and rearrange the rest, to get something with a point.

_____

★★ Got Insurance? by Fred Piscop

ACROSS

1 Golf strokes
6 *The Ghost and Mrs. __*
10 "That can't be!"
14 First-stringers
15 Kournikova of tennis
16 Clear a hurdle
17 Gas-saving plan
19 Title for Agatha Christie
20 Prickly plant
21 Made strong
23 Snake's sound
25 Go ballistic
26 Tone down
30 "__ the night before ..."
32 "Let me think ..."
35 Newsman of old
36 Having great stamina
37 One of "them"
38 Hard to find
39 Radium discoverer
40 Codger
41 Chowed down
42 Thesaurus man
43 Produce Z's
44 Exclamation of amazement
45 [see other side]
46 Allergen from a pet
47 Basilica part
49 Reach across
51 Some treadmill users
54 Numbers to be summed
59 Mideast bigwig
60 Candy in a roll
62 Painter Magritte
63 Yalies
64 Put a cap on
65 "Trick" joint
66 Dial or ring follower
67 Feeds, in a sty

DOWN

1 Hostilities ender
2 Provo's state
3 Actress Hatcher
4 "Lights out" tune
5 Extinguish, as coals
6 Buck and bull
7 Prefix with corn
8 Rustic stopovers
9 Fashion industry, slangily
10 Like days of yore
11 Bean sprouts, tofu, etc.
12 Tattle on
13 Pundit's column
18 Actor Ken or Lena
22 "No problem!"
24 Evil-eye givers
26 Scrawny sort
27 Give a keynote, say
28 Bright red shade
29 Links area
31 Court order
33 Bond after Connery
34 Olympics distance unit
36 Bigger than big
39 Bed accessory
40 Larry King's channel
42 Gad about
43 Beach footwear
46 Most Little League coaches
48 See eye to eye
50 Bel __ cheese
51 Obnoxious one
52 Mystical sign
53 Fodder storehouse
55 Demon's doing
56 *Nautilus* skipper
57 Coffeemaker style
58 Retired speedsters
61 Half a sawbuck

★★ 123

Fill in the diagram so that each rectangular piece has one each of the numbers 1, 2, and 3, under these rules: 1) No two adjacent squares, horizontally or vertically, can have the same number. 2) Each completed row and column of the diagram will have an equal number of 1s, 2s, and 3s.

WRONG IS RIGHT

Which of these four words is misspelled?

A) monicle   B) moniker

C) monetary   D) monastery

★★ Fences

Connect the dots with vertical or horizontal lines, so that a single loop is formed with no crossings or branches. Each number indicates how many lines surround it; squares with no number may be surrounded by any number of lines.

```
2           3 3 2 1

    1 2           2
 1     2 3        3
 2

                       2
 2       2 0         1
 2         1 2
 3 2 0 2           2
```

ADDITION SWITCH

Switch the positions of two of the digits in the incorrect sum at right, to get a correct sum.

```
  5 9 1
+ 4 7 3
-------
  8 6 6
```

★★ Faking It by Randall J. Hartman

ACROSS

1 Stare
5 Short-term worker
9 National Leaguer
14 "Uh ... excuse me"
15 La Scala solo
16 Sky sighting
17 Actress Anderson
18 German philosopher
19 Jazz-club band
20 Mousepad material
23 Take a load off
24 Not him
25 Frequent title starter
28 Former Iranian ruler
31 Influential one
36 __ d'oeuvre
38 Old Testament book
40 Stock-exchange deal
41 Some costume jewelry
44 Summary
45 Marquee name
46 Butcher's stock
47 Chinese zodiac beast
49 Train for a bout
51 Prefix for credit
52 Place in position
54 Building site
56 Funny money
65 Yosemite photographer Adams
66 Economist Greenspan
67 Sandwich cookie
68 McQueen of *Bullitt*
69 Prepare for a portrait
70 Something off-limits
71 Fire-engine accessories
72 Gets it
73 Pass catchers

DOWN

1 Guys' companions
2 Cry from the crow's-nest
3 Ivy League school, for short
4 Sends forth
5 "So there!"
6 Part of QED
7 Short skirt
8 Quilting square
9 Right on the money
10 Messy one
11 Great Pyramid, essentially
12 Unsophisticated sort
13 Aroma
21 "To Each __ Own"
22 Basketball official
25 Like a bronze medalist
26 *Odyssey* creator
27 Susan Lucci TV role
29 French friends
30 Owl sounds
32 Overhead transportation
33 Gave a fig
34 Dwight's two-time opponent
35 Midterms and finals
37 Without a date
39 Piece of cake, so to speak
42 Simon Peter and Bartholomew
43 Pecan treats
48 Originally named
50 Stuff and nonsense
53 Snares
55 Porterhouse alternative
56 Redeem
57 Aware of
58 Puts into service
59 Actress Campbell
60 Arctic Ocean obstacle
61 Life of Riley
62 Resolve, with "out"
63 Give for a while
64 *Gentlemen Prefer Blondes* author

★★ Three-Color Maze

Enter the maze, pass through all the color squares exactly once, then exit, all without retracing your path. You must pass through the color squares in this sequence: red, blue, yellow, red, blue, etc.

SAY IT AGAIN

What four-letter word can mean either "sound quality" or "muscle quality"?

— — — —

bRain BReatHeR
MMM… CINNAMON!

Cinnamon on toast or oatmeal is so yummy, it's hard to believe the brown powder has any health benefits at all, but it's actually one of the most powerful healing spices. It's especially known for its ability to improve blood sugar control in diabetics, with as little as ¼ to ½ teaspoon a day. In addition, it can lower triglyceride and cholesterol levels; it helps to prevent blood clots; it has antibacterial and anti-inflammatory properties; it's rich in antioxidants; it's high in fiber; and it improves memory loss. So shake away! Or, try some of these suggestions:

To perk up chocolate chip cookies or brownies, add ½ teaspoon cinnamon along with the flour.

To flavor up a pot roast, add a cinnamon stick to the braising liquid.

For hot chocolate with a spicy aroma, stir in a pinch of ground cinnamon.

To make rice pilaf with more flavor, add a cinnamon stick to the simmering liquid. This trick is especially ideal for rice that accompanies Indian or Mexican dishes.

For grain salads with a Moroccan flair, add cinnamon and almonds. This tip works well for rice, couscous, barley, and other grain salads, especially if the dressing includes lemon juice and olive oil.

True cinnamon is often labeled as "Ceylon cinnamon" or "Seychelles Islands cinnamon." Most of the cinnamon sold in Western countries is actually cassia— a similar spice with a less complex, yet more pronounced, flavor.

To make spiced coffee, brew 4 cups of strong coffee, adding 1 tablespoon ground cinnamon to the coffee grounds (this works well in a drip-style coffee maker).

For a new twist on baked rigatoni, make the tomato sauce with sausage, onion, garlic, and cinnamon.

To boost the taste of your favorite pie crust, add ½ teaspoon ground cinnamon to the dough for a two-crust pie.

For a great summer-barbecue side dish, grill skewers of sweet potato chunks brushed with a touch of olive oil and sprinkled with cinnamon. Cook on metal skewers: They'll get hot and cook the potato from the inside, while the flame sears the outside.

★ Keyword

Find these 23 words that are hidden in the diagram, either across, down, or diagonally. (Individual words of multiple-word answers are hidden separately.) At first glance, they may appear to be from several different categories, but in fact they are all related—to the multiple meanings of one of the words on the list. What's that keyword?

```
E  T  S  I  S  S  A  E  K  B  H  G  D  S  L
S  T  P  G  V  T  T  Y  C  V  E  L  M  T  A
U  W  I  T  Q  O  E  D  A  U  O  H  A  E  S
S  R  N  R  M  V  J  G  B  H  T  U  I  S  R
T  O  E  O  W  N  O  I  P  M  A  H  C  N  O
A  P  R  S  E  R  B  U  C  B  A  C  P  H  D
I  P  I  N  S  A  E  N  C  O  U  R  A  G  E
N  U  R  O  R  D  G  D  I  S  N  R  O  R  E
N  S  E  P  O  V  G  R  N  W  O  F  E  D  L
R  R  V  S  D  O  E  X  I  U  F  V  I  A  I
R  A  E  R  N  C  R  T  I  W  E  S  G  R  S
E  E  R  T  E  A  H  D  O  R  S  U  M  Z  M
T  E  A  D  S  T  K  W  S  U  P  P  O  R  T
S  N  E  C  D  E  C  E  R  A  C  O  V  D  A
```

ADVOCATE
ASSIST
BACK
CHAMPION
CONFIRM
DORSAL
DORSUM
ENCOURAGE
ENDORSE
GET BEHIND
PROMOTE
REAR
RECEDE
REVERSE
SIDE WITH
SPINE
SPONSOR
STERN
SUPPORT
SUSTAIN
UNDERWRITE
UPHOLD
VOUCH

WHO'S WHAT WHERE?

The correct term for a resident of Great Britain's Isle of Man is:

A) Manislander   B) Mannian

C) Mannite   D) Manx

★★ Hyper-Sudoku

Fill in the blank boxes so that every row, column, 3x3 box, *and* each of the four 3x3 gray regions contains all of the numbers 1 to 9.

	9		8					2
	4				1			
		1	5	9			6	8
						2		
			3					1
					5	3		
7		6			1			
8				2				9
9	1			6	3		8	

MIXAGRAMS

Each line contains a five-letter word and a four-letter word that have been mixed together (the order of the letters in each word has not been changed). Unmix the two words on each line and write them in the spaces provided. When you're done, find a two-part answer to the clue by reading down the letter columns in the answers.

CLUE: Famous Johnson

G O S P O B I L S = _ _ _ _ _ + _ _ _ _

A V I M S T I D A = _ _ _ _ _ + _ _ _ _

S P L A P I D R Y = _ _ _ _ _ + _ _ _ _

B I N E D L A S Y = _ _ _ _ _ + _ _ _ _

★★★ Collectibles by Randall J. Hartman

ACROSS

1 Coal containers
5 Sign of healing
9 Wild
14 Garfield's pal
15 Israeli dance
16 Spin doctor's concern
17 Marcel Marceau, e.g.
18 Geologic divisions
19 Locations
20 Finalizes one's itinerary, maybe
23 Pigs' place
24 Capote, to friends
25 Country crooner Greenwood
26 Put down, in the 'hood
29 Director Craven
30 Wine region of Italy
32 Actor Davis
35 Support
36 Draft rating
37 Lets into the country, perhaps
40 Summer destination
41 Some nest eggs
42 Does damage to
43 Tropical bugs
45 Baby boxer
46 Spanish king
47 Inventor's monogram
48 __ Alamos, NM
49 Trophy shape
52 Creates memorable words
55 Large quantity
58 "Phooey!"
59 Don of morning radio
60 Clear thinking
61 Biblical twin
62 Furniture wood
63 Lorna __
64 Roan's restraint
65 Fellow fighter

DOWN

1 Performs poorly
2 Dostoyevsky title character
3 Spock portrayer
4 Search for
5 They make the cut
6 Greek island
7 Asia's __ Sea
8 Important churches
9 Caught porgy and bass
10 Send forth
11 Stool pigeon
12 Geologic division
13 Guitarist Paul

21 Like the face of El Capitan
22 Nerds
26 Blood-drive participant
27 Nonreactive
28 GNP and CPI
29 Namby-pamby
30 Pablo's potatoes
31 Finish
32 One of a Katharine Hepburn quartet
33 Fixed look
34 Pal of Frank and Dean
35 Boilermaker maker

38 Egyptian peninsula
39 "Be quiet!"
44 Right now
45 Toy with a cork
48 Hawaiian island
49 Saharan transport
50 Quite ordinary
51 Troublesome
52 Something to raise
53 Enclosure with a MS
54 Singer Coolidge
55 Former
56 Whisper sweet nothings
57 It may be inflated with hot air

★★ One-Way Streets

The diagram represents a pattern of streets. P's are parking spaces, and the black squares are stores. Find the route that starts at a parking space, passes through all stores exactly once, and ends at the other parking space. Arrows indicate one-way traffic for that block only. No block or intersection may be entered more than once.

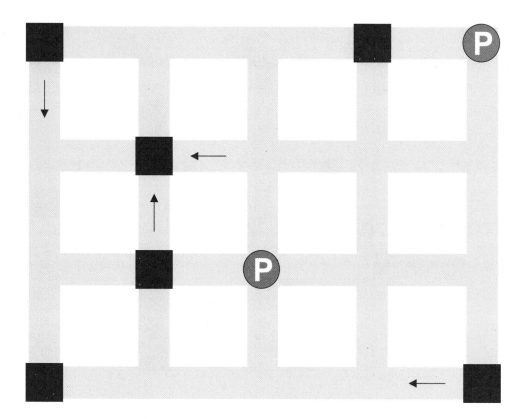

SOUND THINKING

The consonant sounds in the word GARDENIA are G, R, D, and N. What other eight-letter word is pronounced with the same consonant sounds in the same order?

_____

★★ Star Search

Find the stars that are hidden in some of the blank squares. The numbered squares indicate how many stars are hidden in the squares adjacent to them (including diagonally). There is never more than one star in any square.

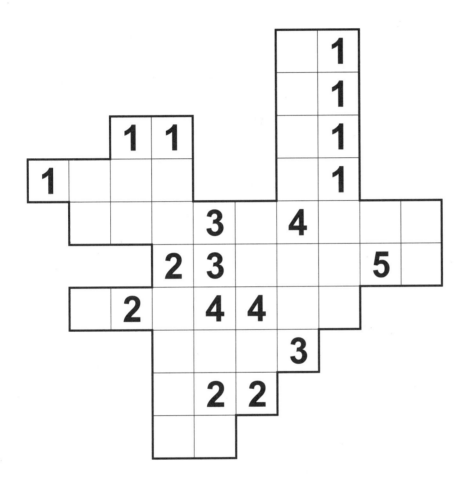

CHOICE WORDS

Form three six-letter words from the same category, by selecting one letter from each column three times. Each letter will be used exactly once.

C	L	L	H	E	D	_ _ _ _ _ _
W	A	S	O	U	T	_ _ _ _ _ _
A	A	M	N	N	W	_ _ _ _ _ _

★★★ In a Wink by Doug Peterson

ACROSS

1 Red Cross supply
6 Paint base
11 Hosp. areas
14 Lei bearer's word
15 Florida city
16 Ran into
17 Sci-fi serial hero
19 Tan in bookstores
20 Corn serving
21 Wisecracks
22 Pluvial month
24 Medieval security device
25 Carol starter
26 When push comes to shove
31 As a companion
32 Attack one's plate
33 Flour holder
36 Dark principle
37 14 Across, at times
41 Wasn't colorfast
42 Not for
44 Mysterious sighting
45 Artless
47 Convenient pick-me-up
51 Tourist draws
53 Get moving
54 Just right
55 Bizet offering
57 Outdo
60 Puncturing tool
61 Level for most seven-year-olds
64 Up to, informally
65 Felt fluish
66 Brave Hall-of-Famer
67 "It's __-brainer!"
68 Like smokestacks
69 Pine (for)

DOWN

1 Unscathed
2 Fitzgerald of jazz
3 Howl with laughter
4 Sounds of hesitation
5 144-tile game
6 Rely upon
7 Farmland parcel
8 Smidgens
9 10 Down rock band
10 Olivia Newton-John film of '80
11 Zhivago portrayer
12 Send, as payment
13 Panache
18 Navy mascot
23 Teacher's faves
24 Game pieces
25 Dilettantish
26 Uxmal resident
27 Actress Lena
28 Five-cent illustration
29 Was nourished by
30 Bar bill
34 Yield to pressure
35 Genuflection joint
38 Inning enders
39 Three-kind connector
40 Historic B-29
43 Ancient Peruvian
46 Samuel Gompers' grp.
48 Zesty dips
49 Hot
50 Parachute pull
51 Mazda model
52 Fictional Drood
55 *Dos* cubed
56 Donne, for one
57 Fictional plantation
58 Polecat's defense
59 Teller partner
62 Earth-friendly prefix
63 *Norma* __

★★ Texas Trail

Enter the maze where indicated at bottom, pass through all the stars exactly once, then exit at top. You may not retrace your path.

SMALL CHANGE

Change one letter in each of these two words, to form a common two-word phrase.

FAIR TOPIC

_____

★★ Sudoku

Fill in the blank boxes so that every row, column, and 3x3 box contains all of the numbers 1 to 9.

					5			
2		7		1		9		8
	4		2		7		6	
6		9				4		
	3						5	
		1				2		6
	9		1		6		3	
4		2		8		7		5
			7					

CENTURY MARKS

Select one number in each of the four columns so that the total adds up to exactly 100.

$$\boxed{\begin{array}{c} 16 \\ \hline 4 \end{array}} + \boxed{\begin{array}{c} 53 \\ \hline 55 \end{array}} + \boxed{\begin{array}{c} 24 \\ \hline 21 \end{array}} + \boxed{\begin{array}{c} 22 \\ \hline 9 \end{array}} = 100$$

★★★ Trash Talk by Doug Peterson

ACROSS

1 Cogent
5 Clickable picture
9 Military bigwigs
14 Partner of heart
15 '96 presidential candidate
16 Tetrad times two
17 High-yield investments
19 Not now
20 Contest of a sort
21 Martial-arts actor
23 Tiny Tim's instrument
24 Taking after
26 Milne character
28 Rams and lambs
30 Cat owner's purchase
34 Island near Bora Bora
35 Rice dish
36 Sign
37 Biscuit topper
39 Colette's chum
43 Proclamation announcer
45 Simple racer
47 Aphorism against extravagance
51 Source of the Mississippi
52 FBI operative
53 African antelope
54 State exec.
55 Let out, maybe
58 Put on the tube
60 Twist
62 Spot for mementos
66 Within the rules
67 Gentle interruption
68 Nike alternative
69 Shangri-las
70 Light-sensitive cells
71 Count (on)

DOWN

1 Financial daily, briefly
2 Marker
3 Work on a tan
4 Sommer of cinema
5 Words of agreement
6 Grifter's game
7 Shoppe adjective
8 Home under an eave
9 South American nation
10 Nipper's co.
11 Bring into harmony
12 Posse member
13 Italicize, perhaps
18 Bohemian topper
22 Loaf
24 Palo __, CA
25 Actor Neeson
27 Far from trite
29 Actually
31 Hints of color
32 Perplexing pictures
33 Sun King's designation
38 '20s auto
40 Swamp tree
41 Unyielding
42 Legendary rebuke
44 Ousters by voters
46 Available
47 Move a little
48 Made amends
49 Uncivilized
50 Did battle
56 Romanov title
57 Reflected sound
59 Construction beam
61 Superintended
63 Pre-noon hrs.
64 __ painting
65 Mrs. Michael Corleone

★★ Split Decisions

In this clueless crossword puzzle, each answer consists of two words whose spellings are the same, except for the consecutive letters given. All answers are common words; no phrases or hyphenated or capitalized words are used. Some of the clues may have more than one solution, but there is only one word pair that will correctly link up with all the other word pairs.

TRANSDELETION

Delete one letter from the word CUBISTIC and rearrange the rest, to get something edible.

★★ Number-Out

Shade squares so that no number appears in any row or column more than once. Shaded squares may not touch each other horizontally or vertically, and all unshaded squares must form a single continuous area.

1	5	6	5	2	2
5	1	6	3	4	2
2	3	5	1	2	4
4	1	1	1	5	3
2	2	6	6	6	5
3	5	2	4	1	6

THINK ALIKE

Unscramble the letters in the phrase TEN CROOKS to form two words with the same or similar meanings.

_____   _____

★★★ Window Dressing by Robert H. Wolfe

ACROSS

1 France, once
5 Neighbor of Armenia
9 *Star Wars* creator
14 Seep (through)
15 Jodie Foster film
16 Habituate
17 Social fix-up
19 Shower time
20 Mariner
21 Full of life
22 Dads
25 Mates of ewes
26 Actress Rowlands
27 Pale
29 Homepage location
32 Turn away from
33 Sweet-talk
36 Negative connector
37 Wee ones
38 Video-game name
39 Lasting impression
40 Museum pieces
41 Became overcast
42 "Ciao!"
43 Gets peeved
45 Ancient Greek physician
46 Civil unrest
47 Play starter
50 Took charge
51 Sugar lumps
53 Writer
55 Fills, as gaps
56 Linden, for one
60 Heavenly one
61 Big book
62 E.A. Robinson title character
63 Insolent
64 Saturates
65 Roll-call shout

DOWN

1 Mariner
2 Part of some e-mail addresses
3 Israeli weapon
4 Microscope part
5 Destination for da Gama
6 Empire
7 Singing voices
8 Met, for one
9 Not bother
10 Lets down, as long hair
11 Acknowledgment of applause
12 Number for one
13 Cash in
18 Mend, as socks
22 Shells and elbows
23 Off the ship
24 Camera enthusiasts
26 Chilly
28 USN rank
29 Had on
30 Just right
31 Task
33 Editing mark
34 Not much
35 Crow relative
39 RR stop
41 In a coarse manner
44 Prolonged attacks
45 Taunt
47 Blessing preceder, perhaps
48 Muscle annoyance
49 Sea fluctuations
51 No. crunchers
52 Arm bone
53 Grounded fleet: Abbr.
54 Engrave
57 Fish eggs
58 Go wrong
59 Take a gander at

★★ ABC

Enter the letters A, B, and C into the diagram so that each row and column has exactly one A, one B, and one C. The letters outside the diagram indicate the first letter encountered, moving in the direction of the arrow. Keep in mind that after all the letters have been filled in, there will be two blank boxes in each row and column.

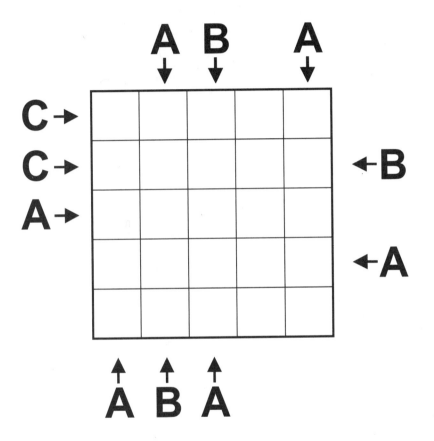

CLUELESS CROSSWORD

Complete the crossword with common uncapitalized seven-letter words, based entirely on the letters already filled in for you.

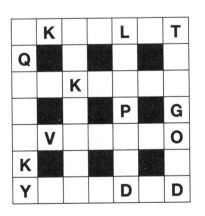

★★ Go With the Flow

Enter the maze where indicated at left, pass through all the yellow circles exactly once, then exit. You must go with the flow, making no sharp turns, and you may use paths more than once.

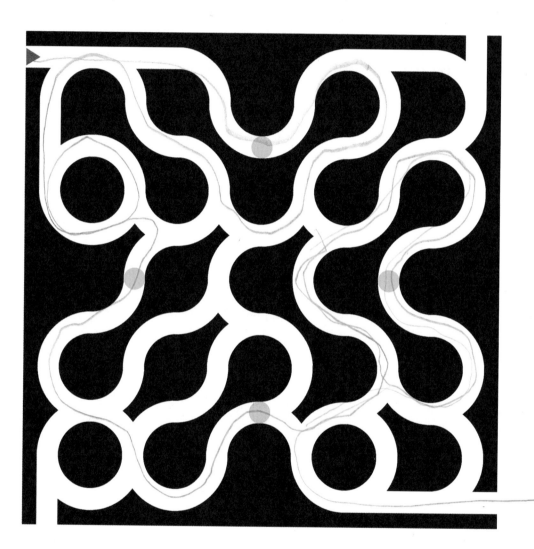

BETWEENER

What four-letter word belongs between the word at left and the word at right, so that the first and second word, and the second and third word, each form a common compound word?

ANT _ _ _ _ TOP

★★★ Line Drawing

Draw two straight lines, each from one edge of the square to another edge, so that the sum of the numbers in each region is the same.

```
┌─────────────────────────────────┐
│                                 │
│   1        3          6         │
│        4              3         │
│                                 │
│                 1               │
│   2                    7        │
│        4        3               │
│                                 │
│                        2        │
│                 1               │
│   3                             │
│        1               10       │
│                                 │
└─────────────────────────────────┘
```

THREE OF A KIND

Find the three hidden words in the sentence that go together in some way.

Go slow, don't be a hero, meditate a little, or just hibernate.

★★★ Food Break by Fred Piscop

ACROSS

1 Fat avoider of rhyme
6 Two-faced god
11 ATM access code
14 Our land, informally
15 Split to wed
16 Planet, to a poet
17 Fountain treat
19 Mad Hatter's beverage
20 Would-be diva
21 Macbeth's title
23 Cooled down
25 Rug cleaner
26 Get going
30 Make mention of
32 Antipasto ingredient
34 Drags to court
35 Nav. rank
38 Sommelier's offering
39 Senator Lott
41 Visit an e-tailer
42 Hang back
43 Narrow margin
44 Attack
46 Slow developer
49 Get mellow
50 Manuscript copyist
52 Mall bag
54 Cohort of Kent and Lane
55 "You're right!"
60 Make illegal
61 Century-old soft-drink brand
65 Timeline division
66 Louisiana waterway
67 Slip by
68 Séance sound
69 Took three of three, say
70 __ salts

DOWN

1 Cylindrical lunches
2 Exam for jrs.
3 Gossipy Barrett
4 Way out there
5 Sunbathing evidence
6 King's amuser
7 Matterhorn, e.g.
8 Cambodian leader Lon __
9 AP rival
10 Some sporting dogs
11 Dip holder
12 Peace goddess
13 Cav or Mav
18 NRC forerunner
22 Something to tip
24 Utah's former name
25 Borscht base
26 Cereal serving
27 Director Kazan
28 Crisp cookie
29 "__ had it!"
31 Games partner
33 Like week-old bread
36 Pig's place
37 Ready for business
40 Blue line on a map: Abbr.
41 __ Lanka
43 Rubs elbows
45 Cloying stuff
47 Compete
48 Inferior liquor
50 Sensible
51 Bow of silents
53 Definite article
56 Links hazard
57 Has a late meal
58 "That __ yesterday!"
59 The other guys
62 Like sashimi
63 Salt's assent
64 Alphabetic trio

★★ Find the Ships

Determine the position of the 10 ships listed to the right of the diagram. The ships may be oriented either horizontally or vertically. A square with wavy lines indicates water and will not contain a ship. The numbers at the edge of the diagram indicate how many squares in that row or column contain parts of ships. When all 10 ships are correctly placed in the diagram, no two of them will touch each other, not even diagonally.

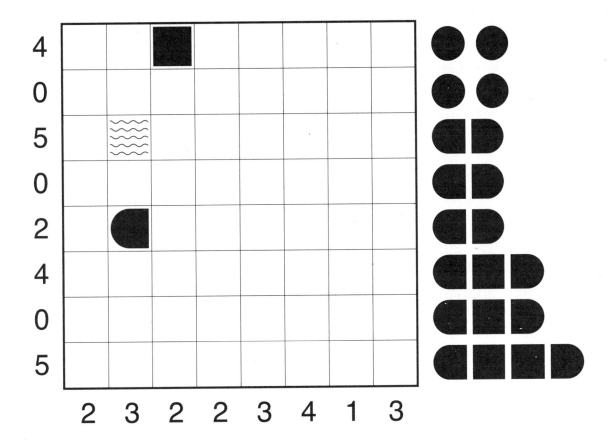

TWO-BY-FOUR

The eight letters in the word WARRANTY can be rearranged to form a pair of common four-letter words in three different ways, if no four-letter word is repeated. Can you find them all?

__ __ __ __   __ __ __ __   __ __ __ __   __ __ __ __

__ __ __ __   __ __ __ __

★★★ Hyper-Sudoku

Fill in the blank boxes so that every row, column, 3x3 box, *and* each of the four 3x3 gray regions contains all of the numbers 1 to 9.

			3	4			2	6
	4					5		
6			8	7				1
	1							
								7
	8		5		2			
		7			8		3	
3			9	1	7	8		

MIXAGRAMS

Each line contains a five-letter word and a four-letter word that have been mixed together (the order of the letters in each word has not been changed). Unmix the two words on each line and write them in the spaces provided. When you're done, find a two-part answer to the clue by reading down the letter columns in the answers.

CLUE: Chuck Berry's specialty

D A M E N C O W E = _ _ _ _ _ + _ _ _ _

F U N L E T A I L = _ _ _ _ _ + _ _ _ _

C O U R S R E A L = _ _ _ _ _ + _ _ _ _

K O K O H A K K I = _ _ _ _ _ + _ _ _ _

★★★ Large-Scale by Shirley Soloway

ACROSS

1 Playing-card spots
5 Avant-__
10 Letters on some radios
14 Mass conclusion
15 Unfamiliar
16 Farm bundle
17 Carson successor
18 Sire
19 Reason for cramming
20 Clearly visible
23 Wall St. introduction
24 Sign of displeasure
25 Pops up again
27 Highest level
30 Dresses down
33 Likened
38 Out of the way
39 Always
40 Packing container
43 *Waltons* daughter
44 Kids' blocks
46 Stopped
48 Hypnotic states
51 Captain Nemo's harpooner
52 Kid's cap
54 *Rigoletto*, for one
59 South African antelope
61 20-screen cinemas
64 Nessie's home
66 Conserve, in a way
67 Neckwear
68 "Times of Your Life" singer
69 Terminator
70 Parisian pronoun
71 A majority
72 Declivitous
73 Chill out

DOWN

1 Coconut sources
2 Clarification introducer
3 Pound fractions
4 It might wake you up
5 Chatters
6 Obi-Wan portrayer
7 Severity
8 Not as superficial
9 Lead on
10 Former Japanese prime minister
11 Shin hider
12 Plane-wing part
13 Note from the boss
21 Black-and-white dolphin
22 Onetime Hemingway home
26 Pretexts
28 Eyebrow shape
29 According to
31 Nicollette Sheridan TV role
32 With 34 Down, make a referral
33 NBA player
34 See 32 Down
35 Lottery prize, perhaps
36 Liable (to)
37 Scoutmaster, often
41 X
42 Language ending
45 Shell game
47 Inspirational figure
49 Accustoms (to)
50 Mum
53 Chopin piece
55 Last Supper diner
56 Napoleon's fate
57 Sees stars
58 Resourcefulness, e.g.
59 Alluring, for short
60 Something banned
62 Phrase of acknowledgment
63 Cop's quarry
65 __ in hand (humbly)

★★★ Fences

Connect the dots with vertical or horizontal lines, so that a single loop is formed with no crossings or branches. Each number indicates how many lines surround it; squares with no number may be surrounded by any number of lines.

```
2    2    3  3  2

  2     3

3          0     3  2

      3              3

2                1

1  2    3           2

         3     3

  3  1  2     2    3
```

WRONG IS RIGHT

Which of these four words is misspelled?

A) gaiety

B) galleon

C) gabardine

D) gaddabout

★★ Dotty

Draw a line from square to square, moving either horizontally and vertically, so that all squares have been visited once. You may pass from one square to another only if it contains a dot of the same color and size. Note that many squares have small dots on top of large dots.

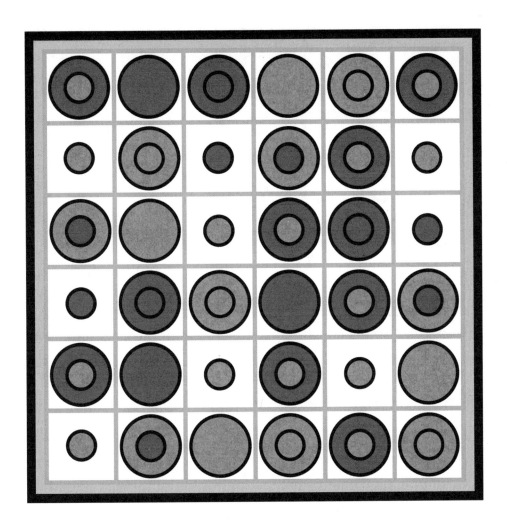

SAY IT AGAIN

What four-letter word can be either a type of thread or a type of tale?

— — — —

★★ Number-Out

Shade squares so that no number appears in any row or column more than once. Shaded squares may not touch each other horizontally or vertically, and all unshaded squares must form a single continuous area.

6	1	5	5	2	4
3	3	3	5	6	2
1	5	4	5	3	2
4	6	6	2	4	3
3	2	2	6	4	1
5	5	2	4	4	6

THINK ALIKE

Unscramble the letters in the phrase FEEDS PATSY to form two words with the same or similar meanings.

_____   _____

★★★ Good Thinking by Shirley Soloway

ACROSS

1 A little wet
5 Tree surgeon's concern
10 "Mi __ es su ..."
14 Phrase of acknowledgment
15 Indian prince
16 General Bradley
17 Part of Orion's belt
18 Really angry
19 Clothes-dryer collection
20 Bet with care
23 '40s wunderkind Welles
24 Chinese money
25 Small amphibians
29 Beer expert
33 Hot tub
36 Megalomaniac's desire
38 Past due
39 Conclude deliberations
43 Poetic adverb
44 Dieter's lunch
45 Blasting need
46 Fortune-teller
49 Parachute material
51 Source of some retirement income
53 Run out
57 Be unswayable
63 Green fruit
64 Celebrities
65 Working hard
66 Gate material
67 Collect
68 Hosiery shade
69 Mao successor
70 Spotted steed
71 Phone letters

DOWN

1 '70s music fad
2 American Fur Company founder
3 Has in mind
4 Soul
5 Electric-power network
6 Seldom encountered
7 Not fully closed
8 Of no use to Jack Sprat
9 Boston nickname
10 "Bird" officers
11 Mixed in with
12 Glassmaking material
13 Creative pursuits
21 Not competent
22 Pitcher handle
26 Try to win
27 Christmas poem start
28 Family car
30 Hold on
31 British prep school
32 Pay for the use of
33 Ripoff
34 Kid's mount
35 "Famous" entrepreneur
37 Hinge (on)
40 Attractive
41 Meas. of heat
42 Objects of devotion
47 Peeve
48 Sort of break
50 '98 Winter Olympics locale
52 "Ditto!"
54 Abide, with "with"
55 Nasty
56 Organic compound
57 Slip and slide
58 Become bored
59 Victor's declaration
60 Saudi Arabia neighbor
61 Snug spot
62 Oil giant of yore

★★★ 123

Fill in the diagram so that each rectangular piece has one each of the numbers 1, 2, and 3, under these rules: 1) No two adjacent squares, horizontally or vertically, can have the same number. 2) Each completed row and column of the diagram will have an equal number of 1s, 2s, and 3s.

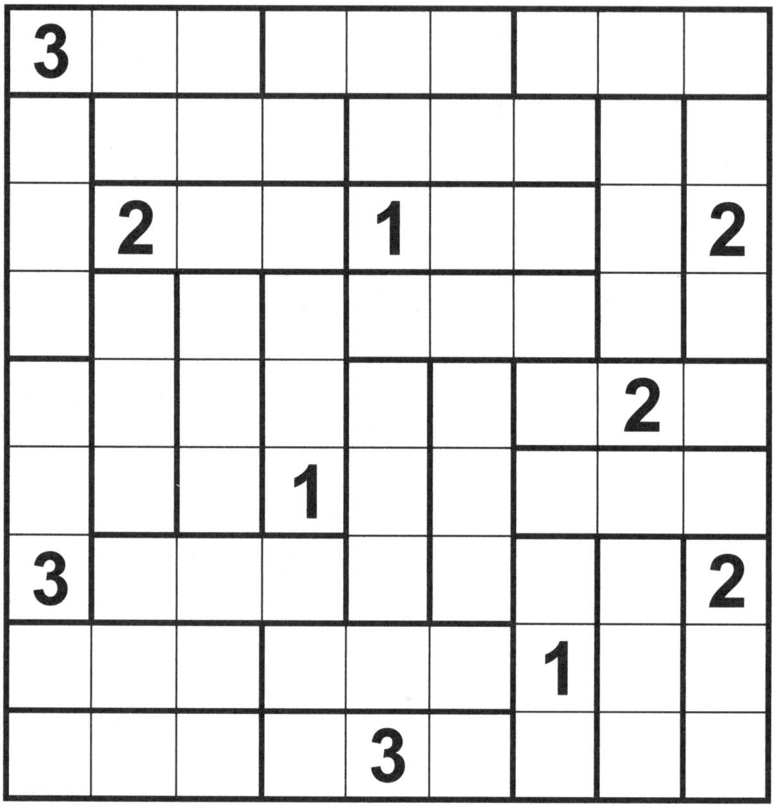

3								
	2			**1**				**2**
							2	
			1					
3								**2**
						1		
				3				

SUDOKU SUM

Fill in the missing numbers from 1 to 9, so that the sum of each row and column is as indicated.

	12	**17**	**16**
21			8
11	1		
13		6	

★★★ Find the Ships

Determine the position of the 10 ships listed to the right of the diagram. The ships may be oriented either horizontally or vertically. A square with wavy lines indicates water and will not contain a ship. The numbers at the edge of the diagram indicate how many squares in that row or column contain parts of ships. When all 10 ships are correctly placed in the diagram, no two of them will touch each other, not even diagonally.

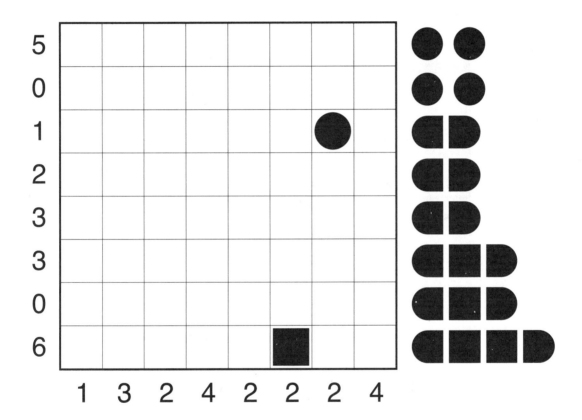

TWO-BY-FOUR

The eight letters in the word ACCREDIT can be rearranged to form a pair of common four-letter words in two different ways, if no four-letter word is repeated. Can you find both pairs of words?

_ _ _ _   _ _ _ _

_ _ _ _   _ _ _ _

★★★ Pocket Change by Doug Peterson

ACROSS

1 Big Apple restaurateur
6 Leather shade
11 Pullman, for one
14 Wielded
15 *Peer Gynt* playwright
16 Eye, in Ecuador
17 Coin first minted in 1909
19 Snooze
20 Smirnoff competitor
21 Use a wok
23 Seating section
24 Decks, briefly
26 __ Aviv
27 Coin first minted in 1916
32 Needs
36 German article
37 "Get lost!"
38 Not behind
40 Stone discovery site
42 Hold sway
43 Oklahoma Indian
45 Canvas holder
46 Coin first minted in 1921
49 Race, as an engine
50 Costa __ Sol
51 Prefix for 55 Across
55 Fermi's field
59 Coin-operated eatery
61 Camcorder abbreviation
62 Person interested in 17, 27 and 46 Across
64 Important time
65 "I Got a Name" singer
66 River feature
67 Electrical jolt
68 Barely beat
69 More cunning

DOWN

1 Pie-in-the-face sound
2 Arrestee's excuse
3 Washer cycle
4 Furnishings and such
5 Screen favorite
6 Venetian Mannerist painter
7 Epitome of easiness
8 Puts into action
9 Confined
10 Being
11 Prolonged struggles
12 Open a crack
13 Well-sinewed
18 Leia's brother
22 Obstacle in Exodus
25 55 Across, for example: Abbr.
27 Topography abbr.
28 Not publicly available
29 Antique auto
30 Captain's underling
31 List ender
32 Angelic strings
33 Flu symptom
34 Earnings limit
35 Family-tree entries
39 Turf section
41 Sun. speech
44 Former
47 Make clear
48 Grad
51 Vacation stop
52 One of the Brontës
53 Discernment
54 Perfumery oil
55 Informal DC title
56 Olympian queen
57 Cottage-cheese morsel
58 Urban blight
60 Smidgens
63 Bar supply

★ Where in the World?

Find these unusual place names that are hidden in the diagram, either across, down, or diagonally. These places are all in the same country, whose name is also hidden in the diagram.

```
O O R A L L A W E O P X A J A
K M A N L W Y A J W D K G T A
N R T O L L B X H M O Y T I L
Z V O O P C I Y A O D A S N O
C O O N A W A R R A D Y S T O
P G P L I L A A A A E K Q I R
A B M V L N W F N G I U T N A
R A O A A O O D A G N A L A K
I L P N R W O O M E R A F R R
N H G M T O U T S T A Z K A A
G A I R S A K L U M A R R U C
A N B N U N D R O O K R R T Q
Q N H N A N G W A R R Y L U C
I A W I L L U N G A H C G E B
A H A G N O P Y M U L W N W E
```

ARKAROOLA
BALHANNAH
BURRA
COONAWARRA
CURRAMULKA
GOOLWA
KALANGADOO
KANGARILLA
MARANANGA
MYPONGA
NANGWARRY
NUNDROO
OODNADATTA
PARINGA
POMPOOTA
TARLEE
TINTINARA
WALLAROO
WAROOKA
WHYALLA
WILLUNGA
WOOMERA

IN OTHER WORDS

There is only one common uncapitalized word that contains the consecutive letters NNK. What is it?

_____

★★ Alternating Tiles

Starting at a red tile somewhere at top and moving either horizontally or vertically, draw a path through the tiles to the bottom. You may not pass through two tiles of the same color consecutively.

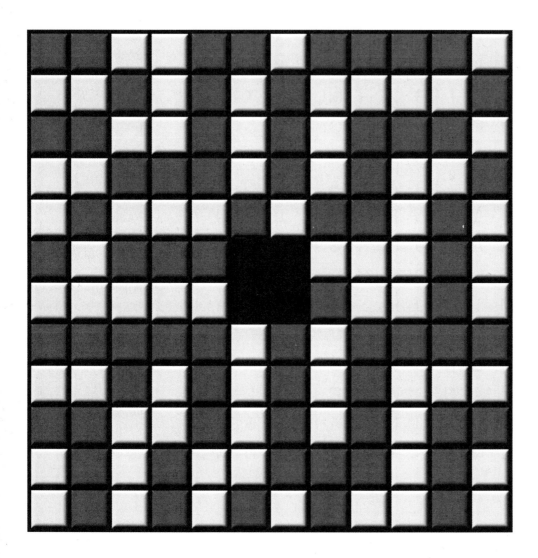

SMALL CHANGE

Change one letter in each of these two words, to form a common two-word phrase.

STEEL CLEAT

★★★ Star Search

Find the stars that are hidden in some of the blank squares. The numbered squares indicate how many stars are hidden in the squares adjacent to them (including diagonally). There is never more than one star in any square.

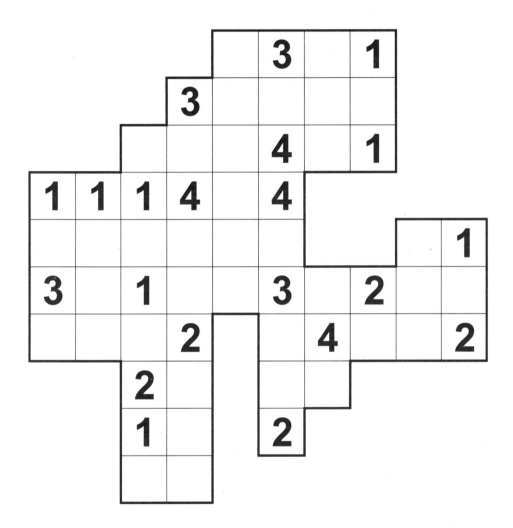

CHOICE WORDS

Form three six-letter words from the same category, by selecting one letter from each column three times. Each letter will be used exactly once.

A	L	T	V	E	D	_ _ _ _ _ _
S	S	E	E	T	E	_ _ _ _ _ _
C	H	R	U	W	R	_ _ _ _ _ _

★★★ Sever-Ance by Robert H. Wolfe

ACROSS

1 Type of train
6 Silicate minerals
11 Weather system
14 Unaccompanied
15 Ranks between viscounts and marquesses
16 Half of *dos*
17 Acted like a hooligan
19 Sgt., for one
20 Nada
21 Early morning hr.
22 Gulf War missile
23 Fit of anger
25 Gives comfort to
27 High spot
30 Stage comment
32 Heavenly body
33 In the neighborhood
35 Sheet-music notations
38 "Orinoco Flow" singer
39 "Peach" dessert
41 Springing movement
42 Chicken feature
44 Nepal's __ Mountains
46 Bewitch
47 1960s protest
48 Ring decisions
49 Hold dear
52 Designer Schiaparelli
54 Towel word
55 Not rude
57 Cuts wood
61 Poetic "before"
62 Cool dessert
64 Heir, often
65 "__ you glad?"
66 Fictional Swiss miss
67 Big-bang material
68 Plaster of Paris
69 Large keyboard key

DOWN

1 Field of grass
2 Breakfast spread
3 St. of the Union
4 Initial chips
5 Virgo preceder
6 Intervening period
7 "It must be something __"
8 Pants line
9 National alternative
10 Ukraine, once: Abbr.
11 Midday time off
12 At precisely the right moment
13 Scenery for Red Riding Hood
18 Malodorous
22 Slow walk
24 Informal turndown
26 "Wow!"
27 Over again
28 Singer Horne
29 Avoid eviction
31 Indian city
34 Star bestowers
35 __ Parker Bowles
36 Belafonte tune
37 Hot spots
40 Start eating, as an apple
43 61, once
45 Q&A part
47 Excels
49 Where the heart is
50 Wading bird
51 Close call
53 Poplar tree
56 Cargo movers
58 Came down
59 Broad
60 Bartending direction
62 Suitcase
63 "Steady as __ goes!"

★★★ Sudoku

Fill in the blank boxes so that every row, column, and 3x3 box contains all of the numbers 1 to 9.

2	1	4	3	7	6	5	2	
4	5	2	6	8	1	7	9	3
8	3	7	9	2	5	6	4	
3	5	6	4	5	2	1	8	
5	8	1	0	6	7	3	9	2
2	7	3	1	4	8	0		
1	6	9	5	3	2	4		
8	4	5	2	0	3	9		
6	3	8	0	1	9	2	7	

MIXAGRAMS

Each line contains a five-letter word and a four-letter word that have been mixed together (the order of the letters in each word has not been changed). Unmix the two words on each line and write them in the spaces provided. When you're done, find a two-part answer to the clue by reading down the letter columns in the answers.

CLUE: Kern classic

D U S K E M B E T = _ _ _ _ _ + _ _ _ _

S H O O T L E L O = _ _ _ _ _ + _ _ _ _

T O D U D B E A R = _ _ _ _ _ + _ _ _ _

W H O V O S E N T = _ _ _ _ _ + _ _ _ _

★★★ One-Way Streets

The diagram represents a pattern of streets. A and B are parking spaces, and the black squares are stores. Find the route that starts at A, passes through all stores exactly once, and ends at B. Arrows indicate one-way traffic for that block only. No block or intersection may be entered more than once.

SOUND THINKING

There is only one common uncapitalized word whose consonant sounds are H, Y, and J, in that order. What is it?

_____

★★★ ABC

Enter the letters A, B, and C into the diagram so that each row and column has exactly one A, one B, and one C. The letters outside the diagram indicate the first letter encountered, moving in the direction of the arrow. Keep in mind that after all the letters have been filled in, there will be two blank boxes in each row and column.

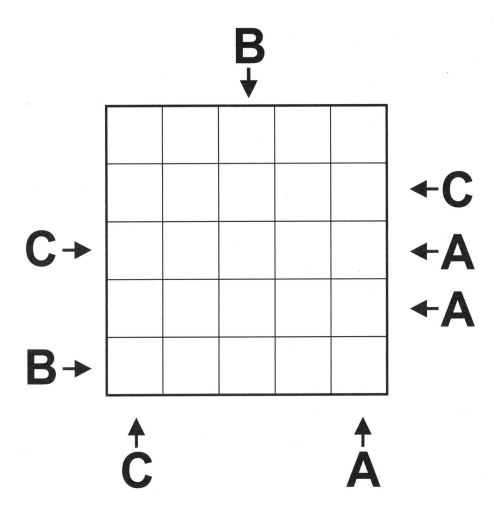

NATIONAL TREASURE

Rearrange the letters in the word AMERICAN to get a capitalized term in the film industry.

— — — — — — — —

★★★ The Bright Stuff by Shirley Soloway

ACROSS

1 Folk singer at Woodstock
5 Residence, slangily
9 *Psycho* character
14 Gymnast Korbut
15 Creative spark
16 Residence
17 Storm signal
19 Oslo's land, to natives
20 PDQ
21 Heads for the supermarket
23 Business partner, sometimes
24 Go wrong
26 Court ritual
27 Mills Brothers song subject
30 Tree product
33 Incredibly bad
36 Florence's river
37 Time-honored stories
38 Pays a visit
39 Spike Lee alma mater
40 Part of SST
41 Get into a corner
42 Pablo Neruda works
43 Roman senators' garb
44 Corp. officers
45 Gets angry
47 Fabled racer
49 Deplorable
50 Tool with teeth
53 Patriotic symbol
57 Austin Powers adversary
59 Saudi currency
60 Mocked, in a way
62 Buckeye city
63 Tough test
64 Phoned
65 Brought on
66 O positive, for one
67 Assistant

DOWN

1 Gauchos' weapons
2 Justice since 2006
3 Incite
4 Former CNN anchor
5 Bucks
6 A mean Amin
7 Pentagon VIP
8 Kitchen herb
9 Small fowl
10 Here and there
11 Sinatra specialty
12 Competitive __
13 Observes
18 Immune-system components
22 Picador's opponent
25 Uganda neighbor
27 Sound scared
28 Comparatively contrary
29 Heavy weights
31 Oratorio piece
32 Chest muscles
33 Last part of *Hamlet*
34 Distort
35 Memory-drill device
37 Closed circuit
40 Place to paint
42 Flamenco cheers
45 __ Yosemite International Airport
46 Specimen
48 Parcel out
50 Region east of Suez
51 Rectify
52 Piece of pie
53 River to the Caspian
54 Winged goddess
55 Tremendously
56 Gardener of rhyme
58 *A Doll's House* protagonist
61 Almanac feature

★★ Wheels and Cogs

When Santa turns the handle as shown, will the wheel point to chimney 1 or chimney 2?

BETWEENER

What four-letter word belongs between the word at left and the word at right, so that the first and second word, and the second and third word, each form a common compound word?

TENDER __ __ __ __ BALL

★★★ Find the Ships

Determine the position of the 10 ships listed to the right of the diagram. The ships may be oriented either horizontally or vertically. A square with wavy lines indicates water and will not contain a ship. The numbers at the edge of the diagram indicate how many squares in that row or column contain parts of ships. When all 10 ships are correctly placed in the diagram, no two of them will touch each other, not even diagonally.

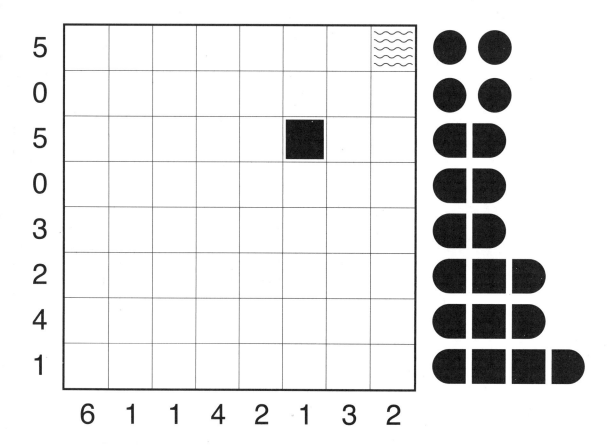

TWO-BY-FOUR

The eight letters in the word BRETHREN can be rearranged to form a pair of common four-letter words in only one way, if no four-letter word is repeated. Can you find the two words?

__ __ __ __   __ __ __ __

★★★ 123

Fill in the diagram so that each rectangular piece has one each of the numbers 1, 2, and 3, under these rules: 1) No two adjacent squares, horizontally or vertically, can have the same number. 2) Each completed row and column of the diagram will have an equal number of 1s, 2s, and 3s.

ADDITION SWITCH

Switch the positions of two of the digits in the incorrect sum at right, to get a correct sum.

```
  6 2 6
+ 2 4 8
-------
  9 1 0
```

bRain BREAtHEr
BAKING SODA AROUND THE HOUSE

If you're like most people, you probably have a carton of baking soda in the fridge. But this versatile product has loads of uses even if you never set foot in the kitchen. Consider these:

Remove crayon marks from walls
Have the kids or grandkids redecorated your walls or wallpaper with some original artwork in crayon? Stay calm! Just grab a damp rag, dip it in some baking soda, and lightly scrub the marks. They should come off with a minimal amount of effort.

Remove musty odors from books
If those books you just took out of storage emerge with a musty smell, place each one in a brown paper bag with 2 tablespoons baking soda. No need to shake the bag; just tie it up and let it sit in a dry environment for about a week. When you open the bags, shake any remaining powder off the books, and the smell should be gone.

Get yellow stains off piano keys
That old upright may still play great, but those yellowed keys definitely hit a sour note. Remove age stains on your ivories by mixing a solution of ¼ cup baking soda in 1 quart warm water. Apply to each key with a dampened cloth (you can place a thin piece of cardboard between the keys to avoid seepage). Wipe again with a cloth dampened with plain water, and then buff dry with a clean cloth.

Remove white marks from wood surfaces
Get those white marks—caused by hot cups or sweating glasses—off your coffee table or other wooden furniture by making a paste of 1 tablespoon baking soda and 1 teaspoon water. Gently rub each spot in a circular motion until it disappears. Remember not to use too much water.

Absorb bathroom odors
Frustrated by having to mask bathroom odors with yucky, overly-sweet aerosol sprays? Keep your bathroom smelling fresh and clean by placing a decorative dish filled with ½ cup baking soda either on top of the toilet tank or on the floor behind the bowl. You can also make your own bathroom deodorizers by setting out dishes containing equal parts baking soda and your favorite scented bath salts.

Baking Soda Shelf Life
How can you tell if the baking soda you've had stashed away in the back of your pantry is still good? Just pour out a small amount—a little less than a teaspoon—and add a few drops of vinegar or fresh lemon juice. If it doesn't fizz, it's time to replace it. A sealed box should last about 18 months; an opened one, about six months.

★★★★ Trading Places by Norma Steinberg

ACROSS

1 Actress Polo
5 Clump
9 Salad ingredient
14 Yoked beasts
15 Crunchy ice-cream ingredient
16 Minds
17 Took off
18 Kitchen herb
19 Overcharges
20 Mrs. Fields' riches
23 Contingencies
24 Snack on
25 Engage
29 Smithsonian's locale
31 Sesame St. home
34 Bucks, e.g.
35 __ Valley, CA
36 Leave in a hurry
37 Comprehensive protection system
40 Ivy Leaguers
41 Legal claim
42 Henri's good health
43 Cozy room
44 Engine sound
45 Caustic
46 Bloom-to-be
47 Freight unit
48 Art thieves
55 Calculator key
56 High spot
57 Mardi __
59 Domicile
60 Fabricated
61 Patio plant
62 Like the SATs
63 Molt
64 88 days on Mercury

DOWN

1 Drag behind
2 Board member
3 Ashcroft predecessor
4 Passionate about
5 Tweak
6 Sign of spring
7 Sense of __
8 Unassisted
9 Type of money order
10 Give or take
11 Irish John
12 Shaver
13 The law, per Dickens
21 Newsstand structure
22 Memento
25 Implant
26 *My Dinner with Andre* director
27 Simple
28 Pince-nez component
29 Marner, for one
30 "What he said!"
31 Work in oils
32 Please, in Potsdam
33 More calculated
35 Brouhaha
36 Impudent one
38 Dodge
39 With
44 Like taffy
45 Reserved
46 Cutting edge
47 Clientele
48 Asian wasteland
49 Small part
50 Turntable settings
51 "What he said!"
52 Mean, as some crowds
53 Sight from Sandusky
54 Part of a *casa*
55 Half a proverbial exchange
58 It's NW of Iraq

★★★ Fences

Connect the dots with vertical or horizontal lines, so that a single loop is formed with no crossings or branches. Each number indicates how many lines surround it; squares with no number may be surrounded by any number of lines.

```
2  2    3    3  1  1

2  3                1
        3  0    2  3
3  3    3  2
2               2  3

3  2  2    3    2  2
```

WRONG IS RIGHT

Which of these four words is misspelled?

A) cocoon   B) bufoon

C) tycoon   D) baboon

★★★ Number-Out

Shade squares so that no number appears in any row or column more than once. Shaded squares may not touch each other horizontally or vertically, and all unshaded squares must form a single continuous area.

5	6	2	2	1	4
6	5	3	5	5	1
4	1	6	3	6	5
3	5	6	4	4	2
2	4	5	1	3	3
3	5	6	4	2	2

THINK ALIKE

Unscramble the letters in the phrase ETCHED SINK to form two words with the same or similar meanings.

_____   _____

★★★★ What's the Damage? by Kevin Donovan

ACROSS

1 Gdansk guy
5 Map ratio indicator
10 Monty Python putdown
14 Decorative vessel
15 Hunter constellation
16 General helper
17 Sudden soaker
19 Lower joint
20 Japanese fencing
21 Stag, say
22 Dutch treat
23 Munich mugs
25 Meat-seasoning mixture
27 Sign of distress, perhaps
29 Spring time
32 Red Wing of renown
35 It usually ends up in hot water
39 Add to barely, with "out"
40 Parisian pal
41 Wine-label info
42 Pershing's command, for short
43 McCourt memoir
44 Ward worker
45 Game with 32 cards
46 Pipe parts
48 Useful seaweed
50 *Your Show of Shows* star
54 Blue-ribbon
58 Versifier
60 Most populous place
62 Ahead of one's time
63 Bring up
64 Crispy cookie
66 High-seas heavyweight
67 '50s Ford
68 Put to work
69 Yan's pans
70 Plant starters
71 Senate approvals

DOWN

1 Small smooches
2 Junior hooter
3 Sierra __
4 Well-educated
5 Cry convulsively
6 Gunky stuff
7 Put on the tube
8 Also-ran
9 Way in
10 Start to discuss
11 Protective hedge
12 Problem solver, perhaps
13 Abound
18 Wrapped up
24 Tie material
26 Current fad
28 Flat rate
30 Chain from Europe
31 It's not right
32 They're often checked
33 Take out
34 Comic's remark
36 Took in
37 Hound sound
38 Moorehead of *Bewitched*
41 Holding device
45 Ostentatious
47 Indian fabric
49 Evil look
51 The Magi, for example
52 Words to the audience
53 Washer cycle
55 Bert's buddy
56 Santa __, CA
57 Varieties
58 Furrowed feature
59 Dynamic starter
61 Matured
65 South African golfer

★★ Horsing Around

Enter the maze where indicated at bottom, pass through all the stars exactly
once, then exit at bottom. You may not retrace your path.

BETWEENER

What five-letter word belongs between the word at left and the word at right, so that the first
and second word, and the second and third word, each form a common compound word?

SUN __ __ __ __ __ MAKER

★★★ Hyper-Sudoku

Fill in the blank boxes so that every row, column, 3x3 box, *and* each of the four
3x3 gray regions contains all of the numbers 1 to 9.

6		5					9	4
	1	9			8	5	2	
	7							
	6			2			3	
					1			
2			4		9			1
	3							
5				4				
				7		3		

MIXAGRAMS

Each line contains a five-letter word and a four-letter word that have been mixed together (the
order of the letters in each word has not been changed). Unmix the two words on each line and
write them in the spaces provided. When you're done, find a two-part answer to the clue by
reading down the letter columns in the answers.

CLUE: Letter opener

E L E X S U E D E	=	_ _ _ _ _	+	_ _ _ _
B I S H I P N E D	=	_ _ _ _ _	+	_ _ _ _
C U R E P A R B Y	=	_ _ _ _ _	+	_ _ _ _
S N O R O S R E Y	=	_ _ _ _ _	+	_ _ _ _

★★ Paint Boxes

Find these colors that are arranged in various box shapes in the diagram.
One answer is shown to get you started.

```
J E R R U Q S L G N V X E C M Z I O
D H W S S X C O B K D J U R B B L F
B R O E T O T L A S N A B K J E U T
E Z N A W E T U N B Y V R U H G S S
U J N F F S E T V C V H J K O T U R
W S K K H F A X F H O I N D S O U Q
M A K J V N W Z A N L O G I U I S E
N G D Y E L D P L I U Y T E W W R H
O L L W O L A S C B U K K H F D S S
A I J G D S P I M G R J M A D C E F
A U J G R X K N M U N U O R A I R G
U B J Y A Z V B M Y D I O N S S E F
R N J G O R A X V B N M L L P I Y R
E W S F E G N F D C N P U R R D S F
G K J F A S D V B J U E L P F H J I
```

ANIL
AUBURN
BLUE
BRONZE
BURGUNDY
CERISE
COBALT
ECRU
FAWN
GRAY
INDIGO
MAGNOLIA
MAROON
NAVY
ORANGE
PINK
PURPLE
RUSSET
TURQUOISE
YELLOW

INITIAL REACTION

Identify the well-known proverb from the first letters in each of its words.

G. T. C. I. S. P. _____

★★★★ Branching Out by Donna Levin

ACROSS

1 Spiced tea
5 Griffin of TV
9 No longer fizzy
13 Snob's put-on
14 Grammy winner India.__
15 Pageant winner's headpiece
16 Inferior
18 Nigeria neighbor
19 With 23 Across, a timely thought for the last Friday in April
21 "Xanadu" band, for short
22 7-Up's nickname, with "the"
23 See 19 Across
29 Stayed home for dinner
30 Jackson predecessor
31 Corp. honchos
34 Tells stories
35 Eleniak of *Baywatch*
36 Part of ISBN
37 Invite
38 *Le Louvre*, e.g.
39 4 Seasons leader
40 Originator of the occasion celebrated here
42 Remarkable
45 Agcy. that regulates explosives
46 40 Across was his Secretary of Agriculture
53 Try again to squelch squeaks
54 One who sleeps in
55 Opinion piece
56 Presently
57 Narcissus admirer
58 Author Silverstein
59 Department-store department

60 Transport

DOWN

1 Early feminist Carrie
2 "Farmer in the Dell" syllables
3 Like the Gobi
4 Knesset members
5 John Wayne's real first name
6 Geologic periods
7 Comic Rudner
8 Swerve suddenly
9 Savage
10 __ Calrissian (Han Solo pal)
11 Typeface choice
12 Country singer Tucker
15 Steakhouse specialties
17 "Blowin' in the Wind" writer
20 Myanmar, once
23 Fabulous fest
24 Singer Redding
25 Sneak a look
26 Anklebones
27 French farewell
28 Seizes
31 Electrical unit
32 Casual top
33 Largest human organ
35 Swiss mathematician
36 Tavern habitués
38 Without a word
39 Poll participant
40 Santalike
41 Experts
42 Fairy-tale villains
43 Just arrived
44 Lasso loop
47 Uncommunicative one
48 *Superman Returns* character
49 Harrow rival
50 *The Apostle* author
51 Radar O'Reilly's beverage
52 Decrease

★★ Triad Split Decisions

In this clueless crossword puzzle, each answer consists of two words whose spellings are the same, except for the consecutive letters given. All answers are common words; no phrases or hyphenated or capitalized words are used. Some of the clues may have more than one solution, but there is only one word pair that will correctly link up with all the other word pairs.

TRANSDELETION

Delete one letter from the word CHICKENS and rearrange the rest, to get a two-word travel term.

_____

★★★ One-Way Streets

The diagram represents a pattern of streets. A and B are parking spaces, and the black squares are stores. Find the route that starts at A, passes through all stores exactly once, and ends at B. Arrows indicate one-way traffic for that block only. No block or intersection may be entered more than once.

SOUND THINKING

There is only one common uncapitalized word whose consonant sounds are J, N, R, and S, in that order. What is it?

_____

★★★★ In Concert by Doug Peterson

ACROSS

1 Translucent mineral
5 Numbered rds.
9 DC-based broadcaster
14 Inventor Sikorsky
15 Grp. for seniors
16 Without company
17 It's no secret
20 CD-__
21 Citrus drink
22 Narrative
23 Son-gun link
24 In good shape
26 Lack of gravitas
30 Rochester's boss
32 Chinese principle
34 Blue material
35 Vortex
36 Brad of *The Client*
38 Air-quality org.
39 Part of some portfolios
42 White House nickname
44 Type of inspection
45 Warsaw Pact land
48 Fencing technique
50 Laconic assent
51 Volleyball star Gabrielle
52 Savvy
54 Former CW sitcom
56 Second Amendment grp.
57 Standard
59 Take most of
60 Cargo unit
61 Act approved by both houses
66 Calf-roping venue
67 Burnt-coal residue
68 Blow one's top
69 Reinforce, with "up"
70 Makes inquiries
71 *Family Ties* character

DOWN

1 Minuscule life form
2 "My bad!"
3 Decalogue element
4 Escort's offer
5 Time off
6 Enjoy 5 Down
7 Directional suffix
8 Catch sight of
9 Paid a visit to
10 LP holder
11 Protective container
12 Director Lee
13 Once known as
18 Adjective for Cheerios
19 __-Mart
25 Less like a milquetoast
27 Not required
28 Helpful hint
29 Singer Sumac
31 Big Apple sch.
33 No longer in trouble
36 Appear in print
37 Kick oneself for
40 In direct opposition
41 Expected to come in
42 Taking after
43 City vehicle
46 Marley partner
47 Appropriate again, as land
49 Artilleryman
51 Newman's Own competitor
53 Drop the ball
55 Leaves suddenly
58 City near Phoenix
61 Yearbook sect.
62 "I'm impressed!"
63 Words before a kiss
64 Plea at sea
65 Ditty syllable

★★★ Solitaire Poker

Group the 40 cards into eight poker hands of five cards each, so that each hand contains two pairs or better. The cards in each hand must be connected to each other by a common horizontal or vertical side.

SAY IT AGAIN

What five-letter word can mean either "very bad" or just "very"?

— — — — —

★★★ Star Search

Find the stars that are hidden in some of the blank squares. The numbered squares indicate how many stars are hidden in the squares adjacent to them (including diagonally). There is never more than one star in any square.

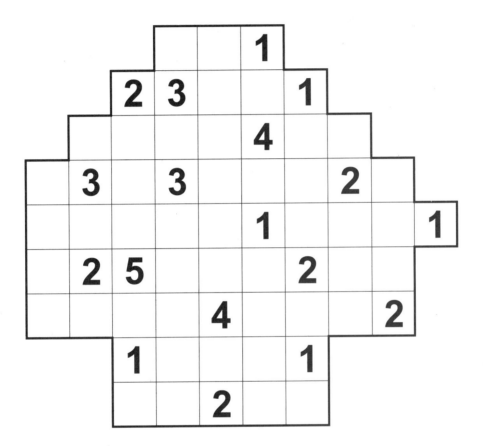

CHOICE WORDS

Form three six-letter words from the same category, by selecting one letter from each column three times. Each letter will be used exactly once.

L	H	S	I	C	E	_ _ _ _ _ _
S	E	D	U	E	K	_ _ _ _ _ _
R	R	R	S	N	N	_ _ _ _ _ _

★★★ Sudoku

Fill in the blank boxes so that every row, column, and 3x3 box contains all of the numbers 1 to 9.

		3	2	8	6	9		
	2						6	
9	6						5	7
					5			
		2				1		
			3					
4	3						9	2
	5						8	
		6	1	2	7	5		

CENTURY MARKS

Select one number in each of the four columns so that the total adds up to exactly 100.

$$\begin{array}{c} 27 \\ \hline 13 \end{array} + \begin{array}{c} 28 \\ \hline 31 \end{array} + \begin{array}{c} 19 \\ \hline 18 \end{array} + \begin{array}{c} 29 \\ \hline 40 \end{array} = 100$$

★★★★ Horsing Around by Raymond Hamel

ACROSS

1 Taunting laugh
5 Tricky move
9 A smaller number
14 Sauce thickener
15 Hero of Hindu epics
16 Sorbonne, *par exemple*
17 On
18 Cart pullers
19 Unrestrained
20 Part of the Indian Ocean
23 "__ you know ..."
24 One making predictions
25 Takes a moment
27 Approach maturity
30 Raisin-center city
32 __-Wan Kenobi
33 Cracker eponym
36 *My Friend* __
39 Colony founder
41 Where Greeks did business
42 Stumble
43 Sundance's girlfriend
44 Presidential middle name
46 San Francisco-to-Las Vegas dir.
47 Kind of football kick
49 Spring flower
51 Occult matter
53 "__ victory!"
55 Wear and tear
56 Well-worn cliché
62 Swindles
64 Important periods
65 Great review
66 Salt quantity
67 K follower
68 No longer in doubt
69 Milquetoast
70 Has debts
71 University position

DOWN

1 Snatch
2 Tiny amount
3 Ocean marker
4 Make known
5 Investigation
6 More lenient
7 Sign
8 Masculine principle
9 Guys
10 Tourism prefix
11 Plant with heart-shaped leaves
12 Beast of Borden
13 Exemplars of thinness
21 __ shui
22 Missing link, maybe
26 Military group
27 Burn cause, at times
28 "That'll be the day!"
29 Fiber-rich side dish
30 Violin opening
31 __ avis
34 Kind of tire
35 Brought to maturity
37 Asian soup ingredient
38 Tiptop
40 Émile Zola novel
45 Chooses, with "for"
48 Beginning to melt
50 Dragster
51 Crescent points
52 Computer-data acronym
53 Midway alternative
54 Squirrels' constructions
57 Floor model
58 Bird's belly
59 Cathedral area
60 Eye layer
61 Seabird
63 Show hosts

★★★ ABC

Enter the letters A, B, and C into the diagram so that each row and column has exactly one A, one B, and one C. The letters outside the diagram indicate the first letter encountered, moving in the direction of the arrow. Keep in mind that after all the letters have been filled in, there will be two blank boxes in each row and column.

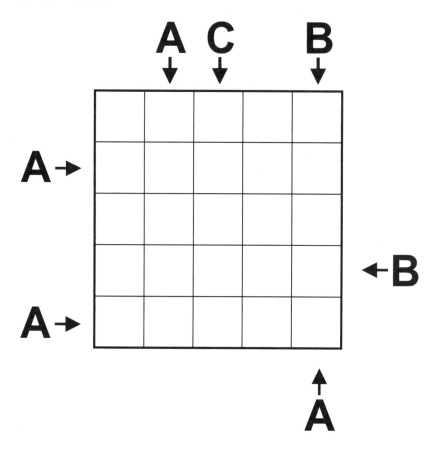

CLUELESS CROSSWORD

Complete the crossword with common uncapitalized seven-letter words, based entirely on the letters already filled in for you.

G		A	N			R
	■		■		■	
A					F	A
	■		■		■	
M		X				M
	■		■	M	■	I
R		D		A	N	

★★★ Find the Ships

Determine the position of the 10 ships listed to the right of the diagram. The ships may be oriented either horizontally or vertically. A square with wavy lines indicates water and will not contain a ship. The numbers at the edge of the diagram indicate how many squares in that row or column contain parts of ships. When all 10 ships are correctly placed in the diagram, no two of them will touch each other, not even diagonally.

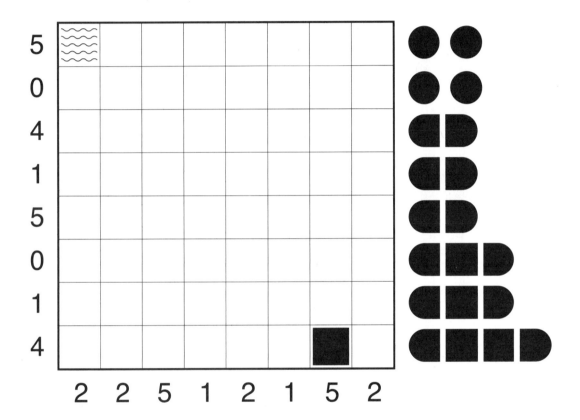

TWO-BY-FOUR

The eight letters in the word CONTEMPT can be rearranged to form a pair of common four-letter words in only one way. Can you find the two words?

__ __ __ __   __ __ __ __

★★★★ Variations on a Name by Donna Levin

ACROSS

1 Caribbean island
6 Stride
10 Entry requirement, at times
14 Greek letters
15 Southern pronoun
16 Golden calf
17 Take forcibly
18 March Madness org.
19 Fortune 500 abbr.
20 Hagrid portrayer in the *Harry Potter* films
23 Sweetie pies
24 Seussian reptile
26 Insult in the 'hood
27 Manilow song setting
29 Army rank: Abbr.
30 Get a short coif
34 Gallaudet University subj.
35 Burden
36 Diving bird
37 "... __ saw Elba"
38 Syr. + Egypt, once
39 Hop participants
43 Hi-def buys
44 __ *Diary* (Twain book)
45 High-rise res.
46 Parlor seat
48 Molts
51 Something on the Merry Men's agenda
56 Hemingway nickname
57 Biblical pottage purchaser
58 Petrol unit
59 New-__ (Enya fan, perhaps)
60 Old one, in Aachen
61 Tiny bits
62 Desires
63 Throw out
64 Feature of just-baked cookies

DOWN

1 Coastal color, in Cap d'Antibes
2 Lay new turf
3 Horseshoe-shaped lab item
4 Caribbean island
5 Ache remedy
6 Harmony
7 Tex-Mex nosh
8 Ben-Gurion Airport client
9 Toothless mammals
10 Goldsmith title character
11 "Whatever"
12 Ungracious one
13 Jungfrau, for one
21 Latin 101 verb
22 Dorsal
25 Branford and Wynton's dad
27 Freshwater fish
28 Like some Chardonnays
30 Matches
31 Typically
32 Bloom suddenly
33 Kemo __
37 Outside
39 Cause for complaint
40 Pig out
41 Robe tie
42 Daughter of Polonius
47 Some ski lifts
49 "Likewise!"
50 Vamoose
52 Home of the Norsk Folkemuseum
53 Framer's inventory
54 Calendar abbr.
55 "__ Rebel" ('62 tune)
56 Settle up

★★ Dot to Dot

Draw five squares in the diagram so that each corner of each square is on a dot. The squares may be at any angle. Dots may be used for more than one square, or not be used at all.

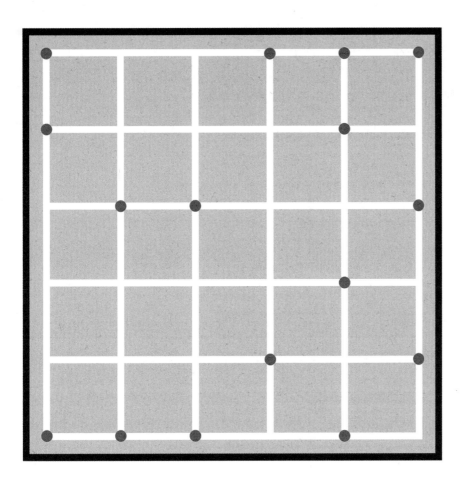

SMALL CHANGE

Change one letter in each of these two words, to form a common two-word phrase.

BEAT DISHES

★★★ 123

Fill in the diagram so that each rectangular piece has one each of the numbers 1, 2, and 3, under these rules: 1) No two adjacent squares, horizontally or vertically, can have the same number. 2) Each completed row and column of the diagram will have an equal number of 1s, 2s, and 3s.

SUDOKU SUM

Fill in the missing numbers from 1 to 9, so that the sum of each row and column is as indicated.

	15	15	15
16		1	
11	2		
18			3

★★★ Fences

Connect the dots with vertical or horizontal lines, so that a single loop is formed with no crossings or branches. Each number indicates how many lines surround it; squares with no number may be surrounded by any number of lines.

```
0  2        3
   2        3           3
2        3     2  1  2
   3
                        1
3  1  3     1        1
3           2        3
            2        3  2
```

WRONG IS RIGHT

Which of these four words is misspelled?

     A) granery   B) grandeur

     C) pomegranate   D) emigrant

★★★★ Hidden Extras by Fred Piscop

ACROSS

- **1** Yuletide airs
- **6** Tiny tastes
- **10** Fishing-line problem
- **14** Plumed wader
- **15** Baby-powder mineral
- **16** Deteriorated
- **17** More roguish
- **18** Frankenstein servant
- **19** MBA subj.
- **20** Spy's writing
- **22** Steinbeck title direction
- **23** What Indy found
- **24** Avoids a trial
- **26** Playful, as a kitten
- **30** Bashful companion
- **31** Small, contemptible one
- **32** Draft animals
- **36** Use the drive-thru
- **40** Hint of a gas leak
- **41** Evenings, in ads
- **43** Icicle site
- **44** 20th-century French dramatist
- **46** Screen image
- **47** "You said it!"
- **48** Timeline division
- **50** Sharon successor
- **52** Ecstasy
- **56** Old hand
- **57** Actor Baldwin
- **58** Military youth group
- **64** Construction beam
- **65** Home to most Turks
- **66** Simmering
- **67** Strike out
- **68** Cubicle fixture
- **69** City near Calais
- **70** Feeder filler
- **71** Fraternal fellows
- **72** Knight's mount

DOWN

- **1** Storied loch
- **2** Make goo-goo eyes at
- **3** Idle of Monty Python
- **4** Impolite look
- **5** Sign of speed
- **6** Adhere
- **7** *Othello* villain
- **8** Walks with effort
- **9** Diatribe
- **10** Dairy product
- **11** Diet-drink label
- **12** Part of a Stein line
- **13** Men

- **21** Check for fit
- **25** As well
- **26** Tadpole, in time
- **27** Inelegant
- **28** Privy to
- **29** 'Hood acceptance
- **33** Sundial number
- **34** "Hidden" theme of the puzzle
- **35** Opposite of paleo-
- **37** Dench's title
- **38** Anon's partner
- **39** Monopoly payment
- **42** Sound of contempt
- **45** Play about Capote

- **49** Video-game site
- **51** Townies
- **52** Fridge incursions
- **53** *Zoo Story* playwright
- **54** Portraitists' family name
- **55** Flip-chart supporter
- **56** Reaches a high
- **59** Tiddlywink, e.g.
- **60** Sort of newspaper bio
- **61** Function
- **62** Tidy sum
- **63** Gravity-driven vehicle

★★★ Hyper-Sudoku

Fill in the blank boxes so that every row, column, 3x3 box, *and* each of the four 3x3 gray regions contains all of the numbers 1 to 9.

5			7			3		4
	6		5					
3			4	9				2
				7				5
1				6				
	2							
		5			1	2	3	
							9	
		6		3			4	

MIXAGRAMS

Each line contains a five-letter word and a four-letter word that have been mixed together (the order of the letters in each word has not been changed). Unmix the two words on each line and write them in the spaces provided. When you're done, find a multipart answer to the clue by reading down the letter columns in the answers.

CLUE: Get hired

A F I C E R Y E S = _ _ _ _ _ + _ _ _ _

J O I N K E R E T = _ _ _ _ _ + _ _ _ _

O K N I C R A H E = _ _ _ _ _ + _ _ _ _

B U D F E F F E R = _ _ _ _ _ + _ _ _ _

★★ Split Decisions

In this clueless crossword puzzle, each answer consists of two words whose spellings are the same, except for the consecutive letters given. All answers are common words; no phrases or hyphenated or capitalized words are used. Some of the clues may have more than one solution, but there is only one word pair that will correctly link up with all the other word pairs.

TRANSDELETION

Delete one letter from the word EXISTENT and rearrange the rest, to get something that may be "sweet."

_____

★★★★ Driving Buggy by Merle Baker

ACROSS

1 Complain
5 "When We Was __" (George Harrison tune)
8 Spending plan
14 Mister abroad
15 Baton Rouge sch.
16 Burger topping
17 Levitated
19 Time piece?
20 Former Dallas Cowboys leader
22 Keeps a low profile
23 Spanish mark
24 Neurology abbreviation
27 George's brother
28 Lincoln or Madison
29 Gospel singer Winans
30 Newcomer's helper
34 Break away
37 Overwhelm
38 Certain British noble
42 Arduous journey
43 Snack since 1912
44 Karate level
47 Special entrées
48 Peach __
50 Speak one's mind
52 Elite clientele
55 Sailor's patron
57 Put into order
58 Poem divisions
59 Printers' widths
60 Little pest
61 Eventually
62 No. on a map
63 Wine prefix

DOWN

1 Ostentatious
2 *In the Meadow* artist
3 Military fleet
4 Streisand role
5 Hoo-ha
6 Like a part of Russia
7 Folded food
8 Displayed displeasure
9 Reunion attendee
10 Soup flavoring
11 Zero
12 SASE, for example
13 "For shame!"
18 Some AL batters
21 *Return of the Native* character
25 Earth sci.
26 Thing in a pool
28 Staff symbol
29 Sly
30 "Bubbles in the Wine" musician
31 Tokyo, formerly
32 Spanish river
33 Misfortune
34 Space-signal searcher's acronym
35 Bring in
36 Roll shape
39 Recital numbers
40 More suave
41 Chemical used in analysis
44 Senator Feinstein
45 Like llamas
46 Are forced
48 Michael Keaton comedy
49 Irregularly notched
50 Giant great
51 "You're welcome," in Milano
53 Prefix meaning "height"
54 Naturalness
55 Part of MS
56 Trig function

★★★ Color Paths

Find the shortest path through the maze from the bottom to the top, by using paths in this color order: red, blue, yellow, red, blue, etc. Change path colors through the white squares. It is okay to retrace your path.

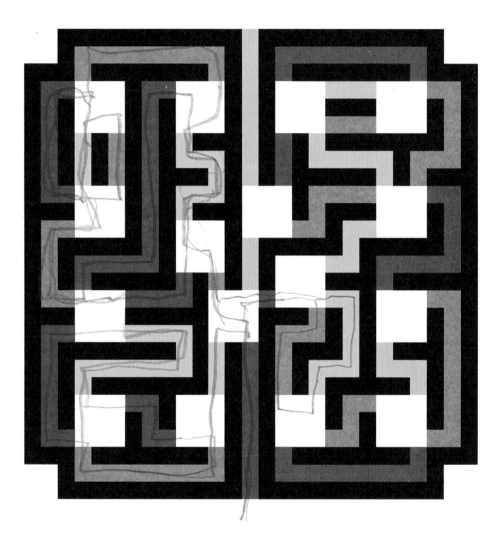

BETWEENER

What five-letter word belongs between the word at left and the word at right, so that the first and second word, and the second and third word, each form a common compound word?

BACK _ _ _ _ _ YARD

★★★ Number-Out

Shade squares so that no number appears in any row or column more than once. Shaded squares may not touch each other horizontally or vertically, and all unshaded squares must form a single continuous area.

3	3	1	2	5	2
4	4	2	1	6	1
2	4	3	6	3	3
5	2	3	5	4	6
1	3	4	3	3	5
3	6	1	4	1	2

THINK ALIKE

Unscramble the letters in the phrase TURNIP WHIM to form two words with the same or similar meanings.

_____   _____

★★★ One-Way Streets

The diagram represents a pattern of streets. A and B are parking spaces, and the black squares are stores. Find the route that starts at A, passes through all stores exactly once, and ends at B. Arrows indicate one-way traffic for that block only. No block or intersection may be entered more than once.

SOUND THINKING

Common words whose consonant sounds are K, L, and D include COLD and CLOUD. The longest such word has eight letters. What is it?

_____

★★★★ Laugh Lines by Doug Peterson

ACROSS

1 Type of electrical coupling
5 Handy
10 Unorthodox sect
14 Make changes to
15 West Coast gridder
16 Mayberry redhead
17 Is indifferent
20 Gold, to Guadalupe
21 "Now __ done it!"
22 Metaphysical poet
23 Mythical hybrid
25 Audiophile's assortment
26 Need in the worst way
32 '70s TV cop
35 Dive like an owl
36 Altar constellation
37 Persian poet
38 Turns over temporarily
39 Sort of signal
40 Doozy
41 Competition on horseback
42 Small craft
43 Make tracks
46 Leave dumbstruck
47 Attaches firmly
51 Pluvial month
54 Everglades bird
56 Moo goo __ pan
57 Gives a tongue-lashing
60 Crèche trio
61 Country estate
62 Goddess of victory
63 Leave dumbstruck
64 Thread holder
65 Santa's sackful

DOWN

1 French wine region
2 Like a lot
3 Rest atop
4 *Star Wars* extras
5 Traveling and performing
6 Deciphers
7 Part of UTEP
8 Golfer Ballesteros
9 Middle of a Napoleonic palindrome
10 Kelly, to Regis
11 Familiar with
12 Sphinx, in part
13 Henri's head
18 Town on the Hudson
19 Make sense
24 Erstwhile Russian sovereign
25 Talks fondly
27 Covered
28 European resort
29 *The Marble __* (Hawthorne novel)
30 Rice-shaped pasta
31 Flatten
32 Keystone group
33 Leave unmentioned
34 Wisecrack
38 One and only
39 Part of a pedestal
41 Bloodhound features
42 Small carving
44 Anted up
45 Friendly
48 Marsh of mysteries
49 Cheap-looking
50 Venues
51 Blouse parts
52 Fuel from fens
53 Prego alternative
54 Furniture flaw
55 Move, briefly
58 Remote targets
59 Demolition letters

doku

blank boxes so that every row, column, and 3x3 box contains all of the numbers 1 to 9.

			2	7	8			
7	4						3	1
3	8						7	9
			9	1	5			
6	9						1	2
4	5						6	3
			5	8	1			

MIXAGRAMS

Each line contains a five-letter word and a four-letter word that have been mixed together (the order of the letters in each word has not been changed). Unmix the two words on each line and write them in the spaces provided. When you're done, find a two-part answer to the clue by reading down the letter columns in the answers.

CLUE: *Shane* star

P E D U C A N A L = _ _ _ _ _ + _ _ _ _

T U S P I B A L L = _ _ _ _ _ + _ _ _ _

R E F E L O D A T = _ _ _ _ _ + _ _ _ _

S E V E Y D I N G = _ _ _ _ _ + _ _ _ _

★★★ Star Search

Find the stars that are hidden in some of the blank squares. The numbered squares indicate how many stars are hidden in the squares adjacent to them (including diagonally). There is never more than one star in any square.

1	1	1	1	1	1	2	
2	2				2		5
		2		1			
	3		3		3			2
2							2
	1			1	3		
	1						

CHOICE WORDS

Form three six-letter words from the same category, by selecting one letter from each column three times. Each letter will be used exactly once.

```
M   I   N   L   U   O    _ _ _ _ _ _

D   O   M   E   A   M    _ _ _ _ _ _

W   A   O   P   R   H    _ _ _ _ _ _
```

★★★★ Former First Family? by S.N.

ACROSS

1 Biopic about Ritchie Valens
8 Stem (from)
15 Cell-door component
16 Of tenths
17 *Lipstick Jungle* author
19 Swiss-born artist
20 Diane's *Godfather* role
21 Spirit-raising session
22 Paid spots
24 Wool-coat owner
26 Small pianos
30 First-year Kennedy Center Honors recipient
36 Vandal
37 Parting words
39 Stage platform
40 *Nancy* cartoonist
43 Orchestra section
44 Not well made
45 Seth's mom
46 Inconsistent
48 Sounded annoyed
50 Pig stealer of rhyme
52 Oath affirmation
53 Rectangular shape
58 Fella
60 Skater Lipinski
64 Star of the silent *Ben-Hur*
67 Auction-house category
68 Entered illegally
69 European potted plant
70 "Make up your mind!"

DOWN

1 Defeat, so to speak
2 Asian inland sea
3 Exemplar of dryness
4 Like llamas
5 Finance deg.
6 Be treacherous
7 Zone
8 www.texastech.__
9 They cry out for cleanup
10 Pine (for)
11 Jazz singer Simone
12 Solemn assent
13 Soft mineral
14 Parisian pronoun
18 "See ya!"
23 Have no use for
25 Gets ready for dinner
26 __ Khan (Kipling tiger)
27 More noble
28 Circle or city preceder
29 House finish
31 Easel support
32 Need bed rest
33 Castaway's home
34 Canadian village official
35 Misspoke
38 Gray shade
41 Gilbert & Sullivan princess
42 Salon service
47 Clara Bow nickname, with "the"
49 Abstract expressionist
51 Vancouver Winter Olympics year
53 Extinguishes
54 Cracker topping
55 Superboy's girlfriend
56 About 3,300 feet, to runners
57 University sports org.
59 First name in advice
61 Part of AFL
62 Yard-sale spoiler
63 A, as in AD
65 Fr. holy woman
66 Signal for help

★★★ Civil War Soldier

Enter the maze where indicated at bottom, pass through all the stars exactly once, then exit at top. You may not retrace your path.

SAY IT AGAIN

What five-letter word can mean either "rend" or "rest"?

_ _ _ _ _

★★★ Shady Spirals

These trees are arranged in spirals in the diagram, either starting or finishing in the center, either clockwise or counterclockwise. Some of the spirals may overlap. One answer is shown to get you started.

```
J A C Q B R E E E R C
D A A M L M A E L T W
N A R F A P D M O N I
E E R T L F R U H W F
O C T V S E E I P L A
R A L S I R T T E E N
A L L E E R N V R T E
A S I A C T E X K G J
P O D R O B B A L V G
K A O I N D I R S A R
E K S I G I F M A S F
R M E F N A B L S S A
L T U Y R O S C O U D
I A P P L E E I L R O
T E E L P P A R A B H
J R T E I F P K M L A
C A R S C A N Q V I P
Y R R D U T D Y O R Y
A H E E N E L A I M Z
C K B C B R R A M A W
M J D W Q Q U C A D N
S U O B D O O M F L A
E D U S L B W A E E M
C I D T A C K B R T E
C Z V A C A P J O O K
A L O H A M U P L A N
A C B N E C A S O D C
R A M T Z N A U O W E
U H X X A I R A A Y G
```

APPLE TREE
BALSAM FIR
BLACKWOOD
BREAD PALM
CANDLENUT
CARAMBOLA
CAROB TREE
CASUARINA
CORAL TREE
COURBARIL
DECIDUOUS
FLAME TREE
FRUIT TREE
HACKBERRY
INDIAN FIG
IVORY PALM
JACARANDA
KERMES OAK
LANCEWOOD
LEMON TREE
MACADAMIA
PLANE TREE
ROSE APPLE
SAPODILLA
SASSAFRAS
TACAMAHAC

WHO'S WHAT WHERE?

The correct term for a resident of Cedar Rapids, Iowa, is:

A) Cedarian   B) Rapidite

C) Rapider   D) Cedar Rapidian

★★★ ABC

Enter the letters A, B, and C into the diagram so that each row and column has exactly one A, one B, and one C. The letters outside the diagram indicate the first letter encountered, moving in the direction of the arrow. Keep in mind that after all the letters have been filled in, there will be two blank boxes in each row and column.

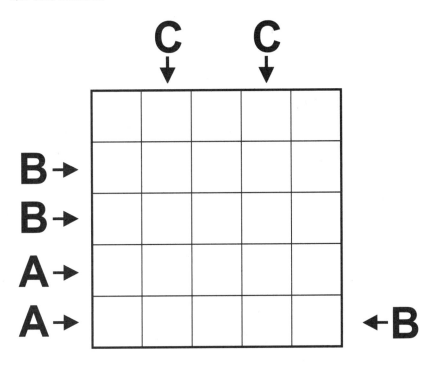

CLUELESS CROSSWORD

Complete the crossword with common uncapitalized seven-letter words, based entirely on the letters already filled in for you.

★★★★★ Themeless Toughie by Doug Peterson

ACROSS

1 Antonio usurped his dukedom
9 Make oneself scarce
14 Put back on the range
15 Picasso's birthplace
16 Flying Fortress feature
18 Alphabet run
19 Program proposed by RWR
20 Available, in a way
21 "__ Si Bon" (Eartha Kitt song)
23 Suit
25 Indications
26 Popular sides
28 B, to Bohr
30 No mixer
31 Rose lover
32 Ancient literary work
36 Recklessly foolish
38 Made a raid
40 Rat tail
41 Vic's wife
43 Bond number
44 Undermine
46 Rouse to action
47 Grand Canyon denizen
50 Construction-site sight
52 Sticking point
53 Mustard-family member
55 __ Luis, Brazil
57 Parisian possessive
58 Exemplars of devotion
61 Concept in astronomy
62 Embitter
63 Old autocrats
64 Cast away

DOWN

1 The King's ex
2 Let
3 Forty-niner's anthem
4 Fixed
5 Green figures
6 Some exercises
7 Edit, in a way
8 Dedicated lines
9 "Hymn to Aphrodite" poet
10 Woody Allen, for one
11 Arrested
12 Go-between
13 Soda jerk's creations
15 Topography abbr.
17 Salad variety
22 Globe habitué
24 Fall away
27 Morsel
29 Motoring monogram
31 Evangeline, notably
33 Hospital staffer
34 Describe precisely
35 Dealt with
37 Metric lead-in
39 Toasting candidate
42 Receiving-line figure
45 Magazine contents
46 47 Across, e.g.
47 Without a faculty for
48 Mineral-rich range
49 Big Band music
51 Org. concerned with equines
54 Asian tongue
56 Another, overseas
59 Stop up
60 Cable letters

bRain BReatHer
WELL-VERSED: MUSINGS ABOUT POETRY

Even if poetry isn't your cup of tea, you'll probably enjoy at least a few of these observations. Some are serious, others lighthearted. Some come from poets, others from fans of poetry.

If I feel physically as if the top of my head were taken off, I know that is poetry.

—EMILY DICKINSON

Everywhere I go I find a poet has been there before me.

—SIGMUND FREUD

Always be a poet, even in prose.

—CHARLES BAUDELAIRE

A poet who reads his verse in public may have other nasty habits.

—ROBERT A. HEINLEIN

I gave up on new poetry myself thirty years ago, when most of it began to read like coded messages passing between lonely aliens on a hostile world.

—RUSSELL BAKER

You don't have to suffer to be a poet; adolescence is enough suffering for anyone. —JOHN CIARDI

"The Ancient Mariner" would not have taken so well if it had been called "The Old Sailor."

—SAMUEL BUTLER

I've read some of your modern free verse and wonder who set it free.

—JOHN BARRYMORE

Publishing a volume of verse is like dropping a rose petal down the Grand Canyon and waiting for the echo.

—DON MARQUIS

★★★★ Find the Ships

Determine the position of the 10 ships listed to the right of the diagram. The ships may be oriented either horizontally or vertically. A square with wavy lines indicates water and will not contain a ship. The numbers at the edge of the diagram indicate how many squares in that row or column contain parts of ships. When all 10 ships are correctly placed in the diagram, no two of them will touch each other, not even diagonally.

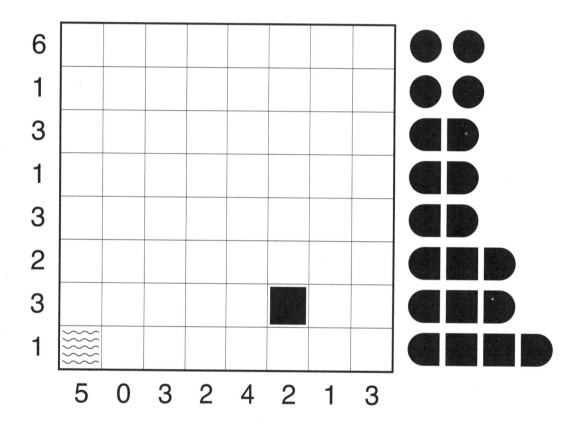

TWO-BY-FOUR

The eight letters in the word DIALOGUE can be rearranged to form a pair of common four-letter words in only one way. Can you find the two words?

— — — —   — — — —

★★★★ Hyper-Sudoku

Fill in the blank boxes so that every row, column, 3x3 box, *and* each of the four 3x3 gray regions contains all of the numbers 1 to 9.

				1				
							6	3
		3					7	
8	1	6	5					9
			4		1			
		1	8					4
	9	2					3	
					3	5		

BETWEENER

What six-letter word belongs between the word at left and the word at right, so that the first and second word, and the second and third word, each form a common compound word?

HEAD __ __ __ __ __ __ BOX

★★★★★ Themeless Toughie by Anna Stiga

ACROSS

1 Glove-compartment item
8 Certain southernmost state
15 HBO series
16 Place without snakes
17 Tipped off
18 Board
19 Stylish and elegant
20 Test versions
22 Antepenultimate word of the Declaration of Independence
23 Failed 27th Amendment
24 Troupe instruction
26 *Carousel* song subject
27 Wite-Out owner
28 Wetland predator
29 See 47 Across
30 Aesopian animal
31 Presently
32 Kid
33 Coasts
39 Like some bolts
40 Queens crew
41 __ hall
42 One in charge
45 Daughter of Tantalus
46 Radar reading
47 With 29 Across, orchestral adjuncts
48 Steve Jobs is on its board
49 Fast flight
50 Popular telecommunications device
51 Rand fractions
52 Further
53 Rule
55 Reason for leaving
58 It has an onion-shaped crown
59 Euro predecessor

60 Use centrifugal force, in a way
61 They're unconquerable

DOWN

1 Lawyer's hurdle
2 Green gas
3 Does over
4 Off
5 Place with snakes
6 Long intro
7 "Flying Circus" nickname
8 Illinois, Wisconsin, etc.
9 Open spaces

10 Checks
11 Ring master of yore
12 Emptied
13 Sounding fine
14 Eats up
21 Bank of Sweden Prize honoree
24 Weapon of the future
25 Tanglewood Festival locale
26 Literally, "soft way"
29 Oscar nominee as Lincoln
32 Don't bother
34 Far from plentiful
35 Promotional device

36 Carrying capacities
37 Verbal skill
38 Spreads, so to speak
42 Big gaps
43 Information source
44 Black Label name
45 A score
48 Check
51 Milk product
52 __ *Modiste* (Victor Herbert operetta)
54 *The Opposite of Fate* author
56 Datebook letters
57 Theoretical trial, for short

★★ Cut That Out

Which of the numbered pieces of wrapping paper has been cut from the sheet?

SMALL CHANGE

Change one letter in each of these two words, to form a common two-word phrase.

WINDING STREAM

_____

★★★★ Fences

Connect the dots with vertical or horizontal lines, so that a single loop is formed with no crossings or branches. Each number indicates how many lines surround it; squares with no number may be surrounded by any number of lines.

```
  3         2 0     1
 2   3             2
 1           3     2
 2     1
                 2       2
 3     2                 3
 3             3     3
 2     2 3         1
```

ADDITION SWITCH

Switch the positions of two of the digits in the incorrect sum at right, to get a correct sum.

```
  1 3 7
+ 2 4 5
───────
  4 8 2
```

★★★★★ Themeless Toughie by Daniel R. Stark

ACROSS

1 Pungent plant
8 Clinks
15 Property of matter
16 Typically
17 Russian vessel
18 Enchanting
19 Emmy actress, '80 and '82
20 It means "trillion"
22 It bites the dust
23 *The Bonesetter's Daughter* author
24 Commanded
25 Manx tongue
27 Gets rid of
29 Exactly
31 Kit and caboodle
32 Imminent risk
33 First Physics Nobelist
35 Land on the Pacific and Caribbean
37 It may be hostile
39 Beatrice, to Charles
43 Knoxville athlete
44 Struggles
45 Motion detector
46 Up
48 Body art, familiarly
50 Spike's former name
51 Ancient mariner
52 Inst. on the Hudson
53 Going __
54 Pump parts
57 Late news
59 Unproductive
60 Mild and pleasant
61 Inexpensive digs
62 Maintains

DOWN

1 Make a false move
2 In the dark
3 Advanced course
4 Quick pace
5 Dune-buggy kin
6 Dogie catchers
7 Was fearless enough
8 Drs.' mag
9 Rose-rose link
10 Emulate Xanthippe
11 Laundry challenge
12 B.B. King's guitar
13 Thrill
14 Take
21 Starts another canopy
24 Feel
25 Crew
26 Gets that syncing feeling?
28 Invest, so to speak
30 Cornwall's father-in-law
33 Show approval, or disapproval
34 Progress
36 Cupronickel creation
37 NBA city
38 Rap-sheet info
40 Properties, in law
41 Makeup
42 2006 hurricane
43 Become invisible
45 Flour or sugar
47 Not quite enough
49 Frenzily
52 Spends
53 Accelerate, with "up"
55 Go beyond embroidery
56 Bracket type
58 Scottish river to the North Sea

★★★★ 123

Fill in the diagram so that each rectangular piece has one each of the numbers 1, 2, and 3, under these rules: 1) No two adjacent squares, horizontally or vertically, can have the same number. 2) Each completed row and column of the diagram will have an equal number of 1s, 2s, and 3s.

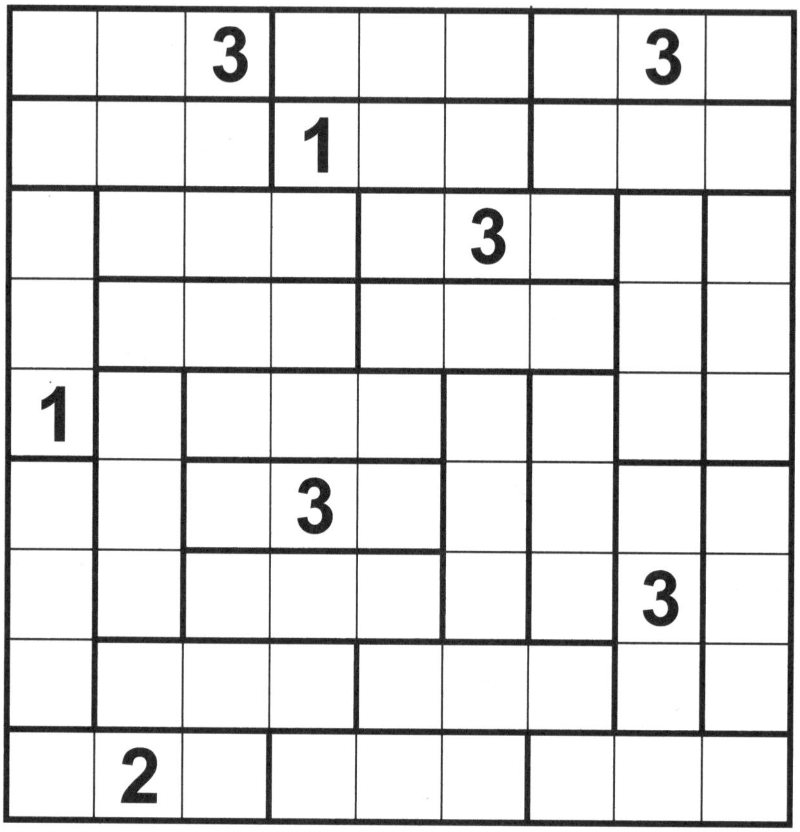

WRONG IS RIGHT

Which of these four words is misspelled?

A) irrecoverable   B) covenant

C) covetted   D) covey

★★★ Number-Out

Shade squares so that no number appears in any row or column more than once. Shaded squares may not touch each other horizontally or vertically, and all unshaded squares must form a single continuous area.

6	5	2	3	3	1
4	4	5	3	4	6
5	4	3	3	1	2
6	2	5	1	5	3
3	4	6	4	2	2
2	3	1	4	6	4

THINK ALIKE

Unscramble the letters in the phrase IDLE WELDERS to form two words with the same or similar meanings.

_____　　_____

★★★★★ Themeless Toughie by S.N.

ACROSS

1 Paint descriptor
9 Something sugary
15 Not free to go
16 Hobbyist's scale
17 Casual greeting
18 Relieves
19 What 1 may mean: Abbr.
20 Was foolhardy
22 Till
24 Tower's job, perhaps
25 Broadway's first Sweeney
26 Something sugary
28 Wasn't true
32 Cut out
34 5th-century invader
35 Best by a 9 Down
37 Soft touch
41 Drift
43 Crab __
44 Something to beat
48 Limit, at times
49 Relieve
50 Biosphere subj.
52 Call
53 Hardly remarkable
58 Proper
59 Quantity calculators
60 1913 Liberty Head, e.g.
62 Shots
63 Waggish to the max
64 Least content
65 Artistes

DOWN

1 Diner drink
2 Better than ever
3 Turning bad
4 "Welcome to" sign letters
5 "Beware __ you lose the substance by grasping at the shadow": Aesop
6 It may be under 26 Across
7 Fulminic acid, to cyanic acid
8 Synagogue canopies
9 See 35 Across
10 Conan Doyle exclamation
11 Young giraffe
12 Smallest UN member by population
13 When boys join the Vienna Boys Choir
14 E-mail command
21 Pitched
23 Thresholds
27 Like 26 Across
29 Electrical conductor
30 Traverses
31 At all
33 Brooks
36 Bore
38 They're often white in warm weather
39 Good egg
40 Outgo
42 Puts down
44 Some steamers
45 Cab Calloway's "kingdom"
46 Copy __
47 Oscar-nominated role of '84
51 *The Wizard of Oz* producer
54 Parcel
55 *Aeneid* character
56 Backup: Abbr.
57 Dickens heroine
61 Second-century date

★★★ River Trail

Beginning with BREEDE, then moving up, down, left, or right, one letter at a time, trace a path of these African rivers.

```
B R E L A O L I G E E N E W H
E E G L O P A F I R U I L T I
D T U U A O N T N B L A U E N
E A W G N P L A Y A A L L L I
R U G A M M I O U T B A O E O
I F G E B I A L U B A R P A R
J A M R G E C U O M H A O N G
I Z B A B R N A W A O O L O E
I Z E T O U Z A K N G U M M M
S E N L O A G A A B U R E A O
M A E G V B L N N G O R B I U
A D N A K C A A G N E N U K N
N B A L U B A S I O C E N O T
Y N A G C E N G O M A P U T A
A O B G O L E B A E L I N N I
N G A O O U E S H L O M A M I
```

ATBARAH	MOLOPO
BANDAMA	MOULOUYA
BLACK VOLTA	MOUNTAIN NILE
BLUE NILE	NIGER
BOU REGREG	NYANGA
~~BREEDE~~	OGOOUE
CONGO	OLIFANT
CUANZA	ORANGE
CUBANGO	OUM ER-RBIA
GABON	RUFIJI
GAMBIA	SANAGA
KUNENE	SENEGAL
KWANGO	SHABELE
LIMPOPO	TUGELA
LOMAMI	UBANGI
LUALABA	WHITE NILE
LUANGWA	ZAMBEZI
MAPUTO	

IN OTHER WORDS

There is only one common uncapitalized word that contains the consecutive letters OIB. What is it?

_____

★★★★ Straight Ahead

Enter the grid where indicated at top; pass through all of the blue squares, then exit at right. You must travel horizontally or vertically in a straight line, and turn only to avoid passing through a black square. It is okay to retrace your path.

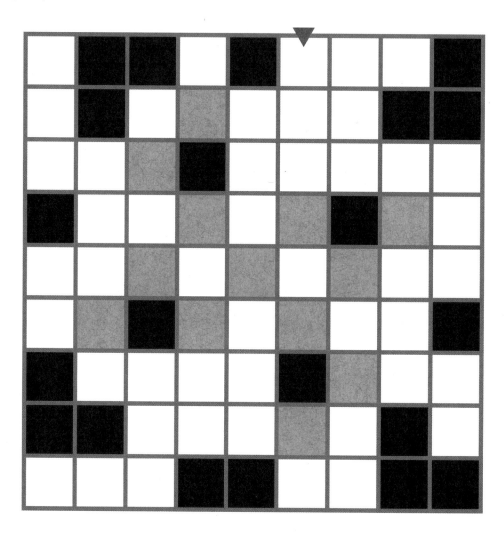

SAY IT AGAIN

What six-letter word can mean either "solidify" or "immobilize"?

— — — — — —

★★★★★ Themeless Toughie by Daniel R. Stark

ACROSS

1 Sees the judge
7 *Greatest Songs of the Sixties* artist
14 Oratorio master
15 Caltech locale
16 Odysseus' advisor
17 It may come with a stamp
18 Continent divider
19 Dweeb
21 Paper processor
22 Seashore denizens
24 Is wavering
26 Near the floor
27 Indelicate
28 Black-and-white animal
29 Name of four Hungarian kings
30 Best groomed
32 Without reservation
34 Back the wrong horse
35 Far from genteel
36 Stress
39 Identifying signs
43 Measure of potential difference
44 Stays in the shadows
46 Historic caravel
47 Scored with three sharps
48 Literary type
49 Mended, in a way
50 Inner self
52 __ Siddons Award
54 Modicum
55 Santa of the screen
57 Abutting
59 Fuse problem
60 Causes wear to
61 Continental foe
62 Strand

DOWN

1 Sci-fi stunners
2 Type of pass
3 Heighten
4 *Fables in Slang* author
5 Bumper damage
6 Shredded side dish
7 Surveyed
8 Warbucks servant, with "the"
9 Sniffing dogs' companions
10 Big favorite
11 Flattened
12 Hot
13 Passage
15 Bring up
20 Help the teacher
23 Shoe part
25 Brewpub display
28 Spice grinder
29 __ split
31 Heyerdahl title starter
33 Quick exit
35 Home add-on
36 Crop duster, e.g.
37 Machinate
38 Put forth
39 Quick trip
40 Dangerous current
41 Ceramist, at times
42 Most woeful
45 Boot
48 Masson rival
49 Word of solace
51 Dramatist Connelly
53 Retired
56 Mauna __
58 Brillo rival

★★★★ ABCD

Enter the letters A, B, C, and D into the diagram so that each row and column has exactly one A, one B, one C, and one D. The letters outside the diagram indicate the first letter encountered, moving in the direction of the arrow. Keep in mind that after all the letters have been filled in, there will be two blank boxes in each row and column.

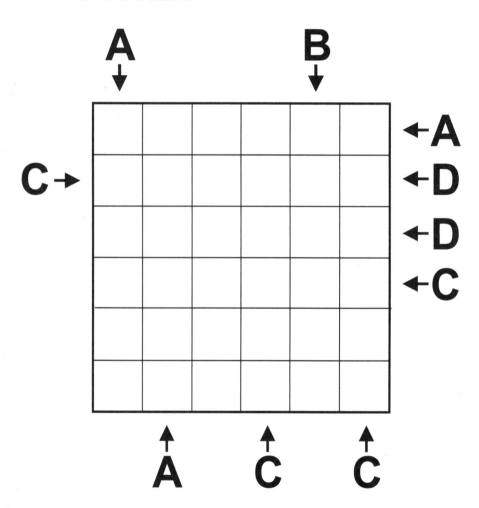

NATIONAL TREASURE

The words VAINEST and EASEMENT can be formed from the letters of what Asian language?

_____

★★★★ Sudoku

Fill in the blank boxes so that every row, column, and 3x3 box contains all of the numbers 1 to 9.

5								1
1			6		3			4
		7			2	5		
	5	8					6	
	9					3	1	
		6	9			7		
4			3		7			2
2								3

MIXAGRAMS

Each line contains a five-letter word and a four-letter word that have been mixed together (the order of the letters in each word has not been changed). Unmix the two words on each line and write them in the spaces provided. When you're done, find a two-part answer to the clue by reading down the letter columns in the answers.

CLUE: Ebert excerpt

O W A U F C H E R = _ _ _ _ _ + _ _ _ _

H U C R I L K E D = _ _ _ _ _ + _ _ _ _

M O M A L I A R M = _ _ _ _ _ + _ _ _ _

C O R M A B O P T = _ _ _ _ _ + _ _ _ _

★★★★★ Themeless Toughie by Merle Baker

ACROSS

1 Bach composition
8 Like a wind-turbine generator
14 Weary
15 Aristotle subject
16 Daydreamer's activity, maybe
18 Like flies
19 Father of American puppetry
20 Tropical fish
21 Not working
23 Long and spindly
25 Karate outfits
26 Walking with a swagger
28 Petition
29 *The Eve __ Agnes* (Keats poem)
30 Not like at all, with "a"
33 Without obligations
35 Software installation direction
36 Landings: Abbr.
37 Insert
38 Send back
43 *Simpsons* bartender
44 1948 Literature Nobelist
46 Pump part
47 Orch. member
49 First name in architecture
51 Zip
52 Become angry
55 Humbled oneself
56 Balaam, e.g.
57 Hardly dry
58 Became expressionless

DOWN

1 *Merchant of Venice* character
2 Doesn't pursue
3 Dissolve again
4 Western movie entrepreneur
5 BBC competitor
6 Does lacework
7 Of a graph line
8 Literary pseudonym
9 Rich, in a way
10 Salt Lake County resort
11 Ministering to
12 Definite lack of modesty
13 Hereditary ruler
15 Ancient temple tower
17 Built up
22 Rears
24 Hot spot
27 Foot bone
29 It means "mouth"
31 Least full-voiced
32 Sea or way follower
33 Brought to a standstill
34 French possessive
35 Frequently using
36 *Comadres*
39 Some Louvre works
40 Early personal computers
41 Root growth
42 Fell carelessly
44 "Rubber Duckie" singer
45 *Perry Mason* police lieutenant
48 Taylor's third
50 Scott Turow novel
53 Directional suffix
54 __ testing

★★★★ One-Way Streets

The diagram represents a pattern of streets. P's are parking spaces, and the black squares are stores. Find the route that starts at a parking space, passes through all stores exactly once, and ends at the other parking space. Arrows indicate one-way traffic for that block only. No block or intersection may be entered more than once.

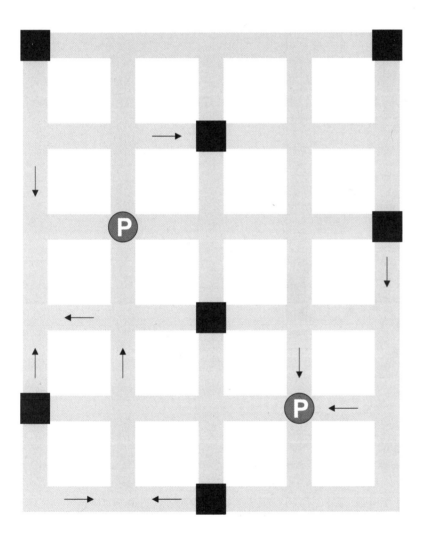

SOUND THINKING

There is only one common uncapitalized word whose consonant sounds are L, T, W, and T, in that order. What is it?

_____

★★ Split Decisions

In this clueless crossword puzzle, each answer consists of two words whose spellings are the same, except for the consecutive letters given. All answers are common words; no phrases or hyphenated or capitalized words are used. Some of the clues may have more than one solution, but there is only one word pair that will correctly link up with all the other word pairs.

TRANSDELETION

Delete one letter from the word EARTHLING and rearrange the rest, to get a kind of shape.

_____

★★★★★ Themeless Toughie by Doug Peterson

ACROSS

1 Proven profit center
8 One doing endorsements
15 Call into question
16 *Mr. Pim Passes By* playwright
17 Hunt cry
18 Ties
19 Largest known dwarf planet
20 *Ulysses* star
22 Prune copy
23 Became established
25 Army unit estd. in 1942
26 Pets
27 Noted animal shelter
30 Tap output
31 Christina's stepmom
34 *The Facts of Life* actress
35 Lima relative
36 Pit player
37 Evil influences
39 USCG bigwig
40 Man. neighbor
42 Arrangement of services
43 Nice name
44 Short-lived insects
46 Irish Rebellion leader
48 Snap
49 "Battle of the Sexes" loser
53 Paul Bunyan's watchdog
54 Silence
56 NBAer
57 Waterproof outerwear
59 Big Brother's state
61 Cheesy snack
62 Serving, in a way
63 General Grant's publisher
64 Green stone

DOWN

1 Tickets
2 To love, in Livorno
3 Lane bane
4 1952 Summer Olympics site
5 Speck of land
6 __ Rios
7 List of leading lights
8 Sight at Indy
9 Superman's mother
10 Meryl's *Prime* costar
11 Assumption
12 Oscar winner of 2000
13 Authorizing
14 Hasn't a care
21 Keeps
24 Malodorous
26 Summertime pest, so to speak
28 CIGNA competitor
29 Arm bones
31 Shaw title character
32 Type of muscle
33 *Star Trek* bigwig
38 Tuneful event
41 Dictators' aides
42 Performer born James Todd Smith
45 Go together
47 *String Symphony* composer
50 Bottled spirits
51 Flash
52 Series unit
54 Pelt
55 Flying Wedge Award org.
58 Japanese leader elected in 2006
60 Teacher's deg.

★★★★ Your Turn

Entering at the bottom and exiting at the top, find the shortest path through the maze, following these turn rules: You must turn right on red squares, turn left on blue squares, and go straight through yellow squares. Your path may retrace itself and cross at intersections, but you may not reverse your direction at any point.

SAY IT AGAIN

What six-letter word can mean either "movement" or "proposal"?

— — — — — —

★★★★ Star Search

Find the stars that are hidden in some of the blank squares. The numbered squares indicate how many stars are hidden in the squares adjacent to them (including diagonally). There is never more than one star in any square.

	2	2	2			
					4	
1		2	4			
1					3	
	2			2		
1		2			3	
	1					
	3		2			

CHOICE WORDS

Form three six-letter words from the same category, by selecting one letter from each column three times. Each letter will be used exactly once.

B	I	L	A	A	T	_ _ _ _ _ _
S	O	N	U	T	D	_ _ _ _ _ _
M	A	N	L	E	A	_ _ _ _ _ _

★★★★★ Themeless Toughie by Anna Stiga

ACROSS

1 It may suit you
6 Ralph Bunche went there
10 Certain student
14 Man with a horn
15 GM brand
16 Walking-shoe name
17 Seat of Summit County
18 Harsh quality
20 Percolate
21 Driver's bane
22 Stuck together
24 __ rule
25 Farther astray
26 *The Simpsons* character
29 Digital-camera unit
30 Some pants
33 Site of a 1799 discovery
36 Eastern European
37 Snobbish
38 Exclamation of triumph
39 Kind of competition
40 Quiet now, perhaps
41 Part of some portfolios
44 Queen Silvia's husband
49 Went back
51 "Somebody's Miracle" singer
52 Poet inspired by Eliot
53 *Atlantic City* director
54 Times
55 Evinces impertinence
56 Literally, "at another time"
57 Unite
58 Aperture
59 "You can hide __ your covers ..." (Springsteen lyric)

DOWN

1 Embodiment of comedy
2 Rises
3 Goofs
4 Moment in time, in astronomy
5 CBS retiree of '04
6 Certified as fine
7 Yellowish brown
8 "Roamin' in the Gloamin'" writer
9 Britcom, briefly
10 Present-day VIP
11 Surpass
12 Medieval foe of Genoa
13 Padlock partner
19 Big do
23 Just passing
27 Transfix
28 Take unfair advantage of
29 Pritzker Prize winner of '83
30 Set light, for short
31 Kind of crook
32 Artie ex
33 Source of annoyance, or relaxation
34 Unlock, in verse
35 Eerie
36 Most substantial
38 French media giant
40 __ soup
41 Ferrari's home
42 Berate
43 All over
45 Pretentious
46 Remote control
47 They're not serious
48 River-delta material
49 Saturn's second-largest moon
50 Count's equivalent

★★★★ Number-Out

Shade squares so that no number appears in any row or column more than
once. Shaded squares may not touch each other horizontally or vertically,
and all unshaded squares must form a single continuous area.

2	5	4	3	1	4
1	3	6	5	1	3
4	2	3	4	6	5
3	3	5	4	5	1
6	1	2	4	3	6
6	3	5	2	5	6

THINK ALIKE

Unscramble the letters in the phrase HONE QUERIES to form two words with the same or similar
meanings.

_____   _____

★★★★ Line Drawing

Draw two straight lines, each from one edge of the square to another edge, so there are a different number of words in each region, and the words in each region have something in common.

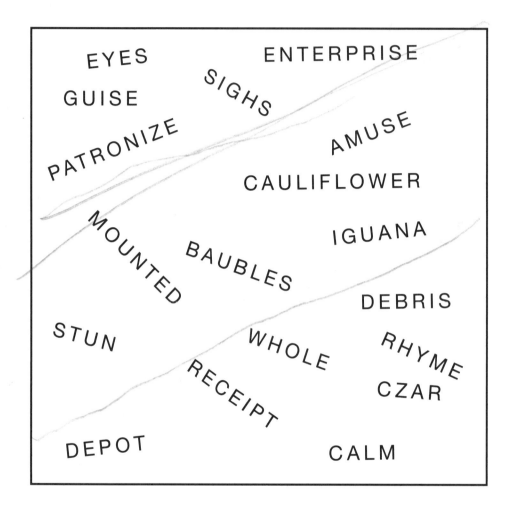

TWO-BY-FOUR

The eight letters in the word EMBLAZON can be rearranged to form a pair of common four-letter words in only one way, if no four-letter word is repeated. Can you find the two words?

ZONE LAMB

★★★★★ Themeless Toughie by Daniel R. Stark

ACROSS

1 Dear
8 Be a schemer
15 In the dark
16 Running amok
17 More than surprised
18 Vivid color
19 Brings on board
20 Purpose
22 Stuffs to the gills
23 Anatomical passage
24 Hockey violation
26 Nothing but
27 Bracket type
28 Like guitars and banjos
30 Hoop site
31 Some eBay auctions
33 Rambles
35 Checking amt.
36 Billion-year period
37 Very fast runner
41 Went up
45 '80s White House dog
46 Evinced an allergy, perhaps
48 Three-*mois* period
49 Roadie gear
51 Makeshift bed, at times
52 Work with a sickle
53 Swift
55 Th.D. student's subject
56 All-Starr Band leader
57 Old photo
59 Uplifts
61 Stands
62 Severely simple
63 Oppressive ones
64 Goes ballistic

DOWN

1 More overgrown
2 Qualify
3 Olympians' quests
4 One with a manual, maybe
5 Airport regulars
6 Air homophone
7 Gathers
8 Stirs up
9 Concert conclusion
10 Badgers
11 Elite squad
12 Too polite
13 Neither forward nor backward
14 Teachers' pets, sometimes
21 Hospitable invitation
24 Cork's home
25 Settle things
28 Certain shoes
29 Sci-fi servant
32 Maggie's grandpa
34 __ mission
37 Made
38 Designer's concern
39 Pays
40 Athina Onassis de Miranda, e.g.
41 Flowering shrubs
42 Even smaller
43 Stand for stuff
44 Brought down
47 Joanne's Oscar role
50 Arrangement
52 Breaks
54 Inexperienced one
56 Ascent
58 Boxer, for example
60 Adequate

★★ Triad Split Decisions

In this clueless crossword puzzle, each answer consists of two words whose spellings are the same, except for the consecutive letters given. All answers are common words; no phrases or hyphenated or capitalized words are used. Some of the clues may have more than one solution, but there is only one word pair that will correctly link up with all the other word pairs.

TRANSDELETION

Delete one letter from the word SEMITROPIC and rearrange the rest, to get an exercise term.

_____

★★★ Piece It Together

Fill in the blue design using pieces with the same shape outlined in black. Some pieces are "mirror-image" versions of the shape shown.

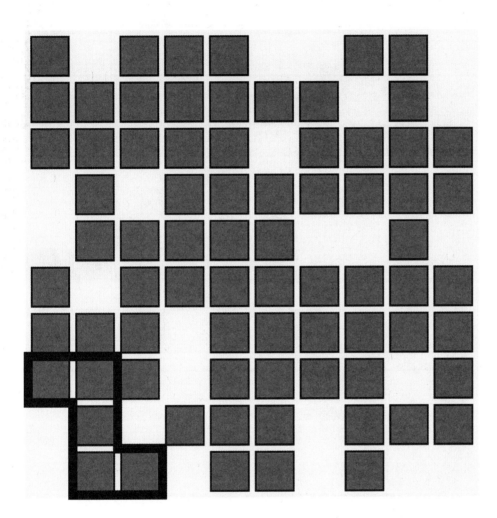

SMALL CHANGE

Change one letter in each of these two words, to form a common two-word phrase.

STRONG QUARTER

_____

★★★★★ Themeless Toughie by Raymond Hamel

ACROSS

1 Window material
11 Attack, with "into"
15 Western winery center
16 Pop group spelled with a backward letter
17 Soundtrack segments
19 Reason for a bouncing
20 Tidal adjective
21 Liszt piece
22 One place to get down
24 __ space
26 Landscape designer's suggestion
32 "__ a Tramp" (Peggy Lee tune)
35 Be very upset
36 Magnetic alloy
37 Symptom suffix
39 Tied
41 *Peut-__* (perhaps, to Pierre)
42 Oscar role of '94
44 Hinge (on)
46 *Westworld* name
47 Collegian's concern
50 Vermeer contemporary
51 Emulates Horton the elephant
55 __ des Beaux-Arts
57 Jerry or Tom
61 Fiery heap
62 Royal representative
65 Trick takers, usually
66 Cool treat
67 "The English Marilyn Monroe"
68 Bee Gees tune of '71

DOWN

1 Farm animals

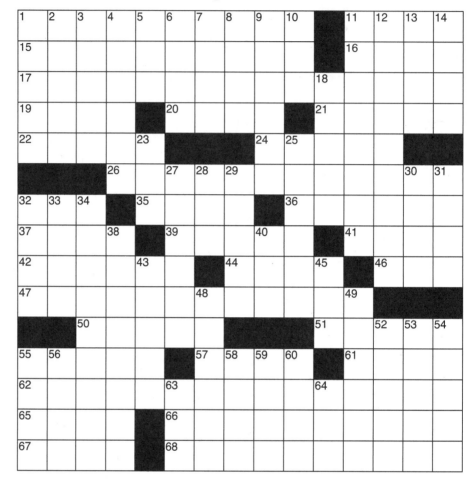

2 City on the Red River
3 Literally, "The Lord"
4 Slurs sounds
5 Thomas Lincoln's nickname
6 First Lola in *Damn Yankees*
7 Memory __
8 Landlocked prov.
9 Apply hastily
10 *On the Road* narrator
11 White wine
12 Silliness
13 Bibliographic abbr.
14 Mantilla material
18 Forging product

23 Difficulty
25 Land on Lake Victoria
27 "The deal is off!"
28 Cocktail with cassis
29 Moon of Jupiter
30 Very light brown
31 Present time
32 Not __ (not really)
33 Small case
34 Cedes
38 Shivering outside, perhaps
40 Humorist Shriner
43 Show scorn
45 __ *Heldenleben* (Strauss tone poem)

48 Fully
49 Place trust
52 Part of the Hittite Empire
53 Sam Catchem's boss
54 Youngest-ever French Open winner
55 "By jove!"
56 *Fame* character
58 *The Plague* setting
59 Eye
60 Former Labour Party leader Kinnock
63 Lacking value
64 Not only that but also

PAGE 17
Nothing to Drink

T	A	L	C	■	T	R	O	D	■	B	A	N	S	■
O	R	E	O	■	R	A	K	E	■	A	L	O	U	D
R	E	S	T	■	I	D	O	L	■	D	I	N	E	R
E	A	S	T	■	B	A	K	I	N	G	S	O	D	A
■	■	■	O	V	E	R	■	■	O	U	T	S	E	T
T	B	O	N	E	S	■	P	I	T	Y	■	■	■	■
R	A	N	G	E	■	W	A	N	E	■	S	N	O	W
A	S	T	I	R	■	H	U	N	■	W	E	I	G	H
P	E	O	N	■	K	I	S	S	■	H	E	L	L	O
■	■	■	S	I	Z	E	■	■	R	E	D	E	E	M
A	S	P	E	C	T	■	■	P	A	N	E	■	■	■
L	E	A	V	E	S	P	O	R	T	■	D	R	U	M
M	A	V	E	N	■	A	L	O	T	■	R	O	N	A
A	L	E	R	T	■	D	E	A	L	■	Y	O	U	R
■	S	S	T	S	■	S	O	M	E	■	E	M	M	Y

PAGE 18
Looped Path

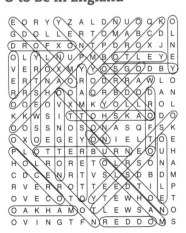

CENTURY MARKS
26, 24, 17, 33

PAGE 19
O to Be in England

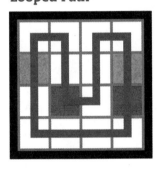

INITIAL REACTION
First Things First

PAGE 20
Sudoku

4	9	8	3	1	6	5	7	2
6	7	5	8	2	9	1	4	3
2	1	3	4	7	5	8	6	9
5	8	9	2	6	3	7	1	4
7	2	6	1	9	4	3	8	5
1	3	4	5	8	7	9	2	6
9	5	7	6	4	1	2	3	8
3	4	2	7	5	8	6	9	1
8	6	1	9	3	2	4	5	7

MIXAGRAMS

E V E N T   B L U E
M A X I M   L I S P
W A I S T   G N U S
B A T C H   S E E S

PAGE 21
Lazy Day

■	A	S	P	■	S	C	R	A	P	■	C	H	I	C
D	U	P	E	■	P	R	O	B	E	■	H	A	N	D
E	R	I	E	■	R	U	L	E	S	■	A	N	T	S
C	O	C	K	T	A	I	L	L	O	U	N	G	E	■
A	R	E	■	H	T	S	■	■	S	T	O	R	M	■
L	A	D	L	E	■	E	E	R	I	E	■	U	N	O
■	■	■	I	R	A	■	L	A	B	■	S	T	E	M
■	G	I	V	E	M	E	T	H	E	R	E	S	T	■
T	O	N	E	■	I	W	O	■	T	O	N	■	■	■
E	L	S	■	E	D	E	N	S	■	A	T	W	A	R
■	A	D	U	L	T	■	■	L	B	S	■	O	D	E
■	S	L	I	C	E	D	M	E	A	T	L	O	A	F
S	T	A	G	■	C	R	E	E	K	■	E	D	G	E
O	A	T	H	■	H	E	A	V	E	■	V	E	E	R
B	R	E	T	■	O	W	N	E	R	■	I	D	S	■

PAGE 22
Fences

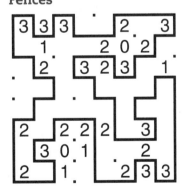

WRONG IS RIGHT
Larinx (should be *larynx*)

PAGE 23
Line Drawing

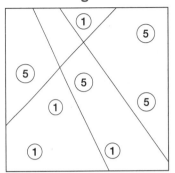

THREE OF A KIND
A SIMPLE ANSWER
SHOWS LIMITED THINKING
ABILITY.

PAGE 24
Dig In!

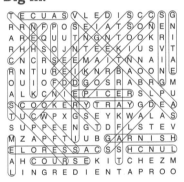

Unlisted word is INGREDIENTS

WHO'S WHAT WHERE?
Dubuquer

PAGE 25
For a Song

M	A	T	S	■	C	O	L	T	■	F	L	A	T	S
O	L	E	O	■	A	F	A	R	■	A	E	I	O	U
N	U	M	B	E	R	O	N	E	■	C	A	R	T	E
A	M	P	■	M	E	L	E	E	■	A	S	C	O	T
■	■	■	A	C	E	D	■	F	I	D	E	L	■	■
A	N	T	L	E	R	■	P	A	N	E	■	E	R	A
S	A	U	T	E	■	■	U	R	N	■	■	F	A	I	R
P	I	N	E	■	H	A	R	M	S	■	A	N	N	E
E	V	E	R	■	A	P	E	■	■	T	R	E	S	S
N	E	A	■	W	I	P	E	■	S	E	C	R	E	T
■	■	P	E	A	R	L	■	S	I	R	E	■	■	■
C	H	I	L	I	■	E	D	I	T	S	■	D	O	E
L	E	A	S	T	■	P	I	E	C	E	M	E	A	L
A	R	N	I	E	■	I	A	G	O	■	A	M	F	M
W	O	O	E	R	■	E	L	E	M	■	R	O	S	S

PAGE 26
Number-Out

4	1	5	5	3
5	4	5	2	4
3	3	1	1	2
5	3	2	1	4
1	3	4	1	5

THINK ALIKE
BAD, EVIL

PAGE 27
Pipe Down

SMALL CHANGE
WISE GUY

PAGE 28
Theme Park

L	P	G	A		P	S	S	T		P	A	N	T	S
A	L	O	T		E	T	T	E		A	D	O	R	E
M	E	A	T		S	U	E	D		L	O	R	E	N
P	A	P	E	R	T	R	A	I	L	S		T	A	D
S	T	E	N	O		G	L	U	E		P	H	D	S
		D	O	M	E		M	O	S	E	S			
A	D	D		F	L	O	E			E	A	T	U	P
S	N	A	K	E	I	N	T	H	E	G	R	A	S	S
P	A	L	E	R		C	A	L	M		R	A	T	
	M	E	S	A	S		M	I	E	N				
S	C	A	N		M	U	N	I		N	U	D	G	E
H	O	T		F	A	M	I	L	Y	T	R	E	E	S
E	M	I	L	E		M	E	T	E		S	A	T	S
E	M	A	I	L		I	C	O	N		E	R	I	E
P	A	N	E	L		T	E	N	S		S	S	T	S

PAGE 29
One-Way Streets

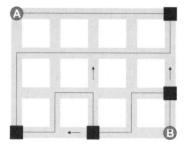

SOUND THINKING
AZALEA

PAGE 30
Split Decisions

TRANSDELETION
SHAWL

PAGE 31
Star Search

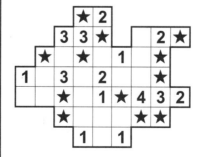

CHOICE WORDS
BANYAN, LINDEN, POPLAR

PAGE 32
"Express" Yourself

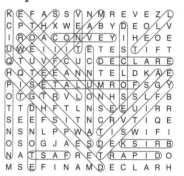

Missing word is STATE

IN OTHER WORDS
BACKACHE

PAGE 33
Rough Road

L	O	S	T		A	T	A	R	I		S	C	A	B
A	B	L	E		B	O	R	E	D		T	U	B	A
G	O	O	S	E	B	U	M	P	S		E	B	B	S
S	E	T	T	L	E	R			S	A	B	R	E	
			B	O	Y	S		M	I	L	K	Y		
	S	W	A	P	S		B	A	B	A		H	A	D
S	P	I	N	E		B	E	R	E	T		O	D	E
K	I	S	S		L	E	A	S	T		G	L	E	N
I	C	E		N	O	R	T	H		P	R	E	P	S
D	E	C		O	U	R	S		F	E	A	S	T	
	R	E	A	D	Y		S	O	O	N				
S	L	A	S	H			T	U	N	D	R	A	S	
P	E	C	S		C	H	E	R	R	Y	P	I	T	S
A	N	K	A		A	B	O	U	T		A	T	O	N
N	O	S	Y		M	O	N	T	H		S	A	P	S

PAGE 34
Hyper-Sudoku

8	6	1	9	4	3	7	5	2
7	3	4	2	8	5	9	6	1
2	9	5	7	6	1	3	8	4
5	8	6	1	3	7	4	2	9
3	2	7	4	5	9	8	1	6
1	4	9	6	2	8	5	7	3
6	7	2	5	9	4	1	3	8
4	1	8	3	7	2	6	9	5
9	5	3	8	1	6	2	4	7

MIXAGRAMS

S H R U G	F I N E
N A T A L	A W A Y
F L U K E	R I S E
A F T E R	E O N S

PAGE 35

Slipper
#7

BETWEENER
CUT

PAGE 36

123

2	3	2	1	3	1
1	2	1	3	2	3
3	1	3	2	1	2
1	3	2	1	2	3
3	2	1	3	1	2
2	1	3	2	3	1

SUDOKU SUM

5	2	3
4	9	7
6	1	8

PAGE 37

No Kidding

PAGE 38

ABC

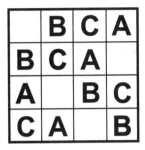

CLUELESS CROSSWORD

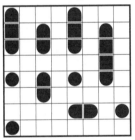

PAGE 39

Find the Ships

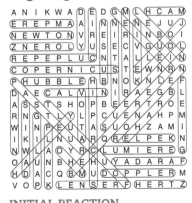

TWO-BY-FOUR
QUID, EVER (or VEER)

PAGE 40

Bright Lights

INITIAL REACTION
Still Waters Run Deep

PAGE 41

Spring Gardening

PAGE 42

Sequence Maze

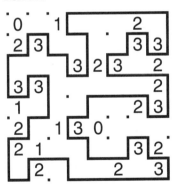

SMALL CHANGE
HOT SEAT

PAGE 43

Fences

WRONG IS RIGHT
Oomf (should be *oomph*)

PAGE 44

Play It Again

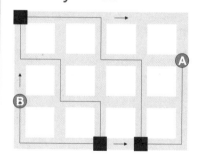

The play is HAMLET

WHO'S WHAT WHERE?
Guamanian

PAGE 45

Patriotic Fish

C	H	I	P		B	O	M	B		E	F	L	A	T
L	A	M	A		A	B	E	L		S	L	I	C	E
A	S	P	S		R	O	L	E		C	O	M	M	A
S	T	E	T		R	E	D	S	N	A	P	P	E	R
P	A	L	A	C	E			S	U	P				
			A	L	O	E		R	E	H	E	A	T	
E	A	R	L	S		A	L	A	S		A	R	I	A
G	R	E	A	T	W	H	I	T	E	S	H	A	R	K
G	L	E	N		A	U	T	O		P	A	S	S	E
S	O	L	E	M	N		E	Z	R	A				
			O	N	E		A	R	D	E	N	T		
B	L	U	E	M	A	R	L	I	N		O	R	E	O
A	I	S	L	E		R	I	S	K		O	R	A	L
R	E	S	I	N		E	L	L	E		R	O	T	E
B	U	R	S	T		D	Y	E	D		S	L	O	T

PAGE 46

Sudoku

5	6	8	9	7	4	1	3	2
4	2	3	8	6	1	9	7	5
7	1	9	3	2	5	4	6	8
6	7	4	5	1	9	2	8	3
9	8	5	2	3	6	7	4	1
2	3	1	7	4	8	6	5	9
3	9	2	6	8	7	5	1	4
1	5	6	4	9	3	8	2	7
8	4	7	1	5	2	3	9	6

MIXAGRAMS

F O C A L   R E A D
W H O O P   A X L E
R E P E L   B I A S
M A Y O R   L E A K

PAGE 47

123

3	2	1	3	1	2
2	1	3	2	3	1
1	3	2	1	2	3
3	2	1	3	1	2
2	1	3	2	3	1
1	3	2	1	2	3

ADDITION SWITCH
4 3 5 + 3 9 1 = 8 2 6

PAGE 48

LP Collection

R	O	S	E		S	T	A	B		C	O	L	T	S
O	R	E	O		N	O	N	O		A	L	O	H	A
L	A	W	N	P	A	R	T	Y		R	I	V	A	L
E	L	S		R	I	T	E	S		E	V	E	N	T
			T	I	L	E		C	H	E	E	P		
	G	L	E	N	S		R	O	A	R		O	N	E
C	R	E	S	T		O	U	T		A	T	O	P	
H	O	S	T		C	H	U	T	E		L	I	T	E
E	A	S	Y		H	A	T		S	T	O	R	E
M	N	O		S	A	M	E		S	H	A	N	E
	N	E	A	R	S		B	E	E	R				
A	P	P	L	Y		A	K	I	T	E		M	A	P
R	E	L	A	Y		L	I	S	T	P	R	I	C	E
I	R	A	T	E		A	L	O	E		O	K	R	A
D	U	N	E	S		D	O	N	E		W	E	E	K

PAGE 49

One-Way Streets

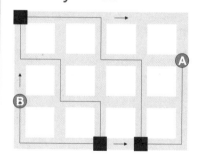

SOUND THINKING
BOYCOTT

PAGE 50

Missing Links

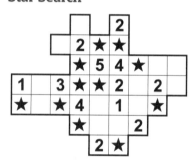

SAY IT AGAIN
BOW

PAGE 51

Star Search

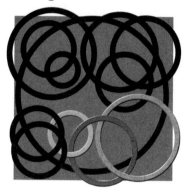

CHOICE WORDS
HAWAII, KANSAS, OREGON

PAGE 52

Capital Idea

P	A	P	A		C	O	L	T		A	S	S	E	T
A	L	A	S		A	R	I	A		S	T	A	R	E
L	A	N	S	I	N	G	M	I	C	H	I	G	A	N
E	N	T	E	R		A	B	L	E		N	E	S	T
			N	E	O	N		S	N	U	G			
R	A	P	T		V	I	A		T	R	E	M	O	R
U	M	A		B	A	S	K	S		G	R	A	T	E
S	T	P	A	U	L	M	I	N	N	E	S	O	T	A
T	O	A	D	S		S	T	A	I	D		R	E	D
S	O	L	V	E	D		A	P	T		A	I	R	Y
			A	S	I	S		P	E	S	T			
S	W	A	N		L	I	I	I		I	L	I	A	D
L	I	N	C	O	L	N	N	E	B	R	A	S	K	A
A	S	T	E	R		U	R	S	A		S	L	I	M
T	H	E	S	E		S	E	T	H		T	E	N	S

PAGE 53

Let's Get Together

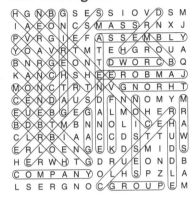

IN OTHER WORDS
BULBS

PAGE 55

Line Drawing

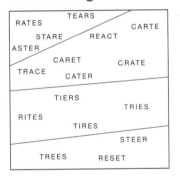

The words in each region are anagrams of each other

THREE OF A KIND
ON A <u>WH</u>IM, I LEARNED
ANOTH<u>ER</u> <u>THEME</u> SONG.

PAGE 56

ABC

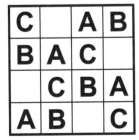

NATIONAL TREASURE
GENIAL

PAGE 57

Celebrities of the Month

PAGE 58

Five by Five

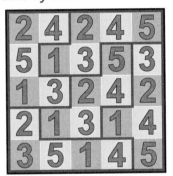

BETWEENER
TOE

PAGE 59

Health Spa Whodunit

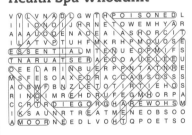

Ralph the Reflexologist did it, with the bathrobe belt, on the couch

INITIAL REACTION
No Pain No Gain

PAGE 60

Find the Ships

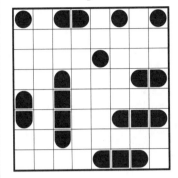

TWO-BY-FOUR
PITY, ARID (or RAID); PAIR, TIDY

PAGE 61

Sudoku

7	1	8	3	5	6	4	9	2
6	9	5	2	4	7	1	3	8
2	3	4	1	9	8	6	7	5
8	4	1	9	3	2	5	6	7
3	5	2	7	6	4	9	8	1
9	7	6	8	1	5	3	2	4
4	6	7	5	2	3	8	1	9
5	8	9	6	7	1	2	4	3
1	2	3	4	8	9	7	5	6

MIXAGRAMS
```
F O C U S    I N C H
L O T T O    P U R E
C O L O R    B E T A
S P I C E    M E L D
```

PAGE 62

Influential

PAGE 63

Fences

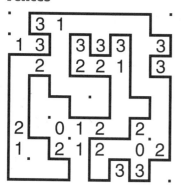

WRONG IS RIGHT
Finickey (should be *finicky*)

PAGE 64

Triad Split Decisions

TRANSDELETION
NURSE

PAGE 65

123

1	3	2	3	1	2
2	1	3	1	2	3
3	2	1	2	3	1
2	1	3	1	2	3
3	2	1	2	3	1
1	3	2	3	1	2

SUDOKU SUM

3	6	1
9	4	5
2	7	8

PAGE 66

Hankerings

R	I	C	E		S	P	A	S		P	E	K	O	E
I	D	O	L		C	A	S	H		L	U	N	G	E
B	E	L	L	Y	A	C	H	E		A	R	O	L	L
S	A	D		O	T	T	E	R		N	O	T	E	S
		N	U	T	S		W	E	E	S	T			
A	B	O	V	E		T	O	O	T		Y	E	S	
C	L	E	V	E	R		W	O	N		O	P	A	L
L	I	F	E		L	I	D		W	I	S	E		
E	C	O	L		P	A	N		S	U	N	N	E	D
O	E	R		B	I	T	E		K	N	E	E	L	
	E	L	A	T	E		H	A	I	R				
S	O	L	E	S		S	C	O	T	T		A	D	S
A	V	O	W	S		H	O	N	E	Y	M	O	O	N
G	E	N	I	E		O	V	E	R		A	N	T	I
A	N	G	S	T		W	E	D	S		P	E	S	T

PAGE 67

Number-Out

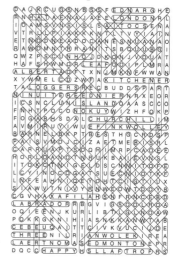

THINK ALIKE
BIG, LARGE

PAGE 68

No Three in a Row

SAY IT AGAIN
FIT

PAGE 69

Northern Exposure

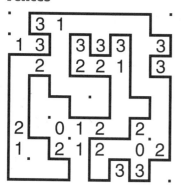

WHO'S WHAT WHERE?
Minneapolitan

PAGE 70

Regret-Full

P	I	P	S		A	L	L	I		A	S	T	A	R
A	L	O	T		P	O	O	R		M	E	R	C	Y
P	L	E	A	S	E	F	O	R	G	I	V	E	M	E
A	S	T	R	O		A	M	E	R		E	K	E	S
			G	O	A	T		G	A	I	N			
A	S	I	A	N	S		F	U	S	S		M	E	T
B	E	N	Z		S	I	L	L		S	P	E	A	R
A	C	C	E	P	T	M	Y	A	P	O	L	O	G	Y
S	T	A	R	E		I	N	R	E		A	W	L	S
E	S	S		A	T	T	N		S	U	N	S	E	T
			A	R	E	A		S	O	M	E			
F	E	E	L		A	T	O	P		P	L	A	C	E
I	M	T	E	R	R	I	B	L	Y	S	O	R	R	Y
S	M	A	R	T		N	O	I	R		A	L	O	E
T	A	S	T	E		G	E	T	S			D	O	C	S

PAGE 71
One-Way Streets

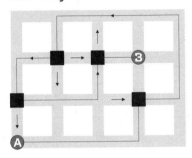

SOUND THINKING
CHOP SUEY

PAGE 72
Hyper-Sudoku

2	1	5	3	8	7	4	6	9
6	8	4	5	9	2	3	7	1
7	3	9	6	4	1	8	5	2
5	7	1	2	3	4	6	9	8
4	2	6	9	7	8	5	1	3
8	9	3	1	5	6	2	4	7
3	5	2	4	1	9	7	8	6
9	6	8	7	2	5	1	3	4
1	4	7	8	6	3	9	2	5

CENTURY MARKS
25, 28, 40, 7

PAGE 73
Star Search

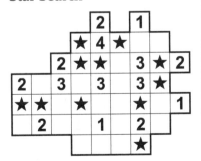

CHOICE WORDS
DESIGN, METHOD, SYSTEM

PAGE 74
Choice Desserts

B	U	F	F		M	E	E	T	S		C	E	L	L
O	H	I	O		O	P	T	I	C		A	R	I	A
S	O	N	Y		P	I	N	C	H		C	R	O	P
C	H	E	E	S	E	C	A	K	E		T	O	N	S
		T	R	A			E	M	A	I	L	S		
Y	O	U		D	E	B	A	T	E	R				
M	A	N	S		L	E	T			A	L	E	R	T
C	H	E	R	R	I	E	S	J	U	B	I	L	E	E
A	U	D	I	O		E	E	G		D	E	A	N	
			B	R	E	A	T	H	E		V	P	S	
	I	N	A	S	E	C		L	E	A				
E	R	A	S		C	H	O	C	O	L	A	T	E	S
T	I	C	K		I	O	W	A	N		R	I	D	E
A	S	H	E		P	E	E	V	E		N	O	N	E
S	H	O	W		E	S	S	E	S		S	N	A	P

PAGE 75
ABC

C	B	A	
B	A		C
	C	B	A
A		C	B

CLUELESS CROSSWORD

C	U	S	T	A	R	D
O		K		D		A
O	V	E	R	J	O	Y
L		T		O		B
E	X	C	L	U	D	E
R		H		R		D
S	A	Y	I	N	G	S

PAGE 76
Tanks a Lot

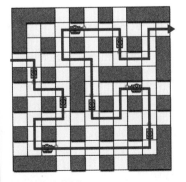

BETWEENER
SEA

PAGE 77
Sudoku

6	9	7	3	1	4	5	8	2
5	3	8	7	9	2	1	4	6
2	1	4	8	6	5	7	9	3
7	5	3	1	8	6	4	2	9
1	8	2	4	7	9	3	6	5
4	6	9	5	2	3	8	7	1
9	7	5	2	3	8	6	1	4
8	4	6	9	5	1	2	3	7
3	2	1	6	4	7	9	5	8

MIXAGRAMS

G U L C H   F I A T
O C E A N   I N K Y
L A D E N   S P U R
D O T T Y   H U R L

PAGE 78
Birthday Offerings

S	O	L	O		L	A	M	B		B	A	S	I	L
A	T	O	P		O	R	E	O		E	M	P	T	Y
G	I	F	T	O	F	G	A	B		G	E	E	S	E
S	S	T		P	A	U	L	S		O	N	L	Y	
			S	A	T	E		L	E	N	D	L		
M	A	J	O	R		S	W	E	D	E		C	P	A
A	B	O	U	T			O	D	D		T	H	A	N
R	A	H	S		H	O	R	S	Y		W	E	S	T
E	T	N	A		A	B	S			C	A	C	T	I
S	E	N		A	S	S	E	T		H	I	K	E	S
			Y	A	C	H	T		W	R	E	N		
	S	C	O	T		A	R	I	E	S		B	O	O
S	P	A	R	S		C	A	R	D	S	H	A	R	K
H	A	S	T	O		L	I	L	Y		U	S	E	R
E	T	H	A	N		E	L	S	E		M	E	S	A

PAGE 79
Line Drawing

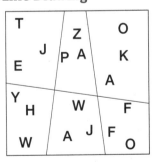

JET, ZAP, OAK, WHY, JAW, OFF

THREE OF A KIND
<u>HONEY</u>, <u>IT WOULD</u> BE GREAT
TO SCUBA DIVE AT
PLYMO<u>UTH REEF</u>.

PAGE 80

Find the Ships

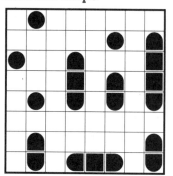

TWO-BY-FOUR
GILT, WITH (or WHIT); TWIG, HILT

PAGE 81

Fences

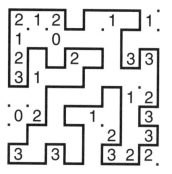

ADDITION SWITCH
708 + 114 = 822

PAGE 82

Urging On

A	S	I	S		S	A	R	I	S		A	C	T	I
M	O	T	H		A	N	O	D	E		C	O	E	D
P	U	S	H	B	U	T	T	O	N	P	H	O	N	E
S	P	Y		A	C	E	S		S	I	E	S	T	A
		A	G	E	S		G	I	G	S				
S	T	A	G	E	S		R	O	B	S		T	D	S
T	O	T	A	L		M	A	L	L		N	E	I	L
P	R	E	S	S	C	O	N	F	E	R	E	N	C	E
A	S	A	P		O	R	B	S		E	A	S	E	D
T	O	T		R	O	S	Y		C	A	R	E	S	S
		P	E	K	E		S	O	D	S				
R	O	M	A	N	O		C	E	N	T		D	O	E
S	P	U	R	O	F	T	H	E	M	O	M	E	N	T
V	A	L	E		F	R	A	M	E		A	L	E	C
P	L	E	D		S	I	R	E	N		D	I	S	H

PAGE 83

Knot or Not?
Knot: 1 and 3, Not: 2 and 4

SMALL CHANGE
FISH CAKE

PAGE 84

123

3	1	2	3	2	1	3	2	1
1	2	3	1	3	2	1	3	2
2	3	1	2	1	3	2	1	3
1	2	3	1	3	2	1	3	2
3	1	2	3	2	1	3	2	1
2	3	1	2	1	3	2	1	3
1	2	3	1	3	2	1	3	2
2	3	1	2	1	3	2	1	3
3	1	2	3	2	1	3	2	1

WRONG IS RIGHT
Compatable (should be *compatible*)

PAGE 85

Number-Out

4	3	2	2	1
5	4	3	1	4
1	4	2	3	5
3	4	5	1	3
4	1	4	5	3

THINK ALIKE
FOE, ENEMY

PAGE 86

Graduation Day

S	O	F	T		A	S	P	C	A		A	J	A	R
W	H	O	A		S	T	A	R	S		L	U	R	E
A	N	A	T		P	O	L	O	S		L	I	E	S
P	O	L	A	R	I	C	E	C	A	P		C	A	T
		A	R	K			I	G	U	E	S	S		
M	A	R	I	N	E		A	T	L	A	S			
A	L	O	N	G		I	L	I	E		A	D	M	S
T	O	A	L	E	S	S	E	R	D	E	G	R	E	E
E	T	R	E		H	E	R	E		Y	E	A	S	T
		T	W	E	E	T		V	I	S	T	A	S	
M	O	R	S	E	L		T	A	N					
E	P	A		E	V	E	N	I	N	G	G	O	W	N
R	A	N	T		I	R	A	N	I		A	R	I	A
G	L	U	E		N	I	N	E	S		S	A	P	S
E	S	P	N		G	N	A	S	H		P	L	E	A

PAGE 87

Sty Writing

SAY IT AGAIN
SAP

PAGE 88

Split Decisions

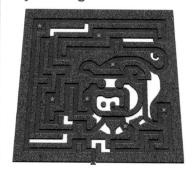

TRANSDELETION
LEADER

PAGE 89

Hyper-Sudoku

5	6	7	1	2	9	3	4	8
8	3	9	7	4	5	2	1	6
1	2	4	6	3	8	7	9	5
9	8	1	5	7	4	6	3	2
3	5	2	8	9	6	1	7	4
4	7	6	2	1	3	5	8	9
2	9	5	3	8	1	4	6	7
6	1	8	4	5	7	9	2	3
7	4	3	9	6	2	8	5	1

MIXAGRAMS

THEIR DEFY
TOPAZ EMIT
ELITE GELS
CYCLE RIME

PAGE 90

What's Now?

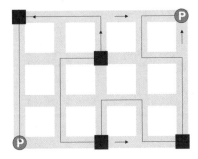

PAGE 91

Tool Time

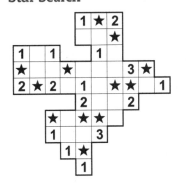

Unlisted words are HAMMER and IMPLEMENT

IN OTHER WORDS
LAMPPOST

PAGE 93

One-Way Streets

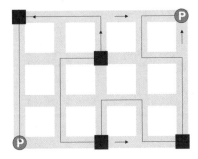

SOUND THINKING
DOORWAY

PAGE 94

Giving Way

PAGE 95

Two-Color Maze

SMALL CHANGE
NIGHT OWL

PAGE 96

Star Search

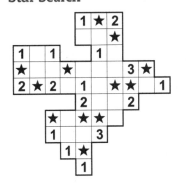

CHOICE WORDS
DAMSEL, LASSIE, MAIDEN

PAGE 97

Triad Split Decisions

TRANSDELETION
COUSIN

PAGE 98

Catch of the Day

PAGE 99

ABC

C		A	B
	B		A	C
A			C	B
	C	B		A
B	A	C	

NATIONAL TREASURE
PIANIST

PAGE 100

Find the Ships

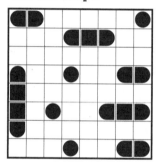

TWO-BY-FOUR
CLUB, NUKE; BUNK, CLUE

PAGE 101

Choose Your Weapon

S	C	A	L	P		A	M	F	M		A	G	E	S
T	A	B	O	O		T	R	A	Y		D	U	N	E
A	R	R	O	W	S	M	I	T	H		I	N	I	T
T	O	A	T	E	E		S	E	C	O	N	D	S	
E	L	M		L	E	O		R	O	S	Y			
		C	L	U	B	R	O	O	M		S	P	F	
S	O	S	O		P	R	E	P		E	M	A	I	L
L	O	W	E	R		I	L	E		R	I	C	C	I
O	Z	O	N	E		E	I	N	S		S	K	A	T
P	E	R		L	A	N	C	E	L	O	T			
	D	D	A	Y		R	I	N		D	O	E		
A	F	F	I	X	E	S		E	A	S	E	L	S	
L	O	I	N		S	P	E	A	R	H	E	A	D	S
D	E	S	K		I	R	K	S		O	L	L	I	E
A	S	H	Y		R	Y	E	S		P	A	T	E	S

PAGE 102

Two Pairs

BETWEENER
PLAY

PAGE 103

Sudoku

7	8	2	9	4	3	1	6	5
4	5	1	6	2	8	9	7	3
6	9	3	1	7	5	4	2	8
3	1	7	2	5	6	8	4	9
9	6	4	8	3	1	2	5	7
5	2	8	7	9	4	3	1	6
1	3	9	5	6	2	7	8	4
2	7	5	4	8	9	6	3	1
8	4	6	3	1	7	5	9	2

MIXAGRAMS

B	O	G	U	S		S	W	A	P
E	R	E	C	T		S	I	L	O
A	N	G	R	Y		T	O	I	L
N	A	I	V	E		C	A	F	E

PAGE 104

Fences

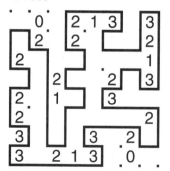

WRONG IS RIGHT
Sparcity (should be *sparsity*)

PAGE 105

Award Winners

C	A	S	T		H	A	S	H		L	U	T	E	S
U	S	E	R		A	C	L	U		E	R	O	D	E
R	I	D	E		S	H	U	N		A	N	N	I	E
E	D	G	A	R	B	E	R	G	E	N		Y	E	N
S	E	E	D	E	R	S		A	T	A	D			
		L	A	O		C	O	R	O	N	A	D	O	
O	T	H	E	R		P	O	R	T		S	N	O	W
L	O	U		S	L	E	I	G	H	T		Z	O	E
D	I	G	S		E	E	L	S		H	E	A	R	D
S	L	O	T	C	A	R	S		D	E	L			
		B	U	L	K		C	A	M	E	R	A	S	
Y	S	L		O	S	C	A	R	L	E	V	A	N	T
M	E	A	T	Y		O	V	A	L		A	N	T	I
C	A	C	H	E		N	O	V	A		T	I	E	R
A	S	K	E	D		E	W	E	S		E	N	D	S

PAGE 106

Number-Out

2	3	5	4	4	4
2	6	5	5	1	3
5	1	3	1	6	1
6	1	4	3	5	6
3	1	6	2	6	5
1	5	2	4	2	6

THINK ALIKE
FINISH, END

PAGE 107

Hyper-Sudoku

2	1	4	7	5	9	3	8	6
8	3	5	4	6	2	9	7	1
9	6	7	1	3	8	5	4	2
7	9	8	2	4	6	1	3	5
3	5	2	9	8	1	7	6	4
6	4	1	5	7	3	2	9	8
5	7	9	8	2	4	6	1	3
4	2	3	6	1	7	8	5	9
1	8	6	3	9	5	4	2	7

CENTURY MARKS
22, 24, 37, 17

PAGE 108
Number Twos

L	I	N	E	N		G	I	N	A		V	A	S	T
A	B	I	D	E		O	R	B	S		E	R	I	E
V	A	C	U	U	M	P	A	C	K		S	O	M	E
E	R	E	C	T	O	R	S		S	I	T	S	O	N
			R	O	O			O	P	E	N	S		
C	R	A	V	A	T		P	H	O	N	O			
R	A	V	E	L		S	A	I	L		C	H	E	W
A	G	E	R		C	U	R	V	E		K	A	L	E
B	A	R	B		B	I	T	E		P	E	R	S	E
	P	A	S	T	Y		H	A	T	T	E	D		
S	O	P	H	S			B	U	R					
T	H	E	R	A	M		M	E	G	A	D	O	S	E
R	A	R	A		V	I	D	E	O	P	O	K	E	R
E	R	O	S		P	O	S	T		E	U	L	E	R
W	A	N	E		S	U	E	S		T	R	A	N	S

PAGE 109
Golden

INITIAL REACTION
Well Begun Is Half Done

PAGE 110
Sets of Three

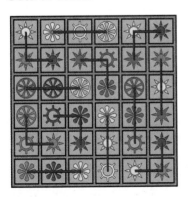

SAY IT AGAIN
PARK

PAGE 111
Shipping News

G	R	A	S	S		C	O	M	A		C	O	M	O
E	E	R	I	E		O	L	I	N		O	R	A	L
M	A	N	T	A		M	A	M	A		M	E	R	E
	P	O	S	T	O	F	F	I	C	E	B	O	X	
			B	A	Y			O	N	O				
L	I	M	B	E	R		W	A	N	D		P	O	T
E	M	A	I	L		H	E	L	D		S	L	U	R
V	A	C	A	T	I	O	N	P	A	C	K	A	G	E
E	G	O	S		N	O	D	S		L	I	T	H	E
L	E	N		E	S	P	Y		D	E	P	O	T	S
			M	A	T			A	N	A				
	P	A	R	T	A	N	D	P	A	R	C	E	L	
C	U	R	B		N	E	A	P		C	A	R	O	L
A	L	L	I		C	A	L	L		U	N	I	T	E
B	L	O	G			E	L	I	E		T	E	N	S	E

PAGE 112
One-Way Streets

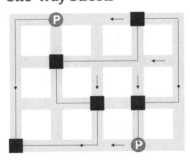

SOUND THINKING
PHARMACY

PAGE 113
123

2	3	1	2	1	3	2	1	3
1	2	3	1	3	2	1	3	2
3	1	2	3	2	1	3	2	1
2	3	1	2	1	3	2	1	3
1	2	3	1	3	2	1	3	2
3	1	2	3	2	1	3	2	1
2	3	1	2	1	3	1	3	2
1	2	3	1	3	2	3	2	1
3	1	2	3	2	1	2	1	3

SUDOKU SUM

7	9	4
5	1	2
8	6	3

PAGE 114
Line Drawing

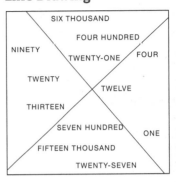

The "numbers" in each region have the same number of syllables

THREE OF A KIND
HEY, GUY<u>S</u>—<u>WANT</u> TO HEAD <u>OVER</u> TO THE B<u>OWL</u>ING ALLEY?

PAGE 115
Find a Seat

H	A	R	P	S		S	T	A	G	S		C	B	S
A	L	O	H	A		L	A	D	L	E		H	U	T
S	T	O	O	L	P	I	G	E	O	N		A	R	E
			T	O	A	D		N	O	D		I	R	E
C	O	C	O	O	N			M	I	R	R	O	R	
E	C	O		N	A	K	E	D		N	A	P		
S	T	U			M	A	L	I		G	R	E	A	T
T	A	C	T		A	R	I	A	S		E	R	G	O
A	D	H	O	C		T	O	R	E		S	A	O	
		P	G	A		S	T	Y	E	S		O	P	T
S	C	O	O	P	S				S	C	E	N	E	S
M	A	T		A	T	A		W	A	R	E			
A	N	A		B	E	N	C	H	W	A	R	M	E	R
L	O	T		L	A	T	H	E		P	I	A	N	O
L	E	O		E	L	S	I	E		S	E	E	D	Y

PAGE 116
Star Search

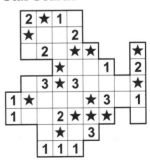

CHOICE WORDS
ELEVEN, TWELVE, NINETY

PAGE 117

Dicey

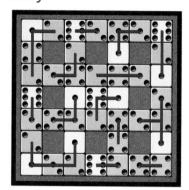

SMALL CHANGE
TREE STUMP

PAGE 118

Up to Speed

C	A	F	E	S		S	L	A	P		F	E	N	G
A	P	A	R	T		H	A	U	L		A	L	A	I
I	S	S	E	I		E	T	N	A		I	L	K	S
N	E	T		F	L	E	E	T	S	T	R	E	E	T
	T	A	L	O	N			T	R	E	N	D	S	
E	N	A	M	E	L		B	R	I	A	R			
M	A	L	I		L	I	L	A	C	S		R	I	D
M	I	K	E	S		L	A	C		H	E	A	D	Y
A	L	S		T	H	E	M	E	S		B	P	O	E
		R	E	E	S	E		A	V	A	I	L	S	
E	N	D	E	A	R		E	M	E	N	D			
Q	U	I	C	K	S	I	L	V	E	R		C	A	P
U	R	G	E		E	D	I	E		S	P	I	R	E
A	S	I	S		L	E	O	N		E	A	T	E	N
L	E	N	S		F	O	N	T		D	R	Y	A	D

PAGE 119

Hyper-Sudoku

4	9	7	8	2	3	6	1	5
8	1	6	5	7	9	2	3	4
5	2	3	4	1	6	7	8	9
2	7	8	9	6	4	1	5	3
6	4	5	1	3	7	9	2	8
9	3	1	2	5	8	4	7	6
3	8	9	7	4	1	5	6	2
7	5	4	6	8	2	3	9	1
1	6	2	3	9	5	8	4	7

MIXAGRAMS

```
R O B E D     S T I R
T H E M E     S O C K
L E A S H     S W I G
L I N E N     A N T E
```

PAGE 120

ABC

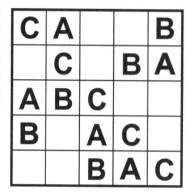

NATIONAL TREASURE
ANNUAL

PAGE 121

Poolside

C	E	N	T	S		N	A	V	E		B	A	A
A	V	I	A	N		O	V	A	L		C	R	A	M
R	A	C	K	O	F	L	A	M	B		H	A	R	E
S	N	E	E	R	A	T		P	A	R	A	G	O	N
			T	I	E	R			E	L	A	N	D	
M	A	T	T	E	R		A	B	A	C	K			
A	C	R	I	D		S	N	A	P		T	A	X	I
S	L	I	M		C	H	A	R	T		A	W	E	D
H	U	G	E		N	A	T	E		C	L	O	N	E
	T	O	N	G	A		T	O	K	L	A	S		
S	O	F	A	R		B	A	E	Z					
T	H	E	B	E	S	T		R	E	U	T	E	R	S
R	A	I	L		T	H	A	T	S	M	Y	C	U	E
U	R	G	E		I	O	N	S		E	R	O	D	E
M	A	N		R	U	D	Y		L	A	N	E	D

PAGE 122

Flaky
A: #10, B: #15, C: #4

BETWEENER
LIFE

PAGE 123

Find the Ships

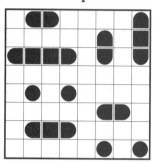

TWO-BY-FOUR
VAIN, GLUT

PAGE 124

Triad Split Decisions

TRANSDELETION
PENCIL

PAGE 125

Got Insurance?

P	U	T	T	S		M	U	I	R		O	H	N	O
A	T	E	A	M		A	N	N	A		L	E	A	P
C	A	R	P	O	O	L	I	N	G		D	A	M	E
T	H	I	S	T	L	E		S	T	E	E	L	E	D
			H	I	S	S		R	A	N	T			
S	O	F	T	E	N		T	W	A	S		H	M	M
C	R	I	E	R		H	A	R	D	Y		F	O	E
R	A	R	E		C	U	R	I	E		C	O	O	T
A	T	E		R	O	G	E	T		S	N	O	R	E
G	E	E		O	V	E	R		D	A	N	D	E	R
		N	A	V	E		S	P	A	N				
J	O	G	G	E	R	S		A	D	D	E	N	D	S
E	M	I	R		L	I	F	E	S	A	V	E	R	S
R	E	N	E		E	L	I	S		L	I	M	I	T
K	N	E	E		T	O	N	E		S	L	O	P	S

PAGE 126

123

1	2	1	3	2	3	1	2	3
2	3	2	1	3	1	3	1	2
3	1	3	2	1	2	1	2	3
2	3	1	3	2	1	2	3	1
3	1	3	2	1	2	3	1	2
2	3	2	1	3	1	2	3	1
1	2	1	3	2	3	1	2	3
3	1	2	1	3	2	3	1	2
1	2	3	2	1	3	2	3	1

WRONG IS RIGHT
Monicle (should be *monocle*)

PAGE 127

Fences

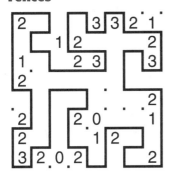

ADDITION SWITCH
3 9 1 + 4 7 5 = 8 6 6

PAGE 128

Faking It

PAGE 129

Three-Color Maze

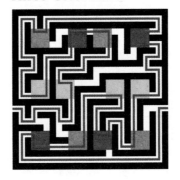

SAY IT AGAIN
TONE

PAGE 131

Keyword

Keyword is BACK

WHO'S WHAT WHERE?
Manx

PAGE 132

Hyper-Sudoku

3	9	5	8	7	6	4	1	2
6	4	8	2	3	1	9	5	7
2	7	1	5	9	4	3	6	8
5	3	9	6	1	7	8	2	4
4	6	2	3	8	5	7	9	1
1	8	7	4	2	9	5	3	6
7	2	6	9	5	8	1	4	3
8	5	3	1	4	2	6	7	9
9	1	4	7	6	3	2	8	5

MIXAGRAMS

S P O I L	G O B S
V I S T A	A M I D
P L A I D	S P R Y
I N L A Y	B E D S

PAGE 133

Collectibles

PAGE 134

One-Way Streets

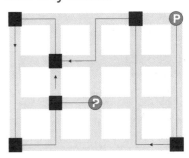

SOUND THINKING
GUARDIAN

PAGE 135

Star Search

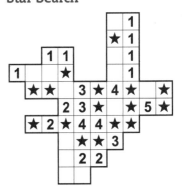

CHOICE WORDS
ALMOND, CASHEW, WALNUT

PAGE 136

In a Wink

S	E	R	U	M		L	A	T	E	X		O	R	S
A	L	O	H	A		O	C	A	L	A		M	E	T
F	L	A	S	H	G	O	R	D	O	N		A	M	Y
E	A	R		J	O	K	E	S		A	P	R	I	L
		M	O	A	T			A	D	E	S	T	E	
M	O	M	E	N	T	O	F	T	R	U	T	H		
A	L	O	N	G		E	A	T		S	A	C	K	
Y	I	N		G	O	O	D	B	Y	E		R	A	N
A	N	T	I		U	F	O		N	A	I	V	E	
	C	R	I	E	R		G	O	C	A	R	T		
M	E	C	C	A	S		R	O	L	L				
I	D	E	A	L		O	P	E	R	A		T	O	P
A	W	L		S	E	C	O	N	D	G	R	A	D	E
T	I	L		A	C	H	E	D		A	A	R	O	N
A	N	O		S	O	O	T	Y		Y	E	A	R	N

PAGE 139

Trash Talk

W	I	S	E		I	C	O	N		B	R	A	S	S
S	O	U	L		D	O	L	E		O	C	T	E	T
J	U	N	K	B	O	N	D	S		L	A	T	E	R
	B	E	E		J	E	T	L	I		U	K	E	
A	L	A		R	O	O		O	V	I	N	E	S	
L	I	T	T	E	R	B	O	X	L	I	N	E	R	S
T	A	H	I	T	I		P	I	L	A	F			
O	M	E	N		G	R	A	V	Y		A	M	I	E
			C	R	I	E	R		G	O	C	A	R	T
W	A	S	T	E	N	O	T	W	A	N	T	N	O	T
I	T	A	S	C	A		A	G	T		G	N	U	
G	O	V		A	L	T	E	R		A	I	R		
G	N	A	R	L		S	C	R	A	P	B	O	O	K
L	E	G	A	L		A	H	E	M		A	V	I	A
E	D	E	N	S		R	O	D	S		R	E	L	Y

PAGE 142

Window Dressing

G	A	U	L		I	R	A	N		L	U	C	A	S
O	O	Z	E		N	E	L	L		E	N	U	R	E
B	L	I	N	D	D	A	T	E		A	P	R	I	L
		S	A	I	L	O	R		V	I	T	A	L	
P	A	S		R	A	M	S		G	E	N	A		
A	S	H	E	N			W	E	B	S	I	T	E	
S	H	U	N		C	A	J	O	L	E		N	O	R
T	O	T	S		A	T	A	R	I		S	C	A	R
A	R	T		G	R	A	Y	E	D		T	A	T	A
S	E	E	S	R	E	D		G	A	L	E	N		
		R	I	O	T		A	C	T	I		L	E	D
C	U	B	E	S		S	C	R	I	B	E			
P	L	U	G	S		S	H	A	D	E	T	R	E	E
A	N	G	E	L		T	O	M	E		C	O	R	Y
S	A	S	S	Y		S	O	P	S		H	E	R	E

PAGE 137

Texas Trail

SMALL CHANGE
HAIR TONIC

PAGE 138

Sudoku

9	1	6	8	4	5	3	7	2
2	5	7	6	1	3	9	4	8
3	4	8	2	9	7	5	6	1
6	2	9	5	7	1	4	8	3
8	3	4	9	6	2	1	5	7
5	7	1	4	3	8	2	9	6
7	9	5	1	2	6	8	3	4
4	6	2	3	8	9	7	1	5
1	8	3	7	5	4	6	2	9

CENTURY MARKS
4, 53, 21, 22

PAGE 140

Split Decisions

TRANSDELETION
BISCUIT

PAGE 141

Number-Out

1	5	6	5	2	2
5	1	6	3	4	2
2	3	5	1	2	4
4	1	1	1	5	3
2	2	6	6	6	5
3	5	2	4	1	6

THINK ALIKE
ROCK, STONE

PAGE 143

ABC

C	B		A
	C	A	B
A		B	C
B	C	A	
A	B		C

CLUELESS CROSSWORD

S	K	I	L	L	E	T
Q		R	E		A	
U	N	K	N	O	W	N
E		S		P		G
A	V	O	C	A	D	O
K		M		R		E
Y	I	E	L	D	E	D

PAGE 144

Go With the Flow

BETWEENER
HILL

PAGE 145

Line Drawing

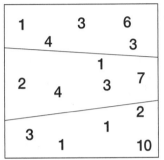

THREE OF A KIND

GO SLOW, DON'T BE A HERO, MEDITATE A LITTLE, OR JUST HIBERNATE.

PAGE 146

Food Break

S	P	R	A	T		J	A	N	U	S		P	I	N
U	S	O	F	A		E	L	O	P	E		O	R	B
B	A	N	A	N	A	S	P	L	I	T		T	E	A
S	T	A	R	L	E	T			T	H	A	N	E	
			I	C	E	D		B	E	A	T	E	R	
B	E	G	I	N		R	E	F	E	R	T	O		
O	L	I	V	E	S		S	U	E	S		C	P	O
W	I	N	E		T	R	E	N	T		S	H	O	P
L	A	G		H	A	I	R		S	T	R	I	K	E
	E	V	O	L	V	E	R		R	I	P	E	N	
S	C	R	I	B	E		T	O	T	E				
O	L	S	E	N			T	H	A	T	S	I	T	
B	A	N		O	R	A	N	G	E	C	R	U	S	H
E	R	A		B	A	Y	O	U		L	A	P	S	E
R	A	P		S	W	E	P	T		E	P	S	O	M

PAGE 147

Find the Ships

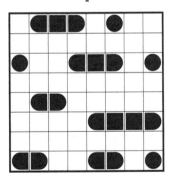

TWO-BY-FOUR

RANT, WARY (or AWRY); WARN, TRAY (or ARTY); WART, YARN (or NARY)

PAGE 148

Hyper-Sudoku

8	7	1	3	4	5	9	2	6
9	4	3	6	2	1	5	7	8
6	2	5	8	7	9	3	4	1
4	1	9	7	5	6	2	8	3
5	6	8	2	9	3	4	1	7
7	3	2	1	8	4	6	5	9
1	8	6	5	3	2	7	9	4
2	9	7	4	6	8	1	3	5
3	5	4	9	1	7	8	6	2

MIXAGRAMS

D A N C E   M E O W
U N T I L   F L E A
C U R S E   O R A L
K H A K I   K O O K

PAGE 149

Large-Scale

P	I	P	S		G	A	R	D	E		A	M	F	M
A	M	E	N		A	L	I	E	N		B	A	L	E
L	E	N	O		B	E	G	E	T		E	X	A	M
M	A	C	R	O	S	C	O	P	I	C		I	P	O
S	N	E	E	R		R	E	C	U	R	S			
			C	A	P		R	E	B	U	K	E	S	
C	O	M	P	A	R	E	D		A	S	I	D	E	
E	V	E	R		C	R	A	T	E		E	R	I	N
L	E	G	O	S		D	E	S	I	S	T	E	D	
T	R	A	N	C	E	S		N	E	D				
	B	E	A	N	I	E		O	P	E	R	A		
G	N	U		M	U	L	T	I	P	L	E	X	E	S
L	O	C	H		R	E	U	S	E		T	I	E	S
A	N	K	A		E	N	D	E	R		E	L	L	E
M	O	S	T		S	T	E	E	P		R	E	S	T

PAGE 150

Fences

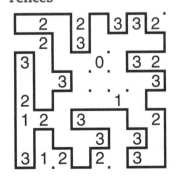

WRONG IS RIGHT

Gaddabout (should be *gadabout*)

PAGE 151

Dotty

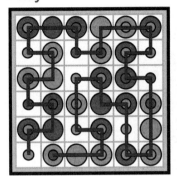

SAY IT AGAIN

YARN

PAGE 152

Number-Out

6	1	5	5	2	4
3	3	3	5	6	2
1	5	4	5	3	2
4	6	6	2	4	3
3	2	2	6	4	1
5	5	2	4	4	6

THINK ALIKE

FAST, SPEEDY

PAGE 153

Good Thinking

D	A	M	P		G	R	A	F	T		C	A	S	A
I	S	E	E		R	A	J	A	H		O	M	A	R
S	T	A	R		I	R	A	T	E		L	I	N	T
C	O	N	S	I	D	E	R	T	H	E	O	D	D	S
O	R	S	O	N			Y	U	A	N				
			N	E	W	T	S		B	R	E	W	E	R
S	P	A		P	O	W	E	R		L	A	T	E	
C	O	M	E	T	O	A	D	E	C	I	S	I	O	N
A	N	O	N		S	A	L	A	D		T	N	T	
M	Y	S	T	I	C		N	Y	L	O	N			
	I	R	A	S			L	A	P	S	E			
S	T	I	C	K	T	O	O	N	E	S	G	U	N	S
K	I	W	I		N	A	M	E	S		A	T	I	T
I	R	O	N		A	M	A	S	S		N	U	D	E
D	E	N	G		P	I	N	T	O		O	P	E	R

PAGE 154

123

3	2	1	3	1	2	3	1	2
1	3	2	1	2	3	1	2	3
3	2	1	3	1	2	3	1	2
2	1	3	2	3	1	2	3	1
1	2	1	3	2	3	1	2	3
2	3	2	1	3	1	2	3	1
3	1	3	2	1	2	3	1	2
1	3	2	1	2	3	1	2	3
2	1	3	2	3	1	2	3	1

SUDOKU SUM

9	4	8
1	7	3
2	6	5

PAGE 155

Find the Ships

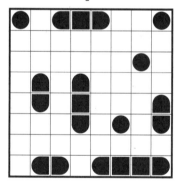

TWO-BY-FOUR
CARD, CITE: CART, DICE
(or ICED)

PAGE 156

Pocket Change

S	A	R	D	I		T	A	U	P	E		C	A	R
P	L	I	E	D		I	B	S	E	N		O	J	O
L	I	N	C	O	L	N	C	E	N	T		N	A	P
A	B	S	O	L	U	T		S	T	I	R	F	R	Y
T	I	E	R		K	O	S		T	E	L			
			M	E	R	C	U	R	Y	D	I	M	E	
H	A	S	N	T		E	I	N	E		S	C	A	T
A	G	A	I	N	S	T		R	O	S	E	T	T	A
R	U	L	E		O	T	O	E		E	A	S	E	L
P	E	A	C	E	D	O	L	L	A	R				
	R	E	V		D	E	L		M	E	T	A		
P	H	Y	S	I	C	S		A	U	T	O	M	A	T
R	E	C		N	U	M	I	S	M	A	T	I	S	T
E	R	A		C	R	O	C	E		D	E	L	T	A
Z	A	P		E	D	G	E	D		S	L	Y	E	R

PAGE 157

Where in the World?

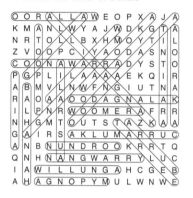

Places are all in AUSTRALIA

IN OTHER WORDS
INNKEEPER

PAGE 158

Alternating Tiles

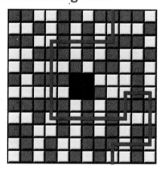

SMALL CHANGE
STEER CLEAR

PAGE 159

Star Search

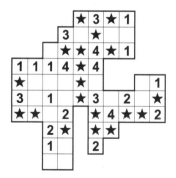

CHOICE WORDS
ASTUTE, CLEVER, SHREWD

PAGE 160

Sever-Ance

L	O	C	A	L		M	I	C	A	S		L	O	W
A	L	O	N	E		E	A	R	L	S		U	N	O
W	E	N	T	O	N	A	T	E	A	R		N	C	O
N	O	N	E		O	N	E	A	M		S	C	U	D
			S	N	I	T		S	O	O	T	H	E	S
A	L	P		A	S	I	D	E		O	R	B		
N	E	A	R	H	O	M	E		C	H	O	R	D	S
E	N	Y	A		M	E	L	B	A		L	E	A	P
W	A	T	T	L	E		H	I	M	A	L	A	Y	A
		H	E	X		S	I	T	I	N		K	O	S
C	H	E	R	I	S	H		E	L	S	A			
H	E	R	S		C	I	V	I	L		S	A	W	S
E	R	E		B	A	N	A	N	A	S	P	L	I	T
S	O	N		A	R	E	N	T		H	E	I	D	I
T	N	T		G	E	S	S	O		E	N	T	E	R

PAGE 161

Sudoku

6	1	8	3	7	4	2	5	9
4	9	2	6	8	5	7	1	3
3	5	7	9	2	1	6	4	8
9	2	4	5	3	6	1	8	7
5	8	6	1	4	7	3	9	2
1	7	3	2	9	8	5	6	4
7	6	9	8	5	2	4	3	1
8	4	1	7	6	3	9	2	5
2	3	5	4	1	9	8	7	6

MIXAGRAMS

S K E E T	D U M B	B
H O T E L	S O L O	O
O D D E R	T U B A	A
W O V E N	H O S T	T

PAGE 162

One-Way Streets

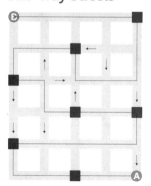

SOUND THINKING
HUGE

PAGE 163

ABC

A	C			B
B	A		C	
C		B	A	
	C	B	A	
	B	A	C	

NATIONAL TREASURE
CINERAMA

PAGE 164

The Bright Stuff

B	A	E	Z		D	I	G	S		B	A	T	E	S
O	L	G	A		I	D	E	A		A	B	O	D	E
L	I	G	H	T	N	I	N	G		N	O	R	G	E
A	T	O	N	C	E		L	E	T	T	U	C	E	S
S	O	N		E	R	R			O	A	T	H		
		G	L	O	W	W	O	R	M		S	A	P	
A	W	F	U	L		A	R	N	O		L	O	R	E
C	A	L	L	S		N	Y	U		S	O	N	I	C
T	R	A	P		O	D	E	S		T	O	G	A	S
V	P	S		F	L	A	R	E	S	U	P			
		H	A	R	E		S	A	D		S	A	W	
U	N	C	L	E	S	A	M		M	I	N	I	M	E
R	I	A	L	S		L	A	M	P	O	O	N	E	D
A	K	R	O	N		O	R	A	L		R	A	N	G
L	E	D	T	O		T	Y	P	E		A	I	D	E

PAGE 165

Wheels and Cogs
Chimney 2

BETWEENER
FOOT

PAGE 166

Find the Ships

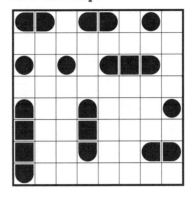

TWO-BY-FOUR
HERB, RENT (or TERN)

PAGE 167

123

2	3	1	2	3	1	3	2	1
1	2	3	1	2	3	2	1	3
3	1	2	3	1	2	1	3	2
1	2	3	1	2	3	2	1	3
2	3	1	2	3	1	3	2	1
3	1	2	3	1	2	1	3	2
1	2	3	1	2	3	2	1	3
2	3	1	2	3	1	3	2	1
3	1	2	3	1	2	1	3	2

ADDITION SWITCH
$626 + 284 = 910$

PAGE 169

Trading Places

T	E	R	I		M	A	S	S		P	A	S	T	A
O	X	E	N		O	R	E	O		O	B	E	Y	S
W	E	N	T		D	I	L	L		S	O	A	K	S
	C	O	O	K	I	E	F	O	R	T	U	N	E	
		I	F	S			E	A	T					
E	M	P	L	O	Y		M	A	L	L		P	B	S
M	A	L	E	S		S	I	M	I		B	A	I	L
B	L	A	N	K	E	T	S	E	C	U	R	I	T	Y
E	L	I	S		L	I	E	N		S	A	N	T	E
D	E	N		P	U	R	R		B	I	T	T	E	R
		B	U	D			T	O	N					
	G	A	L	L	E	R	Y	R	O	G	U	E	S	
T	O	T	A	L		P	E	A	K		G	R	A	S
A	B	O	D	E		M	A	D	E		L	I	L	Y
T	I	M	E	D		S	H	E	D		Y	E	A	R

PAGE 170

Fences

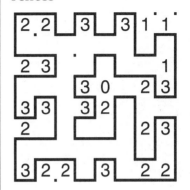

WRONG IS RIGHT
Bufoon (should be *buffoon*)

PAGE 171

Number-Out

5	6	2	2	1	4
6	5	3	5	5	1
4	1	6	3	6	5
3	5	6	4	4	2
2	4	5	1	3	3
3	5	6	4	2	2

THINK ALIKE
THICK, DENSE

PAGE 172

What's the Damage?

P	O	L	E		S	C	A	L	E		T	W	I	T
E	W	E	R		O	R	I	O	N		A	I	D	E
C	L	O	U	D	B	U	R	S	T		K	N	E	E
K	E	N	D	O		D	E	E	R		E	D	A	M
S	T	E	I	N	S		D	R	Y	R	U	B		
			T	E	A	R			A	P	R	I	L	
H	O	W	E		T	E	A	B	A	G		E	K	E
A	M	I		V	I	N	T	A	G	E		A	E	F
T	I	S		I	N	T	E	R	N		S	K	A	T
S	T	E	M	S			K	E	L	P				
	C	A	E	S	A	R		S	E	L	E	C	T	
B	A	R	D		A	S	I	A		E	A	R	L	Y
R	E	A	R		G	I	N	G	E	R	S	N	A	P
O	R	C	A		E	D	S	E	L		H	I	R	E
W	O	K	S		S	E	E	D	S		Y	E	A	S

PAGE 173
Horsing Around

BETWEENER
DRESS

PAGE 174
Hyper-Sudoku

6	3	5	7	1	2	8	9	4
4	1	9	3	6	8	5	2	7
8	7	2	5	9	4	1	6	3
1	6	4	8	2	7	9	3	5
3	9	8	6	5	1	7	4	2
2	5	7	4	3	9	6	8	1
7	2	3	9	8	5	4	1	6
5	8	6	1	4	3	2	7	9
9	4	1	2	7	6	3	5	8

MIXAGRAMS

E X U D E	E L S E
B I P E D	S H I N
R E P A Y	C U R B
S O R R Y	N O S E

PAGE 175
Paint Boxes

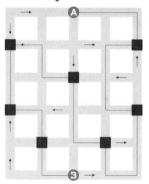

INITIAL REACTION
Good Things Come In Small Packages

PAGE 176
Branching Out

C H A I		M E R V			F L A T
A I R S		A R I E		T I A R A	
T H I R D R A T E			B E N I N	
T O D A Y I S A R B O R D A Y					
	E L O		U N C O L A	
G O P L A N T A T R E E				
A T E I N		A D A M S		V P S
L I E S		E R I K A		B O O K
A S K	M U S E E		V A L L I
	J U L I U S M O R T O N			
O F N O T E		A T F		
G R O V E R C L E V E L A N D				
R E O I L		L A T E R I S E R	
E S S A Y	A N O N		E C H O
S H E L		M E N S		S H I P

PAGE 177
Triad Split Decisions

TRANSDELETION
CHECK IN

PAGE 178
One-Way Streets

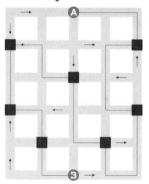

SOUND THINKING
GENEROUS

PAGE 179
In Concert

M I C A		R T E S		C S P A N
I G O R		A A R P		A L O N E
C O M M O N K N O W L E D G E				
R O M	A D E		T A L E	
O F A	T R I M		L E V I T Y
B E N N Y		T A O		D E N I M
E D D Y		R E N F R O		E P A
	M U T U A L F U N D S			
A B E	O N S I T E		U S S R
L U N G E		Y E H		R E E C E
A S T U T E		R E B A		N R A
	N O R M	H O G		T O N
J O I N T R E S O L U T I O N				
R O D E O		S O O T		R A G E
S H O R E		A S K S		A L E X

PAGE 180
Solitaire Poker

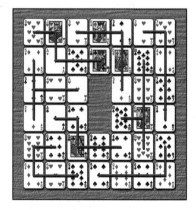

SAY IT AGAIN
AWFUL

PAGE 181

Star Search

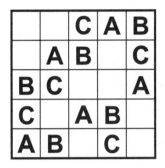

CHOICE WORDS
LESSEN, REDUCE, SHRINK

PAGE 182

Sudoku

5	7	3	2	8	6	9	1	4
1	2	4	7	5	9	3	6	8
9	6	8	4	3	1	2	5	7
3	1	9	8	7	5	4	2	6
7	8	2	6	9	4	1	3	5
6	4	5	3	1	2	8	7	9
4	3	1	5	6	8	7	9	2
2	5	7	9	4	3	6	8	1
8	9	6	1	2	7	5	4	3

CENTURY MARKS
13, 28, 19, 40

PAGE 183

Horsing Around

G	I	B	E		P	L	O	Y		F	E	W	E	R
R	O	U	X		R	A	M	A		E	C	O	L	E
A	T	O	P		O	X	E	N		L	O	O	S	E
B	A	Y	O	F	B	E	N	G	A	L		D	I	D
		S	E	E	R			P	A	U	S	E	S	
R	I	P	E	N		F	R	E	S	N	O			
O	B	I		G	R	A	H	A	M		I	R	M	A
P	E	N	N		A	G	O	R	A		T	R	I	P
E	T	T	A		D	E	L	A	N	O		E	S	E
		O	N	S	I	D	E			P	H	L	O	X
C	A	B	A	L	A			O	N	T	O			
U	S	E		O	L	D	C	H	E	S	T	N	U	T
S	C	A	M	S		E	R	A	S		R	A	V	E
P	I	N	C	H		M	A	R	T		O	V	E	R
S	I	S	S	Y		O	W	E	S		D	E	A	N

PAGE 184

ABC

CLUELESS CROSSWORD

G	R	A	N	D	E	R
R		F		I		E
A	L	F	A	L	F	A
M		I		E		D
M	A	X	I	M	U	M
A		E		M		I
R	A	D	I	A	N	T

PAGE 185

Find the Ships

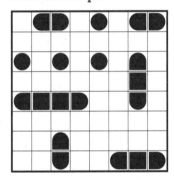

TWO-BY-FOUR
COMP, TENT

PAGE 186

Variations on a Name

A	R	U	B	A		S	T	E	P		V	I	S	A
Z	E	T	A	S		Y	A	L	L		I	D	O	L
U	S	U	R	P		N	C	A	A		C	O	R	P
R	O	B	B	I	E	C	O	L	T	R	A	N	E	
	D	E	A	R	S			Y	E	R	T	L	E	
		D	I	S		C	O	P	A		C	O	L	
B	O	B	O	N	E	S	H	A	I	R		A	S	L
O	N	U	S			A	U	K		E	R	E	I	
U	A	R		B	O	B	B	Y	S	O	X	E	R	S
T	V	S		E	V	E	S		A	P	T			
S	E	T	T	E	E			S	H	E	D	S		
	R	O	B	F	R	O	M	T	H	E	R	I	C	H
P	A	P	A		E	S	A	U		L	I	T	R	E
A	G	E	R		A	L	T	E		I	O	T	A	S
Y	E	N	S		T	O	S	S		A	R	O	M	A

PAGE 187

Dot to Dot

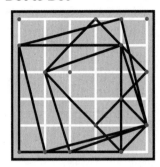

SMALL CHANGE
BEST WISHES

PAGE 188

123

1	2	3	1	2	3	1	3	2
2	3	1	2	3	1	2	1	3
3	1	2	3	1	2	3	2	1
1	2	3	2	3	1	2	1	3
3	1	2	1	2	3	1	3	2
2	3	1	3	1	2	3	2	1
1	2	3	2	3	1	2	1	3
2	3	1	3	1	2	3	2	1
3	1	2	1	2	3	1	3	2

SUDOKU SUM

7	1	8
2	5	4
6	9	3

PAGE 189

Fences

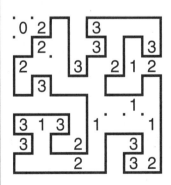

WRONG IS RIGHT
Granery (should be *granary*)

PAGE 190
Hidden Extras

N	O	E	L	S		S	I	P	S		S	N	A	G
E	G	R	E	T		T	A	L	C		W	O	R	E
S	L	I	E	R		I	G	O	R		E	C	O	N
S	E	C	R	E	T	C	O	D	E		E	A	S	T
			A	R	K		S	E	T	T	L	E	S	
F	R	I	S	K	Y			D	O	C				
R	U	N	T		O	X	E	N		O	R	D	E	R
O	D	O	R		N	I	T	E	S		E	A	V	E
G	E	N	E	T		I	C	O	N		A	M	E	N
		E	R	A			O	L	M	E	R	T		
R	A	P	T	U	R	E		P	R	O				
A	L	E	C		C	A	D	E	T	C	O	R	P	S
I	B	A	R		A	S	I	A		A	B	O	I	L
D	E	L	E		D	E	S	K		L	I	L	L	E
S	E	E	D		E	L	K	S		S	T	E	E	D

PAGE 191
Hyper-Sudoku

5	8	9	7	6	2	3	1	4
4	6	2	5	1	3	9	7	8
3	7	1	4	9	8	6	5	2
6	3	8	9	7	4	1	2	5
1	5	4	3	2	6	7	8	9
9	2	7	1	8	5	4	6	3
7	9	5	8	4	1	2	3	6
2	4	3	6	5	7	8	9	1
8	1	6	2	3	9	5	4	7

MIXAGRAMS

F I E R Y   A C E S
I N E R T   J O K E
N I C H E   O K R A
D E F E R   B U F F

PAGE 192
Split Decisions

TRANSDELETION
SIXTEEN

PAGE 193
Driving Buggy

C	R	A	B		F	A	B		B	U	D	G	E	T
H	E	R	R		L	S	U		O	N	I	O	N	S
I	N	M	I	D	A	I	R		O	C	L	O	C	K
C	O	A	C	H	P	A	R	C	E	L	L	S		
H	I	D	E	S		T	I	L	D	E		E	E	G
I	R	A		C	I	T	Y		C	E	C	E		
			W	E	L	C	O	M	E	W	A	G	O	N
S	E	C	E	D	E			B	O	G	G	L	E	
E	A	R	L	O	F	S	U	R	R	E	Y			
T	R	E	K		O	R	E	O		D	A	N		
I	N	S		M	E	L	B	A		O	P	I	N	E
		C	A	R	R	I	A	G	E	T	R	A	D	E
S	T	E	L	M	O		N	E	A	T	E	N	E	D
C	A	N	T	O	S		E	N	S		G	N	A	T
I	N	T	I	M	E		R	T	E		O	E	N	O

PAGE 194
Color Paths

BETWEENER
COURT

PAGE 195
Number-Out

3	3	1	2	5	2
4	4	2	1	6	1
2	4	3	6	3	3
5	2	3	5	4	6
1	3	4	3	3	5
3	6	1	4	1	2

THINK ALIKE
WIN, TRIUMPH

PAGE 196
One-Way Streets

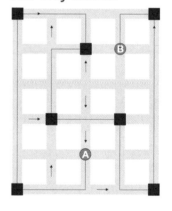

SOUND THINKING
ACCOLADE

PAGE 197
Laugh Lines

M	A	L	E		O	F	U	S	E		C	U	L	T
E	D	I	T		N	I	N	E	R		O	P	I	E
D	O	E	S	N	T	G	I	V	E	A	H	O	O	T
O	R	O		Y	O	U	V	E		D	O	N	N	E
C	E	N	T	A	U	R		C	D	S				
			S	C	R	E	A	M	O	U	T	F	O	R
K	O	J	A	K		S	W	O	O	P		A	R	A
O	M	A	R		L	O	A	N	S		B	U	Z	Z
P	I	P		J	O	U	S	T		C	A	N	O	E
S	T	E	P	O	N	T	H	E	G	A	S			
			A	W	E			C	E	M	E	N	T	S
A	P	R	I	L		C	R	A	N	E		G	A	I
R	E	A	D	S	T	H	E	R	I	O	T	A	C	T
M	A	G	I		V	I	L	L	A		N	I	K	E
S	T	U	N		S	P	O	O	L		T	O	Y	S

PAGE 198

Sudoku

8	6	9	1	4	3	7	2	5
5	1	3	2	7	8	6	9	4
7	4	2	6	5	9	8	3	1
3	8	1	4	2	6	5	7	9
2	7	4	9	1	5	3	8	6
6	9	5	8	3	7	4	1	2
4	5	8	7	9	2	1	6	3
9	3	6	5	8	1	2	4	7
1	2	7	3	6	4	9	5	8

MIXAGRAMS

P E C A N   D U A L
S P I L L   T U B A
F L O A T   R E E D
V Y I N G   S E E D

PAGE 199

Star Search

1	1	1	1	1	1	2
★		★			★	★
2	2			2	★	5
★		2		1		★	★
★	3	★	★	3	★	3			2
2					★		★	2
	★	1		1	3	★
		1

CHOICE WORDS
DINERO, MOOLAH, WAMPUM

PAGE 200

Former First Family?

L	A	B	A	M	B	A	■	E	M	A	N	A	T	E
I	R	O	N	B	A	R	■	D	E	C	I	M	A	L
C	A	N	D	A	C	E	B	U	S	H	N	E	L	L
K	L	E	E	■	K	A	Y	■	S	E	A	N	C	E
		■	A	D	S	■	E	W	E	■			
S	P	I	N	E	T	S	■	A	S	T	A	I	R	E
H	U	N	■	T	A	T	A	S	■	R	I	S	E	R
E	R	N	I	E	B	U	S	H	M	I	L	L	E	R
R	E	E	D	S	■	C	H	E	A	P	■	E	V	E
E	R	R	A	T	I	C	■	S	N	O	R	T	E	D
		■	T	O	M	■	I	D	O	■			
O	B	L	O	N	G	■	M	A	C	■	T	A	R	A
F	R	A	N	C	I	S	X	B	U	S	H	M	A	N
F	I	N	E	A	R	T	■	B	R	O	K	E	I	N
S	E	A	K	A	L	E	■	Y	E	S	O	R	N	O

PAGE 201

Civil War Soldier

SAY IT AGAIN
BREAK

PAGE 202

Shady Spirals

WHO'S WHAT WHERE?
Cedar Rapidian

PAGE 203

ABC

C		A		B
		B	C	A
B	C		A	
A	B			C
	A	C	B	

CLUELESS CROSSWORD

A	N	T	I	Q	U	E
M		A		U		S
A	F	F	A	I	R	S
L		F		Z		A
G	R	I	Z	Z	L	Y
A		E		E		E
M	I	S	U	S	E	D

PAGE 204

Themeless Toughie

P	R	O	S	P	E	R	O	■	■	S	C	R	A	M
R	E	H	E	A	T	E	D	■	M	A	L	A	G	A
I	N	S	T	R	U	M	E	N	T	P	A	N	E	L
S	T	U	■	S	D	I	■	I	N	P	R	I	N	T
C	E	S	T	■	E	X	E	C	■	H	I	N	T	S
I	D	A	H	O	S	■	B	O	R	O	N	■		
L	O	N	E	R	■	A	B	I	E	■	E	D	D	A
L	U	N	A	T	I	C	■	S	O	R	T	I	E	D
A	T	A	T	■	S	A	D	E	■	Y	I	E	L	D
■	■	E	R	O	D	E	■	B	E	S	T	I	R	
B	U	R	R	O	■	I	B	A	R	■	T	I	N	E
A	R	U	G	U	L	A	■	S	A	O	■	T	E	S
D	A	M	O	N	A	N	D	P	Y	T	H	I	A	S
A	L	B	E	D	O	■	A	C	E	R	B	A	T	E
T	S	A	R	S	■	■	M	A	R	O	O	N	E	D

PAGE 206

Find the Ships

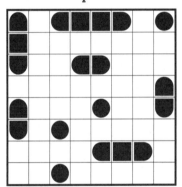

TWO-BY-FOUR
GOAD, LIEU

PAGE 207

Hyper-Sudoku

6	7	5	3	1	9	4	8	2
2	8	9	7	4	5	1	6	3
1	4	3	2	6	8	9	7	5
8	1	6	5	7	2	3	4	9
5	2	4	9	3	6	7	1	8
9	3	7	4	8	1	2	5	6
3	5	1	8	2	7	6	9	4
7	9	2	6	5	4	8	3	1
4	6	8	1	9	3	5	2	7

BETWEENER
STRONG

PAGE 208
Themeless Toughie

S	C	R	A	P	E	R		B	A	V	A	R	I	A
T	H	E	W	I	R	E		I	R	E	L	A	N	D	
A	L	E	R	T	E	D		G	E	T	I	N	T	O	
T	O	N	Y			B	E	T	A	S		O	U	R	
E	R	A		P	L	A	C	E	S		J	U	N	E	
B	I	C		H	E	R	O	N		M	U	T	E	S	
A	N	T		A	N	O	N		L	A	D				
R	E	S	T	S	O	N	O	N	E	S	O	A	R	S	
		H	E	X		M	E	T	S		R	E	C	
C	H	A	I	R		N	I	O	B	E		M	P	H	
H	O	R	N		D	I	S	N	E	Y		L	A	M	
A	T	M		C	E	N	T	S		M	O	R	E	
S	T	A	T	U	T	E		I	T	S	L	A	T	E	
M	I	N	A	R	E	T		G	U	I	L	D	E	R	
S	P	I	N	D	R	Y		N	E	M	E	S	E	S	

PAGE 209
Cut That Out
#3

SMALL CHANGE
WINNING STREAK

PAGE 210
Fences

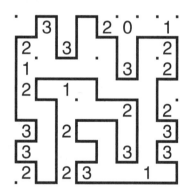

ADDITION SWITCH
1 8 7 + 2 4 5 = 4 3 2

PAGE 211
Themeless Toughie

M	U	S	T	A	R	D		J	I	N	G	L	E	S
I	N	E	R	T	I	A		A	S	A	R	U	L	E
S	A	M	O	V	A	R		M	A	G	I	C	A	L
S	W	I	T		T	E	R	A		M	I	T	E	
T	A	N		B	A	D	E		G	A	E	L	I	C
E	R	A	S	E	S		F	L	A	T		L	O	T
P	E	R	I	L		R	O	E	N	T	G	E	N	
		N	I	C	A	R	A	G	U	A				
	T	A	K	E	O	V	E	R		N	I	E	C	E
V	O	L		V	I	E	S		S	E	N	S	O	R
A	R	I	S	E	N		T	A	T	S		T	N	N
N	O	A	H		U	S	M	A		R	A	T	E	
I	N	S	O	L	E	S		U	P	D	A	T	E	S
S	T	E	R	I	L	E		C	L	E	M	E	N	T
H	O	S	T	E	L	S		K	E	E	P	S	T	O

PAGE 212
123

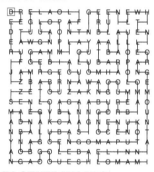

2	1	3	2	1	3	2	3	1
1	3	2	1	3	2	1	2	3
2	1	3	2	1	3	2	3	1
3	2	1	3	2	1	3	1	2
1	3	2	1	3	2	1	2	3
3	2	1	3	2	1	3	1	2
2	1	3	2	1	3	2	3	1
1	3	2	1	3	2	1	2	3
3	2	1	3	2	1	3	1	2

WRONG IS RIGHT
Covetted (should be *coveted*)

PAGE 213
Number-Out

6	5	2	3	3	1
4	4	5	3	4	6
5	4	3	3	1	2
6	2	5	1	5	3
3	4	6	4	2	2
2	3	1	4	6	4

THINK ALIKE
DWELL, RESIDE

PAGE 214
Themeless Toughie

M	E	T	A	L	L	I	C		N	E	C	T	A	R
O	N	A	L	E	A	S	H		O	G	A	U	G	E
O	H	I	T	S	Y	O	U		S	A	L	V	E	S
J	A	N		T	E	M	P	T	E	D	F	A	T	E
U	N	T	O		R	E	P	O			L	E	N	
I	C	I	N	G		R	A	N	A	R	O	U	N	D
C	E	N	S	O	R		S	A	X	O	N			
E	D	G	E	O	U	T		L	O	V	E	T	A	P
		T	E	N	O	R		N	E	B	U	L	A	
T	H	E	S	Y	S	T	E	M		S	I	X	T	Y
R	I	D		E	C	O	L		T	E	R	M	
A	D	I	M	E	A	D	O	Z	E	N		D	U	E
M	E	T	E	R	S		R	A	R	E	C	O	I	N
P	H	O	T	O	S		D	R	O	L	L	E	S	T
S	O	R	E	S	T		S	T	Y	L	I	S	T	S

PAGE 215
River Trail

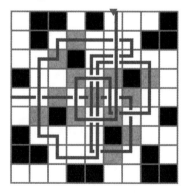

IN OTHER WORDS
FOIBLE

PAGE 216
Straight Ahead

SAY IT AGAIN
FREEZE

PAGE 217
Themeless Toughie

P	L	E	A	D	S			M	A	N	I	L	O	W
H	A	N	D	E	L			P	A	S	A	D	E	N	A
A	T	H	E	N	A			A	P	P	R	O	V	A	L
S	E	A		T	W	E	R	P			C	L	E	R	K
E	R	N	E	S		R	E	E	L	S		L	O	W
R	A	C	Y		P	A	N	D	A		B	E	L	A
S	L	E	E	K	E	S	T		G	L	A	D	L	Y
		L	O	S	E		M	E	A	N				
A	C	C	E	N	T		E	A	R	M	A	R	K	S
V	O	L	T		L	U	R	K	S		N	I	N	A
I	N	A		G	E	N	R	E		T	A	P	E	D
A	N	I	M	A		S	A	R	A	H		T	A	D
T	I	M	A	L	L	E	N		B	E	S	I	D	E
O	V	E	R	L	O	A	D		E	R	O	D	E	S
R	E	D	C	O	A	T		D	E	S	E	R	T

PAGE 218
ABCD

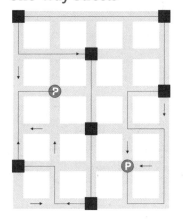

		C	D	B	A
	C	B	A	D	
A			B	C	D
D	B	A	C		
C	D			A	B
B	A	D			C

NATIONAL TREASURE
VIETNAMESE

PAGE 219
Sudoku

5	6	3	4	7	9	8	2	1
1	8	2	6	5	3	9	7	4
9	4	7	8	1	2	5	3	6
3	5	8	1	9	4	2	6	7
6	2	1	7	3	8	4	5	9
7	9	4	2	6	5	3	1	8
8	3	6	9	2	1	7	4	5
4	1	5	3	8	7	6	9	2
2	7	9	5	4	6	1	8	3

MIXAGRAMS
```
WAFER  OUCH
CRIED  HULK
MOLAR  MAIM
COMBO  RAPT
```

PAGE 220
Themeless Toughie

P	A	R	T	I	T	A			B	L	A	D	E	D
O	V	E	R	T	A	X		Z	O	O	L	O	G	Y
R	O	M	A	N	T	I	C	I	Z	A	T	I	O	N
T	I	E	D		S	A	R	G		M	A	N	T	A
I	D	L	E	D		L	E	G	G	Y		G	I	S
A	S	T	R	U	T		S	U	E		O	F	S	T
			F	A	R	C	R	Y	F	R	O	M		
	A	S	F	R	E	E	A	S	A	I	R			
	P	R	E	S	S	E	N	T	E	R				
A	R	R	S		A	D	D		R	E	M	A	N	D
M	O	E		E	L	I	O	T		R	O	T	O	R
I	N	S	T	R		E	E	R	O		N	A	D	A
G	E	T	O	N	E	S	D	A	N	D	E	R	U	P
A	T	E	D	I	R	T		G	E	N	T	I	L	E
S	O	D	D	E	N			G	L	A	S	S	E	D

PAGE 221
One-Way Streets

SOUND THINKING
LIGHTWEIGHT

PAGE 222
Split Decisions

TRANSDELETION
TRIANGLE

PAGE 223
Themeless Toughie

C	A	S	H	C	O	W		P	L	U	G	G	E	R
I	M	P	E	A	C	H		A	A	M	I	L	N	E
T	A	L	L	Y	H	O		C	R	A	V	A	T	S
E	R	I	S		O	S	H	E	A		E	D	I	T
S	E	T	I	N		W	A	C		S	N	I	T	S
			N	O	A	H	S	A	R	K		A	L	E
J	A	C	K	I	E	O		R	A	E		T	I	A
O	B	O	I	S	T				D	E	M	O	N	S
A	D	M		O	N	T		L	I	T	U	R	G	Y
N	O	M		M	A	Y	F	L	I	E	S			
O	M	O	R	E		P	I	C		R	I	G	G	S
F	I	D	O		S	I	T	O	N		C	E	L	T
A	N	O	R	A	K	S		O	C	E	A	N	I	A
R	A	R	E	B	I	T		L	A	D	L	I	N	G
C	L	E	M	E	N	S		J	A	D	E	I	T	E

PAGE 224
Your Turn

SAY IT AGAIN
MOTION

PAGE 225
Star Search

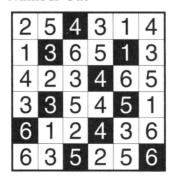

CHOICE WORDS
BALLAD, MINUET, SONATA

PAGE 226
Themeless Toughie

T	W	E	E	D		U	C	L	A		S	O	P	H
H	A	R	P	O		S	A	A	B		A	V	I	A
A	K	R	O	N		G	R	U	F	F	N	E	S	S
L	E	A	C	H		R	A	D	A	R	T	R	A	P
I	N	T	H	E	S	A	M	E	B	O	A	T		
A	S	A		W	I	D	E	R			A	P	U	
		P	I	X	E	L		K	H	A	K	I	S	
R	O	S	E	T	T	A		S	L	O	V	E	N	E
U	P	P	I	T	Y		V	O	I	L	A			
B	E	E			O	I	L	E	D			I	R	A
	C	A	R	L	X	V	I	G	U	S	T	A	F	
R	E	T	R	E	A	T	E	D		P	H	A	I	R
H	A	R	T	C	R	A	N	E		M	A	L	L	E
E	R	A	S		K	I	D	S		A	L	I	A	S
A	L	L	Y		S	L	I	T		N	E	A	T	H

PAGE 227
Number-Out

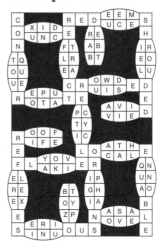

THINK ALIKE
HORSE, EQUINE

PAGE 228
Line Drawing

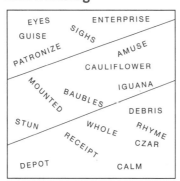

Rhyming words, third letter U, words with silent letters

TWO-BY-FOUR
ZONE, LAMB (or BALM)

PAGE 229
Themeless Toughie

PAGE 230
Triad Split Decisions

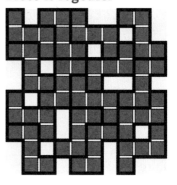

TRANSDELETION
ISOMETRIC

PAGE 231
Piece It Together

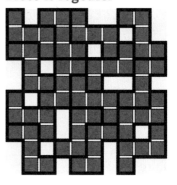

SMALL CHANGE
STRING QUARTET

PAGE 232
Themeless Toughie

S	H	E	E	T	G	L	A	S	S		S	A	I	L
W	A	L	L	A	W	A	L	L	A		A	B	B	A
I	N	C	I	D	E	N	T	A	L	M	U	S	I	C
N	O	I	D		N	E	A	P		E	T	U	D	E
E	I	D	E	R			O	U	T	E	R			
			S	U	N	K	E	N	G	A	R	D	E	N
H	E	S		B	O	I	L		A	L	N	I	C	O
A	T	I	C		D	R	A	W	N		E	T	R	E
L	U	G	O	S	I		R	I	D	E		Y	U	L
F	I	N	A	N	C	I	A	L	A	I	D			
	S	T	E	E	N			N	E	S	T	S		
E	C	O	L	E		T	O	O	N		P	Y	R	E
G	O	V	E	R	N	O	R	G	E	N	E	R	A	L
A	C	E	S		I	T	A	L	I	A	N	I	C	E
D	O	R	S		L	O	N	E	L	Y	D	A	Y	S